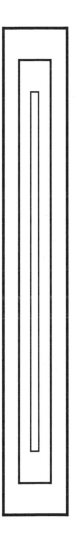

Ethical
and
Legal Issues
in
Counseling
and
Psychotherapy

A
Comprehensive
Guide

William H.
Van Hoose

Jeffrey A.
Kottler

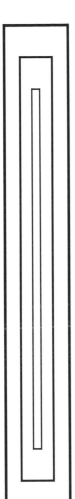

Ethical and Legal Issues in Counseling and Psychotherapy

Second Edition

Jossey-Bass Publishers

San Francisco • Washington • London • 1985

ETHICAL AND LEGAL ISSUES IN COUNSELING AND PSYCHOTHERAPY
A Comprehensive Guide
by William H. Van Hoose and Jeffrey A. Kottler

Library of Congress Cataloging in Publication Data

Van Hoose, William H.
    Ethical and legal issues in counseling and
psychotherapy.

    (Jossey-Bass social and behavioral science series)
    Bibliography: p. 233
    Includes index.
    1. Psychotherapy ethics. 2. Mental health laws—United
States. I. Kottler, Jeffrey A. II. Title. III. Series.
RC455.2.E8V36   1985   174'2   84-43039
ISBN 0-87589-642-1 (alk. paper)

Manufactured in the United States of America

The paper in this book meets the guidelines for
permanence and durability of the Committee on
Production Guidelines for Book Longevity of the
Council on Library Resources.

JACKET DESIGN BY WILLI BAUM

SECOND EDITION

Code 8520

The Jossey-Bass
Social and Behavioral Science Series

Preface to the Second Edition

Since the first edition of *Ethical and Legal Issues in Counseling and Psychotherapy* was published, there have been significant new developments in the field of counseling and psychotherapy. The number of people providing services in these professions—counseling, psychiatry, psychology, and social work—continues to grow. New techniques for helping clients have been developed, old ones have been refined, and a few have been discredited and abandoned. New laws pertaining to various aspects of the helping profession have been enacted, and numerous court decisions that affect the work of practitioners have been handed down. At the same time, practitioners of counseling and psychotherapy appear to have become more sensitive to the ethical and legal implications of their work. Ethics committees are now quite active, and an increasing number of books and journal articles are being devoted to ethical and legal issues.

In our minds, three new developments discussed in this second edition are especially exciting. (1) The implementation of professional standards through program accreditation and credentialing activities: Counselors in particular have made a special effort to improve their training programs through a well-organized process of program review. Psychologists have also refined and updated their accrediting procedures within the past few years. (2) The significant increase in licensure, certification, and registry activities: Counselors maintain that licensure is necessary to secure their right to practice in the public sector; psychologists emphasize quality service to the consumer. Both groups appear to have established their legal right to function in a variety of public settings. (3) The strengthening of professional monitoring: Although many gaps and omissions in professional regulation still persist, progress has been made and many professionals are now serious about accountability. In those states where licensure laws have been recently enacted, progress has been especially dramatic. In this edition, we also include the revised ethical principles of four major associations of helping professionals, and we summarize the implications of recent court decisions in the field of counseling and psychotherapy.

The general purpose of the second edition is to identify and explore some of the major ethical and legal issues facing the helping professions. The underlying tenets of this edition correspond to those of the first edition. Chapter One provides a theoretical background on ethical and legal questions in contemporary society with implications for counseling and psychotherapy. Chapter Two considers three approaches to ethics and discusses ethical decision making. Chapters Three and Four discuss the legal and professional regulation of therapy and describe the responsibilities of therapists. Chapters Five, Six, and Seven identify several special problems in therapy, including value problems, ethical-legal conflicts, and special therapeutic strategies. The final two chapters, Eight and Nine, discuss the marketing of therapeutic services, consumer protection, and the conduct of individual therapists. The four supplemental appendixes provide the current codes of ethics from four major associations of counselors and psychotherapists. The Annotated Bibliography contains brief synopses of 48 of the more than 200 sources used in the preparation of this book.

We believe that the helping professions have a major influence not only on the lives of millions of individuals but also on the way modern society describes and defines human behavior. Any profession that wields such influence must pay close attention to its ethics. We also believe that therapists must understand the extent to which law, community standards, and social custom influence their work. It is our hope that this book will call attention to the major ethical and legal issues confronting helping professionals and will improve their competency and ethical awareness, not only as scholar-professionals generally, but also as specialists in their area of expertise.

We have drawn the material in this book from a variety of sources—professional books and articles, court decisions, laws, and in a few instances, the popular media. We wish to thank all those individuals who granted us access to their materials. We are also most grateful for the many positive reactions to the first edition of this book. The responses from our readers helped stimulate this revision. We also wish to recognize the capable assistance of our copy editor, Dorothy Conway. We alone, of course, are responsible for the final product.

Charlottesville, Virginia William H. Van Hoose
February 1985 Jeffrey A. Kottler

Preface
to the
First
Edition

The title, *Ethical and Legal Issues in Counseling and Psychotherapy,* indicates the general topics covered in our book. A more specific description is that the book is concerned with ethical principles and decision making in therapy and with the legal circumscriptions within which therapists work.

The book provides answers to such questions as: What are some *ethical dilemmas* facing counselors and psychotherapists? How can one decide which *ethical judgments* are acceptable and which are unacceptable? What are some of the *legal issues* in counseling and psychotherapy? What are some *legal pitfalls* in therapy? Illustrative ethical situations and dilemmas are presented and several landmark cases are summarized and analyzed.

During the past three decades, the helping professions have gained a position of prominence in modern society. Counseling and psychotherapy is not only accepted by the general public but also is supported by the state, which relies heavily on such specialists as counselors, psychologists, psychiatrists, and

social workers for ministering to the mental health needs of
large segments of society. Thus, the work of therapists has become more than just a series of services performed by experts in
mental health. Therapy is a major social force and has a profound influence on public beliefs and attitudes as well as on
public policy.

We maintain that any profession so widely practiced, and
having such potential for both positive and negative influences
on people's lives, must pay particular attention to the ethical
principles and issues that find their way into professional practice. Some of the current criticisms and public disclosures of
questionable therapeutic practices suggest that the problem of
ethics has received far too little attention. Unethical behavior is
a major professional problem in counseling and psychotherapy
and, unfortunately, the profession has demonstrated little interest and less capacity for dealing with it. In our book we document practices that cause difficulties for therapists and that
result in criticism and ridicule for the profession. We provide a
thorough analysis of the function of ethics in counseling and
psychotherapy and describe the part that ethical judgments and
concepts play in work with a client.

We are concerned also that counselors and psychotherapists are often unaware of the extent to which laws, court decisions, and regulations influence their work and their profession.
Throughout the book we call attention to legal principles that
have implications for therapy. Such topics, discussed in detail,
are *incompetency, malpractice, licensure and certification, privileged communication,* and *legal obligations* of therapists.

The assistance of many people deserves acknowledgment:
We are grateful to Anna Paradise, Donald Hall, Larry Henning,
Elizabeth Jennings, Henry Rohne, Bruce Walker, Maureen
Worth, and Ingrid Zachary, whose stimulating discussions clarified our thinking on ethical principles, and whose enthusiasm
encouraged us in our beliefs that this work was important. Maureen Worth assisted with much of the library research and was
extremely helpful in securing case material used throughout the
book. Kay Russo spent numerous hours on clerical duties and
helped immensely during several crisis periods.

Special thanks are due Joan Franks and Richard Beard for considerable and valuable professional advice and support over the years. Finally, the senior author expresses personal thanks to Henry Willner for help too varied, complex, and personal to be discussed here.

This book is dedicated to Hazel Van Hoose and Ellen Kottler.

Charlottesville, Virginia   William H. Van Hoose
February 1977   Jeffrey A. Kottler

Contents

Contents

The Authors

William H. Van Hoose has worked as a counselor, psychologist, and teacher for more than twenty-five years. He has taught at four universities in the midwest and southeast and has lectured throughout the United States and in Canada and Europe. Currently he is professor of counselor education, University of Virginia, Charlottesville. Van Hoose received his Ph.D. in counseling and guidance from Ohio State University in 1965. His M.S. is from Indiana University, and his A.B. was awarded by Morehead State University in Kentucky.

Van Hoose is the author and coauthor of more than forty articles and eleven books including *Counseling Adults* (1982, with M. R. Worth), *Adulthood in the Life Cycle* (1982, with M. R. Worth), *Midlife Myths and Realities* (1984), and most recently *Tecumseh: An Indian Moses* (1984).

Jeffrey A. Kottler has worked as a therapist in a variety of settings, including a mental health clinic, a hospital, a city department of human services, and in private practice. He is currently in private practice in Farmington Hills, Michigan. Kottler received his Ph.D. in counselor education from the University of Virginia in 1976. He holds an M.Ed. from Wayne State University and a B.S. from Oakland University in Michigan.

Kottler has been a Fulbright scholar and a senior lecturer in group therapy at Catholic University in Lima, Peru. He has chaired the Ethics Committee of the Association for Specialists in Group Work and is the author of *Pragmatic Group Leadership* (1982).

Ethical
and
Legal Issues
in
Counseling
and
Psychotherapy

A
Comprehensive
Guide

1

Perspectives on Ethical Practice

This chapter provides an overview of the major ethical and legal issues in counseling and psychotherapy today. These introductory statements provide an outline for the content and tone of the entire volume. We begin this undertaking by discussing several of the ambiguous and confusing terms that are common to this subject matter.

A Clarification of Terms

Legal and ethical scholars are concerned with the preciseness of their language. Clinicians, as well, spend a great part of their time splitting linguistic hairs over the relative merits of using one phrase over another, attempting to cultivate an appreciation for the verbal options available in describing one's thoughts and feelings. Therapists and counselors could even be described as "language coaches" whose principal function is to promote greater internal control, self-responsibility, rationality, and clarity by the use of positive, self-enhancing images, meta-phors, descriptors of innermost thoughts.

Since we want to be precise and clear in our own use of language throughout this book, we should at the outset explain our use of certain key terms. First of all, both "counseling" and "psychotherapy" are used in the title of this book because it is difficult for us to make a distinction between them. There is little agreement among authorities in the field on significant dif-ferences between these two terms; and, as Patterson (1980) has noted, definitions of them often overlap. Furthermore, there appear to be no distinct techniques that separate counseling from psychotherapy. Some differences may appear when one considers objectives. That is, counseling often deals with rela-tively "normal" people who are having developmental adjust-ment problems, whereas psychotherapy more closely follows the medical model and is more intensive and lengthy as a treat-ment for neurotic disturbances (Kottler and Brown, 1985). However, since the counselor is not limited to working with normal adjustment conflicts any more than the therapist works only with severely disturbed clients, many of these alleged dif-ferences between the two therapeutic modalities may be un-essential and artificial (Pietrofesa, Hoffman, and Splete, 1984). Therefore, although we recognize some possible differences in the severity of clients' problems, we will—in the interests of practicality—use the terms "counseling" and "psychotherapy" interchangeably throughout this book. For the same reason, we will use the generic term "therapist" to refer to all psychologi-cal helpers and "client" for the people they help.

The terms "ethics" and "morals" also overlap and are often used synonymously—both terms referring to principles concerning what is good and bad or the study of human con-duct and values. Again, shades of difference have been discerned in the terms: Mowrer (1967), for example, suggests that "mo-rality" may imply force or coercion, whereas "ethics" suggests reason and objectivity. In our view, "morality" is a useful and legitimate term for describing some of the issues in counseling and psychotherapy and in many cases may be a satisfactory sub-stitute for "ethics." However, in line with Levy's (1972) definition of "ethics" as standards of conduct or actions in relation to others—these standards arising from some definition of individual or collective responsibility to others and based on the nature of the relationship to them, whether personal, familial, social, or occupational—we believe that the term "ethics" more accurately conveys our intentions. Therefore, we will primarily use the term "ethics" throughout this book.

Ethics is concerned with questions that have no ultimate answers yet are important to planning one's life, justifying one's activities, and deciding what one ought to do. More than psychology and the other social sciences that attempt to describe human behavior, ethical philosophy is concerned with evaluating conduct. "Ethics is not primarily concerned with getting people to do what they believe to be right, but rather with helping them to decide what is right" (Jones, Sontag, Beckner, and Fogelin, 1977, p. 8).

Ethics is generally defined as a philosophical discipline concerned with human conduct and moral decision making. Moral decisions involve judgments that lead to some action and that involve the use of such words as "ought," "should," "right," "good," and their opposites (Brandt, 1959). Unlike a discipline such as mathematics, ethics is normative rather than factual. It is concerned with principles that ought to govern human conduct rather than with those that do govern it. A fundamental and necessary postulate of ethics is that human beings are capable of self-determination; that is, that at least some decisions are freely made and that we—as human beings and professional helpers—are capable of making good and right decisions.

Ethics in the Therapeutic Relationship

Ethics, values, and morality are an intrinsic part of therapy practice. In the therapeutic relationship, the very concept of influence is a moral issue. The basic values of our profession —to protect privacy, to promote autonomy, and to avoid forms of deceit, manipulation, and exploitation—have moral significance.

Bayles (1981) has presented and evaluated several possible models of ethical decision making in the framework of the therapeutic relationship:

1. The client is the one in charge, assumes most of the responsibility and authority for decisions, and relies on the therapist as a neutral consultant. This model is inappropriate because it fails to recognize the client's impaired judgment during periods of emotional crisis and the therapist's expertise in structuring change efforts.
2. Power and authority are equally shared in a contractual arrangement with mutual responsibilities and equal roles. This model is naive because the power between therapist and client is not, in fact, equal. The therapist has more experience, more status, and is operating on home turf.
3. The professional relationship is essentially one of friendship, in which the two participants equally and personally engage one another. This model is not applicable because, in the therapeutic encounter, the flow is unidirectional—only the client receives help.
4. An attitude of benevolent paternalism prevails, in which the professional guards the client's best interests and retains control of decision making. This model is inappropriate because true informed consent is not provided to the client.
5. The therapist's extensive knowledge and skills are recognized, but the client retains ultimate responsibility for decision making. This fiduciary model has the advantages of equal partnership in authority, with the stronger position of expert helper counterbalanced by the client's right to informed consent.

As Bayles' fiduciary model suggests, the therapeutic relationship is different from other human encounters in that there is a contractual arrangement designed to promote the welfare and greater autonomy of the client. Other characteristics include the client's right to informed consent, confidentiality, and competent treatment (Woody and Associates, 1984).

Unlike those relationships that involve other helping professionals, such as physicians, accountants, or attorneys, counseling and psychotherapy often involve the ambiguous enterprise of delivering services that leave no physical evidence. Our treatment strategies are done in privacy with those who come to us in pain, fearful and vulnerable. Integrity, trustworthiness, and, above all, ethical responsibility are even more crucial in a profession that is unclear about its predominant goals.

After agreeing among ourselves that our mission is to promote the welfare of the client, we then drift in different directions. We cannot agree on whether we should be working in the past, present, or future; with thoughts, feelings, or behavior; in group, individual, or family settings; or for weeks, months, or years. We cannot agree on what to call a client's problem, much less the best way to resolve it. Although these differences of opinion implicit in therapeutic work reduce the reliability and validity of our methodologies, they also lead to a certain humility and respect for individual solutions to individual problems. It is our commitment to helping that binds us together—and a special kind of helping that is built on trust, nurturance, and expertise.

Psychotherapy in Modern Society

During the past few decades, the craft of counseling and psychotherapy has attained a prominent place in Western society: "Its professors and practitioners, once contemptuously regarded as eccentrics mumbling arcane obscenities at the fringe of medicine, have advanced from relative obscurity to chairs of eminence and couches of opulence in the finest universities and neighborhoods in the Western world" (London, 1964, p. v). The United States has been a particularly fertile territory for the growth of counseling and psychotherapy. At the turn of the century, professional counselors were unknown, and there were probably fewer than five hundred psychiatrists in the United States. While it is impossible to provide more than a gross estimate of the number of counselors and psychotherapists in this country today, it is certain that the numbers run into hundreds of thousands. London (1964, p. 18) marvels that psychotherapy, in barely three generations, has become an influential and lucrative profession, even without much benefit of scientific validation: "Armed with rationales apparently consonant with scientific inquiry and independent of overtly religious messianism or denominational buffoonery that might supernaturalize its goals, psychotherapy gained increasing appeal among educated people as a potential means of relieving their problems of living even if they are not plainly sick."

We are living in the "age of psychiatry." People suffering from emotional handicaps, as well as normal people seeking optimum development of their personal resources, turn to counseling and psychotherapy because they believe they will be helped. And there is evidence that the helping professions do assist such people. Several critics, however, have raised embarrassing questions about the methods used by professional helpers and have decried the lack of attention to ethical considerations in counseling and psychotherapy.

Several dimensions of this problem require attention. The first is philosophical and has to do with our contention that counseling as a technology and as a science contains many ethical considerations and judgments. Unfortunately, ethical issues have been minimized or ignored in these professions in what may be a naive belief that such matters have no place in a scientific system. Helping professionals may be deluding themselves; for, as Halleck (1971) notes, psychiatry was never an ethically or a politically neutral profession. Value systems, usually implicit, have always dominated the different schools of psychiatry. Every psychiatrist who ever treated a patient has some notion of what kind of life would be best for that patient. And every patient who has benefited from psychiatry has incorporated some of his doctor's values. Furthermore, by the very nature of his practice, the therapist consistently takes positions on issues that involve the distribution of power within social systems—issues that have political implications. Can it be denied that a client's ideas concerning right and wrong, his political beliefs, and his religious views influence his behavior? Do the counselor's views on such social issues as abortion, drug abuse, and law and order influence his behavior with his clients?

In therapy there may be no "correct" decision, no "right" answers; nevertheless, the therapist is committed to helping clients reach a decision and prepare to deal with the inevitable consequences. In short, therapy advocates a metaethic of "rational autonomy"—whereby clients are given the freedom to decide—without the applied ethics of specifying what best form the decision should take (Englehardt, 1982). The therapist's ultimate role is to unleash the client's capacity for making independent and individual decisions within the context of rationality, which involves the ability to reason logically, clearly, and intelligibly; to distinguish means from ends; to use empirical evidence for supporting factual beliefs; to be impartial when judging beliefs; and to hold values conducive to freedom and enlightenment (Edwards, 1982). This metaethic of rational autonomy is one to which we can all ascribe, in spite of the varied differences in theoretical allegiance and personal values.

The second dimension of the problem of ethics pertains to the practice of counseling and psychotherapy and to the handling of client-therapist relationships. The first affirmations of confidentiality and attention to ethical issues between doctor and patient can be traced to the era of Hippocrates (Musto, 1981). The Greek ideals of professional behavior still remain as appropriate as when the father of medicine first coined his now immortal oath: "Whatever houses I may visit, I will come for the benefit of the sick, remaining free of all intentional injustice, of all mischief, and in particular of sexual relations with both female and male persons, be they free or slaves. What I may see or hear in the course of treatment or even outside of the treatment in regard to the life of the man, which on no account one must spread abroad, I will keep to myself, holding such things shameful to be spoken about" (quoted in Edelstein, 1967, p. 17).

The ideals established by Hippocrates are echoed in our professional organizations. The American Psychological Association, the National Association of Social Workers, the American Association for Counseling and Development, and the American Association for Marriage and Family Therapy have developed ethical codes that attempt to regulate professional conduct. (These codes are reprinted at the end of this book.) The codes, unfortunately, are very difficult to enforce; and some practitioners may not espouse them. For them, ethics is a lively topic for professional meetings, but questions of ethical behavior do not concern them.

In the "business" of therapy, those practitioners who hook their clients into dependencies, who can creatively bill insurance companies, who pay favors to referral contacts, who are politically astute and unburdened by scruples, conscience, "and other liabilities" are naturally going to be more financially successful than those who follow the rules of fairness and morality. Yet, in spite of the temptations and obvious benefits of acting in one's own self-interest to the exclusion of others' welfare, there is an impressive body of evidence supporting the natural urge toward altruism. In the animal kingdom, ethical behavior is based on reciprocal arrangements between individuals in a group for their mutual benefit: among chimpanzees, "I'll scratch your back if you'll scratch mine." Other examples go beyond reciprocal altruism, in which animals are genetically programmed to protect and help others of their own species. Singer (1981) lists several kinship pacts that support the sociobiological basis for ethics. Thrushes sound a warning call to their brethren when a hawk is sighted overhead, even though such scouting reports jeopardize their own safety by calling attention to themselves, unselfishly offering themselves as hors d'oeuvres. Many predators share the spoils of a kill with other members of the pack who were not even a part of the hunt. When an elephant suffers injury, other members of the clan stop to help the fallen animal rise again.

Humans, of course, operate according to similar evolutionary schemes, often intuitively choosing to act in the spirit of community welfare. "Human emotional responses and the more general ethical practices based on them have been programmed to a substantial degree by natural selection over thousands of generations" (Wilson, 1979, p. 6). According to sociobiologists such as Edward Wilson and Peter Singer, the pursuit of good and right values is intrinsically adaptive in the human gene pool to preserve continued survival. When the capacity for reasoning is added to the list of human dimensions, the

likelihood of making sound ethical judgments is even further assured. Egoism is ethically irrational from a biological perspective, since selfish individuals would leave behind fewer descend-
ants than those who were helpful to their kin.

Why, then, do we have so much murder, stealing, lying,
deception? Why do we need so many rules and laws and armed
police to enforce them? Or, even more to the point, why do
therapists need a book on ethics if professional behavior ought
to be intrinsically altruistic? The answer is, at least in our case,
that the vast majority of professionals intuitively do what is
right and good for their clients. Sometimes, however, professionals are faced with conflicting loyalties and find it difficult
to know whether their responsibilities are to clients, colleagues,
the profession, or society. In these instances they need guidance, a code of professional ethics or standards, and perhaps a
book such as this one.

Professional Codes

All professions have moral codes, general rules to guide
behavior. For therapists as well as for physicians, lawyers, or
even prostitutes or thieves, there are rules of conduct so that all
may flourish. "Thus, a profession, much more than a knowledge discipline, is concerned with the issues of sanction, legiti-
macy, setting, knowledge, and methods of practice or intervention. In short, a profession seeks to establish a unique set of
symbolic codes for expression and control. It establishes normative structures to develop, test, and control those symbolic
codes" (Bolan, 1980, p. 263).

Basic moral rules are remarkably stable across cultures
and situations; they are absolute, invariant, universal (Wright,
1971). Because of this absolutism, the language of ethics consists of words that grate on the nerves of therapists. We who
stand for freedom, choice, acceptance, flexibility, and relativity bristle at the prospect of defining absolute rules for human
conduct. We who favor phrases such as "It depends," "That's
for *you* to decide," and "I don't know what's best" have consciously deleted the language of ethics from our vocabularies.

Justice, duty, should, ought, obligation, virtue, sin, blame, good, bad, right, wrong, moral, immoral: such things have no meaning in therapeutic sessions except as they limit the individual. We therefore resent committees, overseers, authors, and preachers who tell us what *they* think is best for everyone.

Zemlick (1980) argues that our resentment of professional regulation has led to a pervasive attitude of complacency, permissiveness, and reactivity to ethical problems. Rather than making a serious effort to establish standards of ethics and police our field from within, we make cosmetic changes to pacify the public and lawmakers. Zemlick further suggests that the very autonomy of our field is at stake unless we are more willing to respect the professional codes that regulate counselor conduct. To prevent entanglements with external authorities, Keith-Spiegel (1977) emphasizes the importance of ethical study and universal compliance with consensual norms of professionality. The majority of ethical violations result not from a willful disregard of professional codes but, rather, from ignorance and poor judgment.

All the professions discussed in this book have ethical codes and standards in one form or another. These standards reflect professional concerns and define basic principles that "ought" to guide the professional activity of the therapist. Ethical codes provide a position on standards of practice to aid each member of a profession in deciding what he should do when conflicts arise. They help to clarify the therapist's responsibility to his client and to society. They give the profession some measure of assurance that the behaviors of individual therapists will not be detrimental to the profession. A code of ethics (supposedly) gives society some guarantee that therapists will demonstrate a sensible regard for the social mores and expectations of the community. Finally, a code of ethics gives the therapist himself grounds for safeguarding his professional freedom and integrity.

Codes of ethics are of course helpful—indeed essential—but they do not solve individual problems. Barclay (1968) believes that there are no safeguards in any form of therapy aside from the individual therapist's sense of ethical responsibility.

Once a person enters therapy, he loses some individual autonomy and freedom of choice, for the interaction of human beings in almost any situation militates against absolute freedom.

Wrenn (1966, p. 195) believes that ethical responsibility is related to professional competence: "[The profession is not] in want of a respect for evidence and scientific truth, nor does it lack the desire to serve individuals and society. If this profession is in want of anything, it is a neglect of the proposition that man is spiritual as well as intellectual in nature. . . . The profession has established a code of ethics, but its application calls for decisions that require great courage and depth of conviction. It is at this point that the counselor may have to have recourse to the great values and principles of the human race in order to resolve ethical conflicts." It is the counselor's understanding of these values and principles and his personal courage that provide true professional competence.

Many people believe that ethical standards for professional groups are designed to protect the public from charlatans and incompetents. While they may sometimes have such an effect, that is not the only reason for their existence. More often they are designed to protect the professions from three main dangers. First, ethical standards are designed to protect the profession from the government. All professions desire autonomy and seek to avoid interference and regulation by lawmakers. They would rather regulate themselves through professional codes or standards than risk regulations from legislative bodies. Second, ethical standards protect the professions from the self-destruction of internal bickering. It is unethical to criticize a professional colleague or to entice his clients to leave him. This standard enables therapists to live in harmony with one another. Finally, ethical standards are designed to protect the therapist from the public. If he behaves within the code, he has some protection if he is sued for malpractice (Fish, 1973).

Another problem with ethics in therapy stems from the divergent and competing views concerning what therapy is and what its practitioners ought to do. It has been suggested that there are as many schools of therapy as there are practitioners and that they compete with each other in the style of automobile dealers. Each school has its own set of principles, and each stresses its benefits to divergent client populations. Furthermore, thousands of counselors or therapists are practicing their craft in a variety of settings: elementary schools, colleges and universities, abortion clinics, hospitals, community mental health centers. Roles and responsibilities of therapists are at least as varied as the settings in which they work, and the professional preparation may range from a baccalaureate degree to a Ph.D. or an M.D. As noted earlier, there is little agreement on which is the best therapy in any situation. School counselors, for instance, tend to ignore the ethics of counseling because there is no clear delineation of what is ethical or legal in the profession, and statements from professionals are often ambiguous and contradictory (Huckins, 1968). These conditions make it difficult for the profession to incorporate a general set of ethical principles into its body of knowledge.

Ethical Codes and Conflicting Values

Every practitioner espouses or pretends allegiance to one ethical theory or code but often uses quite another when confronted with problematic situations. This distinction between "espoused theories" and "theories-in-use" was originally made by Argyris and Schön (1974) to describe the incongruence between ethical theory and practice. For instance, although almost all therapists would agree on the importance of client follow-up after sessions have terminated and support such a rule of professional conduct, very few cases actually receive this theoretically prescribed treatment. The same point might be raised for any aspect of ethics or of professional practice.

It is difficult enough for a profession to establish a code of ethical practice to regulate individual behavior when the practitioner's duties can be systematically delineated and scientifically validated. The problem is even more difficult when ambiguities and differences of opinion prevail and when the practitioner's role is not generally understood. The type of service provided by helping professionals, as well as the way they provide it, sets them apart from other professionals. The counselor or psychotherapist deals with sickness of the soul, which cannot be seen through a microscope, cultured in a laboratory, or cured by injection. His methods have little of the concreteness or obvious empiricism of the physician. "He bandages no cuts, administers no pills, and carries no needle. He cures by talking and listening" (London, 1964, p. 3). Thus, the therapist is not a scientist in the true sense, even though he may use scientific methods in helping clients and in his research. He is a clinician and must apply and adapt knowledge and techniques to individual cases. The therapist's interpretation of knowledge available to him and the mode of application of techniques are highly individualized, subject to personal judgment, beliefs, and preferences.

Much of what the therapist does and why he does it cannot be understood outside a context of human values. Psychotherapy is certainly a value-laden activity. We intervene directly in the lives of our clients, often helping them change their behavior, their standards, and their views of themselves. We diagnose and thereby commit Thomas Szasz's sin of perpetuating the "myth of mental illness." We *conditionally* demonstrate our positive regard when clients act cooperatively. We select content for sessions according to our whims and moods. We treat the problems that we regard as important and ignore the ones that we consider unimportant. We work harder for some clients than we do for others. We pretend neutrality, objectivity, detachment—knowing full well that, although such a posture may be desirable and even helpful, many of our biases, personal opinions, and preferences continuously slip through an ambivalent guard who is not sure that being all that vigilant is even necessary.

Partly because of these value differences, some members of other professions view psychotherapists as quacks, practicing the black arts without regard for a knowledge base or for the requirements and expectations of society. This condition may continue until we begin to deal with several internal problems, including attention to ethical issues in the practice of counseling and psychotherapy.

In addition to the value conflicts and differences already noted, there is often a conflict among a therapist's loyalties to his clients, the employing institution, and the larger society. The state allows therapists to exist, social institutions employ them, and society encourages their activities. Because of these sanctions and support, therapists are expected to help people "adjust" to their environment. As Fish (1973, p. 150) notes, "Any therapy which turned people into revolutionaries would be rapidly condemned, discredited, and outlawed." Thus, therapists must conform to the roles and responsibilities assigned by society. They also perform services for the state that may conflict with their own sense of responsibility to the client. Some conflicts—for example, those between the individual and a social institution—cannot be completely reconciled, and the therapist's decision then will be based on his own sense of obligation, as well as on his preference for the standards or values that are in conflict.

We believe, and we will argue throughout this book, that the needs and welfare of clients should be the primary concern of all therapists. While recognizing that their responsibilities as citizens do not end when they put on the white coat, therapists must also recognize that their role does not include supporting and even implementing policies that cause misery for already troubled people. The therapist must work to change policies that restrict individual freedom, ignore human dignity, and deny due process. This may require more courage than some therapists have and involve more personal and professional risks than some therapists wish to chance. We believe, however, that a display of courage and risk taking will help therapists achieve the status they seek and, more important, will add credibility to the helping arts.

Therapy, Ethics, and Law

We do not suggest that therapists become legal experts, nor do we believe that they can look to the law to solve their professional problems. We do believe, however, that all counselors and psychotherapists should be sufficiently familiar with legal principles and legislation affecting their work to understand the legal climate in which they practice. In later chapters we will call attention to and provide illustrations of both illegal and unethical practices.

A precise delineation of all the legal ramifications of counseling and psychotherapy is difficult, because there is no uniform or national code of laws in the United States. Consequently, each state or territory has jurisdiction and regulatory power over the professions practicing within its geographical boundaries. Statutory laws dealing with such matters as licensure, malpractice, and privacy vary greatly from state to state and in some states are nonexistent. In 1985, for example, while all states had laws governing the private practice of psychology, only ten states had laws distinguishing between counseling and psychology and regulating the private practice of counseling.

As noted earlier, inconsistencies among laws pertaining to the helping professions compound the problem. As a consequence of this lack of uniformity, therapists have little to guide them in making decisions or in providing services that may have legal implications. Professional associations have not provided sufficient direction to practitioners in establishing basic principles and guidelines related to professional practice. Standards and codes are often wordy, confusing, and contradictory. Huckins (1968, p. 13), referring to legal issues in counseling, states that "although both law and ethical codes have in mind the assurance of moral and equitable behavior, they sometimes are at variance on how this can be achieved. . . . The practitioner is often caught between forces that seem to be in opposition. The collective conscience of his profession and his own moral convictions as a counselor may not always be in accord with legal dictates."

Consider the issue of confidentiality as an example: A twenty-two-year-old client reveals to a counselor that he is having sexual relations with two fourteen-year-old girls in the park near a school where he frequently pushes drugs. He readily admits that the girls are hooked and have become dependent on him. "They'll do anything I say," he brags. Numerous legal/

ethical issues are raised by this situation. Does the counselor report this client to law enforcement authorities? Ethical codes of
some professional associations are quite specific on this matter.
When a counselor determines that a client's behavior results in
clear and imminent danger to the client or others, the counselor
is expected to take direct action by informing the authorities.
Furthermore, in most states the counselor can be forced to
testify in court regarding information revealed by the client. On
the other hand, the counselor who reveals confidential information may face legal action brought by a client. A few states have
enacted laws enabling a client to sue a counselor for damages
when confidential information is revealed.

Judicial Decisions. The absence of law and unspecific
existing laws and regulations leave interpretation in the hands
of the courts. In the absence of statutes, courts must rely on
precedents or case law. While courts may be influenced by decisions in similar cases, the court is not bound by precedent unless it was established in its own state or unless the ruling principles have been laid down by the U.S. Supreme Court. Given
these conditions—varying statutes, conflicting court decisions,
and confusing professional standards—therapists now function
in a legal no-man's-land.

The effect that courts may have on the practice of counseling is described by Huckins (1968). He states that law is not
fixed and immutable, although its reliance on precedent may
cause it to appear so. Not only do legal bases—that is, legislative
acts and statutes—vary with cultural change, but also judicial decisions tend to reflect prevalent social attitudes. The law is a
part of the social process, subject to change and interpretation.
It affects and is affected by social mores and beliefs. Courts
have broad powers to interpret both the Constitution and legislative acts. This means that courts could, in fact, chart the
course of the helping professions and, furthermore, could promote or retard progress in counseling and psychotherapy.

Effects of Legislation. In an earlier section of this chapter, we described the rapid growth and acceptance of counseling
in our society during this century. Mental health has become a
national concern, and to some extent the provision of mental

health services has become a responsibility of the state. This concern is manifested through the provision of community mental health centers, mobile clinics, family and child counseling services, outreach programs, and various prevention programs. These developments have been accompanied by legislation that has a significant impact on the helping arts. To cite some examples, during the past thirty years Congress has passed the Vocational Rehabilitation Act, the Community Mental Health Centers Act, and acts establishing the Medicare and Medicaid programs. In addition, such legislation as the National Defense Education Act and numerous federal support programs provide assistance for counseling and psychological services for students in elementary and secondary schools. In the past ten years, ten states have enacted counselor licensure laws, describing the actions of counselors and defining the requirements for private practice.

Furthermore, during the past two decades, most states have enacted legislation that provides some support for mental health services in hospitals, schools and colleges, and community agencies. Such legislation has changed the concept of mental health services and has resulted in a shift of funding from private sources to public funds. Consequently, persons outside the profession now have become more involved with these services and have more control over them. Recent legislation and government policy suggest that the public will continue to support the work of counselors in treating such social ills as alcoholism, drug addiction, and crime and violence. All these developments have challenged the traditional role of therapists and have given new responsibilities to all helping professionals. The ensuing role confusion—along with a lack of agreement among professionals on what therapy is and a paucity of evidence on its benefits—has created a complex problem for counseling and psychotherapy. As more therapists move into institutions and programs supported by taxpayers, the profession will have to deal with the question of the effectiveness of therapy if it is to continue to receive financial support and legal acceptance.

A Professional Problem. A consideration of the preceding general problem forces a more ticklish issue into our discussion. The welter of confusion among the divergent schools of therapy, the questionable techniques, and the prevalence of Madison Avenue messiahs constitute not only a professional problem but also a professional embarrassment. Many therapeutic approaches that catch the public fancy have no scientific validity, and many "therapists" meet no recognized professional standards, nor do they appear to adhere to any code of ethics. It is doubtful that they could withstand even a most casual judicial appraisal. Many professionals are embarrassed by this disorderly condition, but few professional or legal moves have been made to improve it. Decisions must soon be made relative to competencies of therapists. The profession will have to decide not only what therapy is but also who can practice it. However the profession decides, or whether it decides to make the decision or leave it up to legislators or judges, it cannot delay the decision much longer.

Summary

Within the past few decades, the helping professions have gained a prominent position in American society. Counseling and psychotherapy, along with other helping crafts, are not only sanctioned by the state but also supported by a public that expects therapists to provide mental health care to large segments of society. Public awareness of and interest in mental health have been major factors in the growth and expansion of counseling and psychotherapy in education, medical treatment facilities, community mental health centers, and other publicly supported institutions. Private practitioners—psychologists, counselors, and psychiatrists—are now found in most American communities.

During the past decade, the state has assumed increasing responsibility for such social problems as drug abuse, alcoholism, and crime and violence and has relied heavily on counselors and psychotherapists as primary professionals in the treatment of these problems. Current trends suggest an expansion of counseling services and increased participation of therapists in all aspects of American life.

In short, society places considerable responsibility on therapists for treatment of a myriad of human and social problems. We believe that most therapists are qualified to deal with human and social problems and, furthermore, that their services are beneficial to individuals and to the larger society. We contend, however, that an analysis of the surfeit of approaches, as well as an examination of some current practices and practitioners, will reveal issues and problems that threaten the survival of the profession. We are concerned that the ethical dimension of counseling and psychotherapy has been too often ignored. Furthermore, the legal climate in which therapists work most certainly has implications for their services to clients.

In the chapters that follow, we examine and explicate these issues and problems and their professional implications.

2

Ethical
Theory
and
Decision
Making

A theory is a systematic way of organizing a body of knowledge into a meaningful perspective. Patterns of behavior and thought are simplified and structured so as to provide guidelines for action and make sense of complex phenomena. Whether operating at implicit or explicit levels, all therapists have an ethical theory. Very rarely is the theory concrete, specific, or clearly defined, but it nevertheless influences the way a therapist characteristically acts, his belief system, goals, strategies selected, and outcomes of his work with a client (Ajzen, 1973). Stefflre and Matheny (1968) also suggest that a client's behavior is affected by the counselor's behavior, which is in turn influenced by the theoretical orientation from which he operates.

There is, of course, a distinction between the theories espoused by a therapist and those actually used in practice. As Argyris and Schön (1974) have shown, any practitioner of architecture or psychotherapy will personally organize the profession's body of knowledge, normative standards, methods of practice, and ethical codes into a publicly espoused theory; when responding to situational cues and professional episodes, however, the practitioner usually will convert this "theoretical" thought into a more pragmatic "theory-in-use."

Perhaps more than a single theory, we are dealing with a collection of theoretical conceptions. Every therapist has an individual theory of metaphysics, or how the world works; a personal understanding of logic, or cause-effect relationships; an ontological theory to describe the meaning of human existence; a theory of epistemology, or how people develop, learn, and change; and a clearly personalized ethical theory about what is good and right and how we ought to act (Kottler, 1983). All therapists are thus practical philosophers, constantly refining their theories in light of new experiences and evidence, changing their beliefs and values as they interact and often clash with those of colleagues and clients. Benjamin (1974, p. 53) has summarized the ever changing nature of a therapist's ethical theory: "Our clients in the helping interview do not leave our values unchallenged. By examining their own, they may be challenging ours. While insisting that we define for them what is right and wrong, they may be groping for their own ethical standards. It is impossible to tell them that we hold no values, for we do. Neither can we legitimately claim that our values are of no concern to them. We may prefer not to disclose them outright, thus leaving our clients to ponder and guess. Alternatively, we may state our values, assuming they will be adopted by our clients, and feel hurt and resentful when they are rejected."

Ethics and Philosophy

Ethics is a branch of philosophy that is concerned primarily with how and why people make moral decisions (Daubner and Daubner, 1970). It is a search for principles to guide decisions concerning what is right and wrong, and it provides guidelines for solving moral problems. Philosophy, as a discipline, can be a very intellectual, abstract, and theoretically dry approach to dealing with conflicts, with little practical value and almost no relevance to the real world. Consequently, the practitioner may justifiably wonder what Aristotle, Thomas Aquinas, or Immanuel Kant has to do with making his world a bit more comprehensible. On the other hand, a discussion of philosophical principles and ethical concepts can be an instructive method for laying a foundation on which to build a personal theory of ethics.

Russell (1959) defines philosophy as the attempt to answer questions critically and explore uncertainty. The knowledge that is studied in philosophy is the core of the study of the sciences. "The essential characteristic of philosophy, which makes it a study distinct from science, is *criticism*. It examines critically the principles employed in science and in daily life; it searches out any inconsistencies there may be in those principles, and it only accepts them when, as the result of a critical inquiry, no reason for rejecting them has appeared" (pp. 149–150).

In his "Call to Armchairs," Miller (1983) reminds us of the value of philosophical inquiry for practicing therapists. Because of our stubborn determination to keep the field empirical, we have sadly neglected ethics as well as other branches of philosophy. First we deluded ourselves that psychotherapy is ethically neutral and so hardly requires a detailed study of moral judgments. Then we acknowledged that moral issues are certainly part of our field but are largely subjective, irrational elements that ought to be disregarded. Miller believes that philosophical analysis, the most rigorous form of intellectual activity, ought once again to come into prominence as the tool for reconciling differing moral and theoretical positions.

All therapists are not only philosophers but *ethical* philosophers, in the sense that they hold beliefs about the nature of human beings, what is good and bad for human beings, and how the "good" can best be promoted. Drane (1982) further stresses the importance of philosophy by showing how the therapist's work intersects with the realm of ethical issues:

1. The therapeutic relationship is a contractual agreement in which the therapist attempts to influence a client, but without making his or her own belief system explicit. When a

therapist is asked by curious clients how he feels or what he thinks or believes, his responses often involve attempts to guard his true values.

2. Therapists use the jargon of ethical philosophy as part of their heritage. In every session attention is paid to choices, beliefs, values, oughts, shoulds, and *being* in the world.

3. Many therapeutic efforts involve the development of character. That is, therapists exhibit the qualities of honesty, trustworthiness, genuineness, sincerity—attributes that they hope a client will choose for himself.

4. Therapists delve into the roots of conscience. They help clients accept responsibility for their acts, to be accountable without destructive guilt.

5. Finally, much of what clients experience as problems are in fact ethical dilemmas regarding "What ought I to do?"

Ethical Versus Legal Approaches

Law, whether enacted by a legislature or established by a court, is designed to govern the affairs of man. Laws tell us what we can and cannot do; and if we do something that is prohibited, and get caught, laws tell us what is likely to happen to us afterward. Every individual is granted the right to challenge a law and act in a way he feels is most appropriate as long as he is willing to suffer the consequences of his actions and accept responsibility for his decisions. In his influential essay "Civil Disobedience" (1849), Henry David Thoreau provides examples of the conflicts between personal ethics and societal law and insists that the principled individual has a duty to disobey unjust laws. Dostoevsky's fictional character Raskolnikov stands in haughty disdain for the law, since his personal sense of rightness is exempt: "Ordinary men have to live in submission, have no right to transgress the law, because, don't you see, they are ordinary. But extraordinary men have a right to commit any crime and to transgress the law in any way, just because they are extraordinary" (Dostoevsky, [1866] 1950, p. 234).

Ethical judgments do not enjoy the degree of precision that legal issues do in deciding what is a correct act and what is not. In a democracy the law is designed to apply to all members of a given population; that is, citizens of a state, county, or country. In contrast, each person has his own set of ethical principles. Although many of the attitudes and feelings about what is right or wrong are inherited from parents, shaped by siblings and peers, modified by experience, taught by teachers and ministers, and imbibed from television, radio, novels, and magazines, an individual, as he matures, ultimately develops a personal "style" of ethics.

Ethics covers the realm of conduct not covered under the law. While there is overlap between them, since immoral acts can be legal or illegal and illegal acts can be moral or immoral, each subject approaches human behavior differently. The law is formally prescribed, enacted, interpreted, enforced. Formal consequences-punishments are imposed when the law is disobeyed. In the realm of ethics, however, violations usually do not entail statutory penalties. There are exceptions, of course. For instance, breaches of ethics may also violate the law; and at institutions such as West Point or the University of Virginia, a student may suffer consequences as the result of honor code violations for cheating or lying or other immoral acts.

Traditionally, the roles of law and ethics as governing rules were both contained in religious bodies. The Old Testament, the Koran, and other religious documents clearly embrace rules that involve legal matters ("Thou shall not kill") and moral issues ("Thou shall not covet thy neighbor's wife"). The "Word of God" was once held to be so sacred and inscrutable that Divine Law functioned as the civil and moral power for instilling a sense of duty, obligation, and obedience in a citizen. Brennan (1973) reminds us that we are living in a secular age, perhaps the first culture in the history of the world that is agnostic. We now have division of labor among legislators, judges, and clergy. And each person is held responsible for developing a unique style of ethics that meets the criteria of various professional, social, religious, and ethnic groups. Nevertheless, personal ethics do intersect with an established societal norm of right and wrong that forbids certain acts and sanctions others (Fried, 1979).

There is not necessarily a perfect correlation between what one believes and how one acts. A therapist may genuinely *believe* that his professional services are a good thing and that economically disadvantaged people as well as his affluent clients should have the opportunity to benefit from his services. But whether he is willing to act on the basis of his moral beliefs is another story. How often do we see a Park Avenue therapist setting up shop in Harlem in lieu of his Tuesday golf game? There is, therefore, a qualitative difference between "attitudinal morality" and "behavioral morality"—a difference between what one believes, what one says he believes, and what one does on the basis of his beliefs. A person who argues for the necessity of human equality and freedom, sexual and racial equality, client rights and therapist responsibilities, and evaluation and accountability sounds impressive on the podiums of convention programs and at political dinners and cocktail parties; but meaningful results are not accomplished unless these theories are put into practice. Similarly, the philosophical issues, ethical conflicts, and legal dilemmas discussed in this book are just so many words unless the reader is sufficiently motivated to do something to change his behavior in the direction of professional growth and ethical development and responsibility.

Three Approaches to Ethics

Ethical theorists and philosophers have struggled with the problems of the human condition throughout the history of civilization. Questions of obligations, conscience, human freedom, and the process by which one ought to act have been debated in the arenas of the Roman Senate and the United States Congress. At this moment, in various spots around the globe, men are killing each other because they believe they are morally justified. Ethical issues are not merely intellectual exercises of academia but often life-and-death struggles. Understanding the work of predecessors will give us a background on which to build an individual course of moral action that will stand the test of time and guide us in our personal and professional lives.

To illustrate the wide range of opinion that exists in the

field on even the most basic of questions—"What is ethics?"—we have chosen three approaches that seem to us especially relevant for contemporary psychology: hedonism, self-realization theories, and moral development theories. For the reader who is interested in pursuing the subject further, an anthology of approaches to ethics has been compiled by Jones, Sontag, Beckner, and Fogelin (1977).

The hedonist position, supported by the utilitarian philosophies of John Stuart Mill, Jeremy Bentham, Henry Sidgwick, and G. E. Moore, and by the instinctual-psychoanalytical influences of Sigmund Freud, is perhaps the best-known approach to ethics: "If it feels good, do it!" One does not have to be well versed in philosophical definitions of absolutism, intentionality, or utility to understand that human beings are motivated by what feels good. The behaviorist applications of reinforced principles are in fact based on the judicious use of rewards to give the subject immediate gratification. Nevertheless, the commonsense hedonist approach to ethics has far-reaching implications for understanding human behavior and making ethical decisions.

The second theoretical orientation presented, self-realization, is enjoying increased popularity since the rebirth of the humanist movement. Essentially viewing man as innately good and creative and able to make ethically right decisions, the self-realizationists encourage the maximization of human freedom, choice making, trust, and optimism. Aristotle, humanists such as Abraham Maslow and Erich Fromm, and existentialists such as Rollo May will be mentioned in this context.

The third theory presented, the moral development position, is no stranger to the fields of education and psychology. Jean Piaget and Lawrence Kohlberg, educators and psychologists by profession, have sought to compose a developmental model for viewing ethical behavior. They have succeeded in integrating moral philosophy, the case-study method, and psychological research into specific stages of ethical development.

Hedonism. The hedonistic approach to ethics encompasses the philosophies of a diverse range of individuals. Essentially, the utilitarians Sidgwick, Mill, Bentham, and Moore, as well as Freud in his instinctual theory, view the worth of an act in terms of its potential to produce pleasure. Sympathy is seen as the basic and universal sentiment that influences man's ethical behavior.

Jeremy Bentham (1748–1832), the first of the utilitarians, developed a problem-solving method for reaching ethically correct decisions based on pain and pleasure as the "two sovereign masters" that govern man's behavior (Bentham, [1810] 1977). Man is guided in what he ought to do by the pursuit of pleasure and the avoidance of pain. Thus, an action is ethically right if it brings pleasure and wrong if it brings pain. This basic statement, the "principle of utility," forms the basis of hedonistic ethics. *Every* human action can be approved or disapproved according to its *utility* in promoting or opposing happiness. This cut-and-dried decision process is a useful concept in analyzing one's behavior and making decisions about how one should act.

Interestingly, Bentham had no concern for "society" or "community" in his ethical theory, because the "community" is nothing but a collection of individuals with interests. The interest of the community, then, is the sum of all the interests of the members that compose it. He therefore attempted to resolve the historic conflict between the One and the Many by protecting the sacred rights of the individual.

In Bentham's model the measurable value of a pleasure or a pain is modified by (1) its intensity; (2) its duration; (3) its certainty or uncertainty; (4) its propinquity or remoteness; (5) its fecundity, or chance of being repeated; (6) its purity, or chance that it will not be followed by its opposite; and (7) its extent, or number of persons involved or affected. By using these variables and their relation to pain and pleasure, one can obtain the sum of all values of pleasure on one side and the values of pain on the other. The balance then indicates the "goodness" or "badness" of the act.

Carkhuff's (1973) problem-solving system seems to be based on Bentham's model. Carkhuff develops value hierarchies from alternative courses, assigns positive and negative quantitative values to a choice, and allows the person to figure a product of the value items for each alternative. One can then assess

how effective each course of action is in facilitating each value
item. The highest positive total equals the preferred choice.

John Stuart Mill (1806–1873) made fundamental revisions in Bentham's work. Mill recognized that not all pleasures
are created equal, and he attempted to correct for this discrep-
ancy. In his view, mental pleasures are superior to bodily pleasures because they are safer, more permanent, and less costly. In
Mill's words, "It is better to be a human being dissatisfied than
a pig satisfied; better to be a Socrates dissatisfied than a fool
satisfied. And if the fool [and] the pig are of a different opinion, it is because they only know their own side of the question.
The other party of the comparison knows both sides" ([1863]
1977, p. 349). Mill also recognized the importance of conscience,
the trait that separates man from the other species, and incorporated it into the utilitarian framework.

Henry Sidgwick's (1838–1900) contribution to utilitarian ethics was his attempt to develop a rational method to determine what individual human beings ought to do. On the basis
of a historical study of ethical theory, he concluded that three
methods exist:

1. *Egoistic hedonism.* Each individual should pursue his own
   pleasure, his own self-interest.
2. *Universalistic hedonism.* Individuals should attempt to secure "the greatest good for the greatest number" (the basic
   utilitarian position).
3. *Intuitionism.* Individuals possess an innate moral sense,
   which should serve as the basis for ethical decisions.

Sidgwick essentially rejected both egoistic hedonism and
intuitionism. He attempted to show, however, that universalistic
hedonism (utilitarianism) has a relationship to intuitionism but
is more basic, since the doctrine of common sense rests on the
principles of utilitarianism.

Sidgwick ([1874] 1977) said that absolute moral truths
exist but are too abstract and need to be made more explicit.
Consider, for example, the axiom that the therapist should
have the client's best interest in mind for any intervention he

may use. Any therapist would regard that as an absolute moral truth relevant to his field, but how may it be interpreted? What does "best interest" mean? Who decides whether a specific action is in a client's "best interest"? To make this universal moral truth more meaningful and capable of being enforced and to enable the actor to know whether he is unethical or ethical, the term must be more explicitly formulated.

G. E. Moore (1873-1958) postulated utilitarian concepts of morality and restated the universal categorical imperative: All men pursue pleasure and avoid pain; therefore, the pursuit of pleasure is the sole good. However, "good" is a simple, indefinable, nonnatural property, and any attempt to define it is impossible. Therefore, like A. J. Ayer (1978) in his theory of logical positivism, Moore concluded that one cannot formulate an all-encompassing ethical theory.

Moore viewed the ethical philosopher not as a dictator who tells humans how they should act or what is right and wrong, good and bad, but as a detective who tries to answer certain fundamental questions: What is an ethical action? What is good or bad? Are there general characteristics of all right actions? What is unique about right action? What is common and unique to all good things?

Moore's precision in defining basic ethical terms was valuable in pinning down many abstract notions. For example, in his explanation of "rightness," he specifically described the characteristics of and differences between right and wrong acts: "A voluntary action is right whenever and only when the agent could *not,* even if he had chosen, have done any other action [that] would have caused more pleasure than the one he did do; and . . . a voluntary action is wrong whenever and only when the agent *could,* if he had chosen, have done some other action instead [that] would have caused more pleasure than the one he did do" (Moore, [1912] 1969, pp. 11-12).

Sigmund Freud (1856-1939) is not remembered particularly for his contributions to ethical philosophy. Primarily concentrating on the fields of medicine and psychology, Freud revolutionized the helping professions. He was, however, influenced by philosophers such as Franz Brentano and Friedrich

Nietzsche, and he did spend a great deal of time attempting to integrate philosophy with medicine. His theory of psychoanalysis includes two moral subconcepts: the "pleasure principle" and the "superego."

According to Freud's instinctual theory, like the theories of the other hedonists, every action may be tested according to the relative level of pleasure that it brings. This pleasure principle (that is, absence of pain and unpleasantness or strong feelings of pleasure) decides the purpose of life and motivates happiness. Man can avoid suffering and attain pleasure by keeping his instinctual (id) drives in check and through the economics of the libido. The superego, the guardian of moral prohibitions, is the moral influence on man's behavior. Acting in a parental and societal role, the superego brings to the surface feelings of guilt and shame as a result of internal struggles and conflicts over ethical issues. "We are threatened with suffering from three directions: from our own body, which is doomed to decay and dissolution and which cannot even do without pain and anxiety as warning signals; from the external world, which may rage against us with overwhelming and merciless forces of destruction; and finally from our relations to other men" (Freud, [1895] 1958, p. 440). Not content with merely identifying the nature of the problem, Freud also sought to contribute suggestions for the solution; that is, he considered several methods by which men pursue pleasure and avoid suffering:

1. Controlling the instincts by higher physical states minimizes lack of pleasure and protects against suffering. (Meditation, aerobics, and running are contemporary examples of systematic attempts to exercise this method.)
2. Shifting instincts through defense mechanisms, such as sublimation, avoids confrontation with frustration. Substitute gratifications of fantasy and imagination are used.
3. Escaping from reality is a means of avoiding suffering. Freud classified religion as an example of mass delusions to escape reality. It depresses the value of life, restricts choice, curtails freedom, and distorts reality.
4. The "art of living" is the most desired mechanism to pur-

sue pleasure. It is the only one that makes the individual independent of the universe and fate and does not avoid or
turn away from the external world. This is, of course, the
main goal of all therapies: to teach the art of living.

Self-Realization Theories. The proponents of the self-
realization approach to ethics view man as an innately good
creature who has the ability to grow naturally into a moral
being and to make ethical decisions that are good and right.
Aristotle (384–322 B.C.) is perhaps the most representative
spokesman of the classical humanistic notion of man's striving
for rightness. He reasoned that "Every art and every inquiry,
and similarly every action and pursuit, is thought to aim at
some good; and for this reason the good has rightly been declared to be that [at] which all things aim" (Ross, 1954, p. 3).
Like the hedonists, Aristotle had a notion of the absolute good
of all men—the attainment of happiness. However, man strives
for the highest good not by egoistic hedonism but by natural
virtues, which are contained, according to Aristotle, in superior
men. Traits such as courage, friendship, and justice are those
that motivate man to act in ethical ways.

     Abraham Maslow (1908–1970) constructed what can be
considered the most complete and relevant self-realization theory of our time. Maslow, perhaps more than any other twentieth-
century theoretician, was responsible for the growth in humanistic science. He believed, as do the sociobiologists, that the inner core of man is instinctively and intrinsically ethical. The
moral principles common to all men naturally lead them to
make good and right decisions. Any badness or immorality is
accounted for by society's triumph over man's instincts. The
virtues intrinsic in human nature, such as truth, beauty, justice,
joy, serenity, love, unselfishness, courage, honesty, and kind-
ness, lead one toward self-actualization and provide the potential for becoming fully human.

     By merging the case-study approach with scientific meth-
odology, Maslow concentrated on studying the "best" people of
the human race—the ethical, successful, striving individuals who
have reached a state of self-actualization. He concluded, as Aris-

totle did, that by such an approach one can determine the ultimate morality that is possible. Thus, the ethical standards of
self-actualized persons, the healthy, are the basis for a naturalistic value system of good and bad: "Instead of cultural relativity,
I am implying that there are basic, underlying, human standards
that are cross-cultural—which transcend cultures and which are
broadly human" (quoted in Goble, 1970, p. 92). These characteristics of man, although unique in their manifestations for
each individual, are all intrinsically good. The individuals who
are fully functioning ethical beings, who have developed their
potential and reached a state of self-actualization, act as models
of morality and success for all of mankind. Such an ethical
being, according to the humanist, looks inward to find the most
natural spiritual guide for behavior. The self-actualized person
is responsible, caring, and immune to others' approval when
making hard decisions.

    In addition to his theoretical formulations, Maslow at-
tempted to support his claims of universal inborn ability, or
"the wisdom of the body," by citing research by Dove (1935),
whose study on the individuality of the nutritive instincts "is
pregnant with implications for value theory" (Maslow, 1962, p.
151). Chickens vary widely in their choices of foods when left
to their own devices. Good choosers become stronger; bad
choosers become weaker. When the food selected by the good
choosers is then forced on the bad choosers, they too become
strong and healthy. "That is, good choosers can choose better
than bad choosers what is better for the bad choosers themselves" (p. 151). Similarly, Maslow suggested, humans who are
good choosers (that is, self-actualized) should be the judges and
developers of morality for the whole human race. Maslow further believed that values are intrinsically developed from within and chosen by the person. Therapy is a search for values, an
attempt to unroot the deepest, most intrinsic values in the
client.

    Erich Fromm (1900–1980), the neopsychoanalytical the-
orist, also contributed to humanistic ethics in his book *Man for
Himself* (1947). Fromm based morality on man's intrinsic ability to reason and postulated that the sources of norms for ethi-

cal conduct are found in human nature, in man's powers to discern good from bad or right from wrong. No external authority can dictate values to an individual. The humanistic conscience, the internalized reaction of the total personality in its capacity to be fully human, is the source of moral regulation and decision making. Fromm's concept of conscience is as "the guardian of integrity." It is the "voice of our true selves which summons us back to ourselves, to live productively, to develop fully and harmoniously—that is, to become what we potentially are" (1947, p. 159).

Running parallel with the humanist school is the existentialist approach to morality. Existentialism as a philosophy that views experience as the core of meaningful existence was first expounded in Europe by such writers as Søren Kierkegaard, Paul Tillich, and Jean-Paul Sartre. Among contemporary Americans, Rollo May (1958, 1967, 1983), Carl Rogers (1951, 1961), Dugald Arbuckle (1965), and Irvin Yalom (1980) are exemplary champions of the existentialist cause as it relates to counseling and psychotherapy.

The existentialist regards man as a responsible being who is born anxious in an unknown world. Confronted by universal laws, ethical codes, and societal rules, the individual feels lost and adrift. He strives for authenticity by feeling, thinking, and acting on the choices available to him. The existentialist position stresses the individual's freedom to choose a course of action. Each person stands free and alone—either before God (according to Kierkegaard, as well as Karl Jaspers, Martin Buber, and Gabriel Marcel) or before his own conscience (according to Sartre and Albert Camus). As Amato (1982) has shown, Camus and Sartre both describe the existentialist being's fight for freedom and autonomy as he resists attempts by others to create a collective ethics and deals instead with his own history and future. "Man is condemned to be free . . . to carry the weight of the whole world on his shoulders; he is responsible for the world and for himself as a way of being" (Sartre , [1943] 1965, p. 277).

Each person gives personal value to things in the world; each therapist gives weight to certain beliefs and concepts deemed more useful and ignores those that are less helpful. Each person, therefore, constructs his own morality by his ethical choices, his options, and the consequences that result.

Rollo May applies the philosophy of existentialism to a theory of morality for the therapist. According to May (1967), all personality problems and emotional disturbances are related to the ultimate moral question "How shall I live?"; therefore, therapy is by its very nature geared toward moral adjustment. When the therapist attempts to cut the therapeutic process short by imposing his own ethical standards on the client, the experience will be short-circuited, because the client is robbed of his inalienable right to develop his own moral system. Thus, clients have the capacity, if allowed, to make their own decisions and choose what is right for them. The therapist's chief role, then, is to facilitate free expression in his clients, as evidenced by spontaneity, originality, genuineness, authenticity, and moral freedom. Ultimately, a creative system of ethics would be evolved to guide the person's behavior.

Moral Development Theories. The moral development point of view is more an outgrowth of psychology than of traditional philosophy. Whenever possible, proponents of this point of view rely on scientific research and case-history observation rather than introspective "armchair" thought. Although certain philosophical aspects of ethics have been merged with the developmental theory, it remains essentially a product of physiology and psychology. This interdisciplinary attack on the problem of ethics is useful in unifying and synthesizing the strengths and contributions from several different fields.

Jean Piaget and Lawrence Kohlberg are the most representative proponents of the moral development view. They believe that morality is not a collection of virtues such as honesty, sincerity, loyalty, and generosity, but an idea of justice that matures as a function of development and experience. The young child relates to the world through a primitive morality, one grounded in absolutes that do not generalize to all circumstances in the real world. Generally, more sophisticated and higher-order stages of morality evolve, until the individual has the capacity to make ethical decisions consistent with his beliefs. This *ethic of justice* is central to the moral stages and principles representative of this position.

Piaget, the influential genetic psychologist, began the study of moral development (which Kohlberg was later to refine) by intensively observing young children. By studying the play, games, and interaction of children and by conducting sensitive interviews, Piaget was able to differentiate the moral thinking of young children from older children. He noticed that the sense of justice became qualitatively more refined as the children grew older. Younger children, who think "heteronomously," tend to obey the rules laid down by external authorities, whereas older children develop personally meaningful moral codes.

Piaget's theory of moral development is one of the components of his total theory of cognitive development and perception. He specifies three factors that retard moral development. First, the child from three to eight years old confuses moral rules with physical laws. He views all rules as absolute, fixed, and external because of his "realism"—his inability to differentiate between subjectivity and objectivity—and his "egocentricity"—viewing himself as the center of the universe. The younger child cannot distinguish between his experiences and those of others. He views parents, adults, and other authorities as omnipotent and sacred, deserving of "unilateral respect." Piaget confirmed his hypotheses in his "marble studies." He found that children believe that the laws and rules of marbles have been handed down by some divine force (God, father, president) since the beginning of time, when, in fact, the game is totally regulated from within the childhood culture.

Piaget specifies six characteristics of moral development that distinguish younger from older children: intentionality, relativism, independence of sanctions, the use of punishment, reciprocity, and a naturalistic view of misfortune. The dimensions increase with age and are constant throughout all cultures. Piaget ingeniously discovered from watching children's play that the game of marbles is one of the few and simplest social interactions in which the morality is created and elaborated entirely by children. In this game adult intervention is held to a minimum, and the child's moral behavior can be studied in its purest form, unpolluted by external parental influence.

On the basis of his investigation, Piaget (1932, p. 13) concluded that "all morality consists in a system of rules, and the essence of all morality is to be sought for in the respect which the individual acquires for these rules." Reflecting on the specific codes of ethics in marble playing, Piaget discovered the distinction between the "consciousness" and the "practice" of ethics: "With regard to game rules, there are two phenomena which it is particularly easy to study: first, the *practice* of rules, the way in which children of different ages effectively apply rules; second, the *consciousness* of rules, the idea which children of different ages form of the character of these game rules, whether of something obligatory and sacred or of something subject to their own choice, whether of heteronomy or autonomy" (pp. 14–15).

In an earlier experimental study of children's moral character and the ethic of honesty, by Hartshorne and May (1928, 1930), this distinction between the theory and the practice of ethics was confounded. The subjects of this study, children in a Sunday school, were given a test that they could pass only if they cheated. The researchers concluded:

1. There are no "honest" or "dishonest" people. Everyone cheats at something some of the time.
2. People who cheat in one situation will not necessarily cheat in any other. There is no character trait indicative of cheating.
3. People's verbalizations of what they believe is ethical have nothing to do with the way they act.
4. Cheating depends on the degree of risk in being caught. Noncheaters are not more honest than cheaters—just more cautious.
5. Honesty is influenced by the situational factors of group approval and sanction of the behavior.
6. Honesty is relative to a particular social class or peer group.

This relativistic view of morality, which remained the accepted belief of the field until Piaget's and, later, Kohlberg's investigations, implied that behavior is determined solely by situational factors and group pressures rather than by internal regulation and conscience. Hartshorne and May concluded that different groups operate from different systems of morality and that there are no universal human values. They further concluded that one cannot predict cheating in various situations and that there is no such thing as an ethical or unethical person, "but rather a normal distribution of honest behavior around an average of moderate cheating" (McCandless and Evans, 1973, p. 275).

Hartshorne and May, concerned with *behavioral* observations of children's moral conduct, sought to determine whether people violate ethical principles and in what circumstances. Piaget, in contradistinction, was interested primarily in the *reasoning* that leads the child to choose a particular course of action. Each of these aspects of the study of morality is important and should not be ignored. Moral *behavior* may be situation specific relative to circumstances involved, whereas moral *reasoning* is composed of invariant developmental stages that remain absolute across cultures and individuals.

Kohlberg (1958, 1964, 1971), strongly influenced by Piaget's developmental theory, continued the refinement of moral theory with many creative innovations of his own. In contrast to the relativist position of Hartshorne and May, Kohlberg's theory of ethics stresses the universal and absolute nature of moral judgments. The same ethics apply to all people in all situations. All humans, including young children, are moral philosophers. Parents and adults rarely listen to a child's ethical theory because they are preoccupied with molding the child to fit into their own standards of ethics. Kohlberg describes the behavior of his four-year-old son, who became a vegetarian for six months in protest over the cruelty of killing animals. In spite of his parents' insistence that there is a qualitative difference between justified and unjustified killing, the child adhered to his personal belief system of internally developed ethical standards.

Kohlberg's greatest contribution to the field of ethics is his construction of moral stages of development. Basing his study on the moral-stage theories of Piaget (1932) and Baldwin

(1906), Kohlberg analyzed the underlying thoughts revealed in children's interactions and validated Piaget's work in a comprehensive system of discrete levels and stages. His interpretation of the evidence is as follows: "The stages of moral thinking may not directly represent learning of patterns of verbalization in the culture. Instead, they may represent spontaneous products of the child's effort to make sense out of his experience in a complex social world, each arising sequentially from its predecessors" (1964, p. 402).

Kohlberg and Piaget agree that moral development, like cognitive development, is a function of maturation within a context of age-related experience. In the tradition of the self-realization theorists, they believe in the innate goodness of man. If the child is allowed to develop naturally, he will become an ethical being. Kohlberg (1971) has converted this premise into an approach to moral education. He suggests that teachers (or therapists) view the child as an individual moral philosopher with an organized pattern of thought. Rather than impose a system on the child, the teacher can stimulate the child's active organization of his own experience.

On the basis of longitudinal and cross-cultural studies of children in a dozen countries as well as in his own experimental "Cluster School," Kohlberg concludes that teachers and counselors can best promote ethical behavior by (1) exposing people to higher stages of moral reasoning; (2) presenting irreconcilable ethical conflicts that lead to dissatisfaction with current, more primitive levels of thinking; and (3) creating a therapeutic atmosphere that permits open dialogue (see Kohlberg and Wasserman, 1980). Ideally, these conditions may be generated within the context of therapy sessions as well.

The "synoptic" approach to ethics proposed by Munk (1977) is also developmental in its conception of moral thinking. Essentially an empirical philosophy, the synoptic position attempts to avoid the fragmentary, reductionistic, nit-picking overemphasis of the logical positivists and language analysts who ignore the realities of moral life. In an effort to be synthesizing, synoptic philosophy combines developmental concepts of the human innate potential for moral decency with the vital enrichment process that can only come from personal effort and discipline. It is thus both humanistic and rational in its scope.

Like Kohlberg, Munk organized the human sense of "oughtness" into a developmental model of conscience, with each stage progressively more sophisticated. At the most advanced stage, the individual is able to use intuitive and reasoning processes to make moral decisions. Without this statement of moral ideal, "especially in terms of sincerity, honesty, truthfulness, and the aim at perfection as excellence, there can be no creativity in any of the great realms of human achievement. . . . Here then, at last, we can safely rest our case for the primacy of the moral factor" (Munk, 1977, p. 389).

McCandless and Evans (1973), in their textbook on human development, state that the concept of reciprocity—that is, mutual respect and trust for the other person's point of view—provides the basis for moral justice. Hoffman (1970), another contemporary developmental theorist, indicates that the healthy, well-adjusted, moral person has the following characteristics: he conforms within "sensible" limits, perceives authority as rational and fair, is able to inhibit inappropriate impulses when necessary, and is considerate of others. Hoffman (1970, pp. 277–278) further specifies the following indicators of moral identification in human development:

1. *Internalized moral code.* The individual has the ability to resist temptation. He will not engage in unethical practices even if he knows that he cannot be detected. He is motivated to please himself rather than others.
2. *Sense of guilt.* The person feels bad when he does something wrong.
3. *Personal standards.* The person relies on his own beliefs and moral standards rather than on an externally imposed set of standards.
4. *Responsibility for actions.* The person accepts responsibility for the consequences of his behavior.

In Search of a Personal Style of Ethics

The regulation of all therapist behavior is based entirely on a belief system concerning what is right for a particular client. Since the core of a therapist's system of what is right and wrong, good and bad, effective and ineffective, appropriate and inappropriate is based on a philosophical ethical system, this value system must be developed to optimal levels.

Kelley (1972) suggests a more challenging way of approaching ethical concerns than establishing minimal levels of acceptable behavior for a given professional practice. For Kelley creative morality goes beyond limits and aims for personal rather than external meaning. The individual thus moves toward "an ethics of risk" and away from an "ethics of caution." Instead of worrying about getting caught for doing something one is not supposed to do, and merely conforming to established standards, therapists should attempt to press for "individual growth and institutional change" (p. 173). Kelley urges the practitioner to consider the importance of individuality, creative expression, and working for change and dynamic growth rather than unconditional passive acceptance of norms.

Browne (1973) deplores the ubiquitous "morality trap" —the irrational belief that one *must* obey an ethical code created by someone else—and encourages the individual to reassess all relevant consequences of personal action and construct a personal morality to guide behavior: "When you decide to take matters into your own hands, someone may ask you, 'Who do you think you are? Who are *you* to decide for yourself in the face of society and centuries of moral teachings?' The answer is simple: You are you, the person who will live with the consequences of what you do. No one else can be responsible, because no one else will experience the consequences of your actions as you will. If you are wrong, *you* will suffer for it. If you're right, you will find happiness. You *have* to be the one to decide. 'Who are you to know?' It's your future at stake. You *have* to know" (p. 59).

The universal or absolute morality created by philosophers, judges, and politicians is not necessarily compatible with a personal morality. To blindly follow ethical codes without questioning their personal relevance is to continually live up to others' expectations for how one ought to act. This blind obedience is responsible for some of the world's most immoral actions, as all wars and mass human atrocities will attest.

To aid an individual in developing a style of ethics, we list here several guidelines—in the form of questions—for examining the moral rules one lives by. These questions have evolved from our own experiences and the many significant contributions made by the philosophers described in this chapter.

1.   Is this moral rule or principle devised by others or society to restrain you, or was it developed by you to better yourself?
2.   Are you acting on the basis of a rule because it has always been there, or is it one you have determined on the basis of your self-awareness, knowledge, and goals?
3.   Are the payoffs you get (rewards and punishments) from obeying a rule undefined, abstract, and intangible, or do they bring you specific happiness?
4.   Is the morality approved by others or tailored to your own needs?
5.   Is the morality aimed against yourself or does it promote your own self-interests?
6.   What would you be willing to do for money? (Agree to see a client even though you cannot help him?)
7.   In what circumstances would you lie to a client?
8.   When would you divulge confidential information? (To save a life?)
9.   To what extent would you practice something that you are not qualified to practice or in which you lack competence?
10.   To what extent will you obey professional codes of ethics, society's laws, or institutional policies if they are incompatible with your own?
11.   Under what circumstances would you divulge test or record information?
12.   How tolerant are you of colleagues' unethical practices? Under what circumstances would you turn someone in?

13. How would you remedy a situation if you found out that you had made a mistake or a wrong diagnosis?
14. To what extent would you accept responsibility for negligence or errors?
15. What do you need to know before you experiment with a new method?
16. To what extent do you impose your own morality on clients?
17. How do you deal with transference and countertransference?
18. How much of yourself do you commit to your work?
19. To what extent do you evaluate your effectiveness?

In addition, as an aid to ethical decision making, a therapist may adopt the following guidelines:

1. List the crises and conflicts that you fear most. (Common fears include breaching confidentiality or becoming emotionally involved with a client. Others are mentioned in subsequent chapters.)
2. Try to work through in your mind or on paper exactly how you would think and feel in those situations and what you would do.
3. Ask yourself whether you are satisfied with your reactions and ability to handle the situations and with your ethical decision-making skills.

We anticipate that most people are not totally proficient in all areas of ethical functioning. There is much work to be done to achieve greater ethical responsibility. The ground rule for the practitioner is: If one has a specific, responsible rationale for a given behavior, can defend it as justifiable under the circumstances, and the results turn out favorably, one is in the clear. If, however, the result turns out poorly and somebody complains or files suit, the same action may be construed as irresponsible, unethical, incompetent, or illegal.

If a person can meaningfully integrate some of the ethical philosophy, theory, and principles contained in this chapter, he should have the necessary knowledge to begin developing a personal style of ethics. By committing himself to upgrade his ethical behavior and working diligently to assess his current levels of functioning, desired goals, and courses of action necessary to meet moral responsibilities to himself, his clients, and his profession, the therapist can refine his competencies and protect himself against outside interference, legal suits, and a guilty conscience.

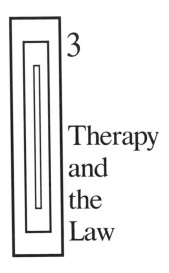

3

Therapy
and
the
Law

During the past decade, the psychological helping professions have grown steadily, both in scope and influence. This growth has resulted in a need to understand the interaction of ethics and law as they affect therapist activities and client-therapist relationships. This chapter examines several legal problems and issues pertinent to the practice of counseling and psychotherapy. We will focus on areas where legal obligations seem clear as well as on those where the boundaries are unmarked and uncertain. We will deal with modes of treatment and therapist-client relationships that may present legal problems for the therapist. This chapter will also suggest some general principles that can be helpful as guidelines for all therapists.

Types of Laws Governing Therapists

Contrary to popular opinion, law is not cut and dried, definite and certain, or clear and precise. To paraphrase Foster (1975), law invariably expresses compromise; it seeks to recognize, reconcile, and delimit competing claims and interests, in accordance with the predominant values of a given place and time. Law provides few definite answers, and almost every rule has its exceptions. Moreover, there is no general body of law covering the helping professions. Several court decisions and pertinent statutes deal directly with special aspects of counseling and psychotherapy and, in some instances, describe how therapists should perform their services. In addition, some general legislation dealing with such social problems as mental health, drug abuse, and commitment has direct implications for the practice of counseling and psychotherapy. Some psychotherapists, namely psychiatrists, are also trained medical doctors and thus are subject to the laws covering physicians and surgeons. Psychotherapists without medical training may be exempt from those laws. However, all psychotherapists, regardless of the type of training, can be legally liable for such infractions as breach of contract and negligence leading to malpractice.

Laws vary from state to state, and court decisions in one jurisdiction are not binding in another. Statutes dealing with the several helping professions also vary from state to state, depending on the profession covered. For example, a social worker engaged in the practice of psychotherapy may not be covered by a state's privileged-communication law, while a psychiatrist using the same mode of treatment with like patients may be granted the privilege.

There are few laws dealing with counseling in schools and community settings, particularly when the counselor has no psychiatric training and holds no license to practice psychology or psychotherapy. While school counselors are generally certified by state boards of education, in most states this certification does not grant them rights accorded to several other helping professionals. For example, they may not be permitted to enter private practice or to serve as expert witnesses unless they are licensed professional counselors. Some counselors employed in public agencies, such as drug centers or community mental health agencies, may possess no license or certification and thus may have no legal recognition as a professional therapist. This does not mean, however, that they are immune from the dictates of law that govern everybody else. In fact, in states that have fairly precise laws regulating the professions, they may find themselves in violation of the criminal code dealing with practicing without a license (see, for example, *City of Cleveland* v. *Cook,* 75-CRB 11478 (Mun. Ct. 1975)).

The Therapist-Client Relationship

The type of therapy discussed in this book requires a relationship built on mutual understandings and two-way agreements between therapist and client. The therapist's primary mode of treatment is talking and listening. Thus, at the inception of the relationship, major reliance must be placed on what is communicated vocally. The client makes judgments and decisions about the therapist's qualifications and skill and about whether to trust the therapist, mainly on the basis of what is communicated to him in the initial interviews. Sullivan (1970) states that the first interview should help clients decide whether they will benefit from therapy.

The therapist structures the relationship by defining the helping situation—by explaining what therapy is and what it is not. Boy and Pine (1982) believe that therapists should explain that they do not have solutions to the client's problems but will help the client search for appropriate solutions. These authors also write that "counseling is structured in terms of time. By adhering to a stated time limit, the counselor contributes to the stability of the encounter." Boy and Pine warn that a lack of structure in therapy may lead to dependency. The client who enters therapy expecting the counselor to provide solutions for his problems and to tell the client exactly what should be done will find it difficult to assume responsibility for self-direction. Some counselors seem quite willing to take control of the client's life, but this attitude is potentially harmful and ethically questionable. According to the *Ethical Standards* of the American Association for Counseling and Development (1981, sec. B), "The member's *primary* obligation is to respect the integrity and promote the welfare of the client(s), whether the client(s) is (are) assisted individually or in a group relationship."

In the relationship we begin to chart both ethical and

legal responsibilities of therapists. Ethically, the therapist must be certain that he is competent and willing to undertake treatment of the client; if he does agree to treat the client, he assumes a degree of loyalty and responsibility for the outcomes of therapy. The therapist must also deal honestly with his feelings about the client. The client has a right to expect that he will be treated as a human being and not as an object of passing importance (Foster, 1975). Legally, the therapist has a duty to communicate to the client an honest representation of his skills and methods, along with the conditions of therapy, fees, appointment schedules, and special obligations of both therapist and client. The understanding that develops during the first contacts becomes, in effect, an unwritten contract. Each party has a responsibility to abide by the contract. If the contract is breached, the remedy may be legal action.

Obligations under such contracts are not entirely mutual. The client may leave therapy without stating reasons and probably without incurring liability for the cost of sessions not attended, although if the therapist can prove that he suffered financial loss as a result of canceled sessions, the client might be liable. Conversely, if a therapist terminates treatment without due cause and if the client is injured by this action, the therapist might thereafter be liable for malpractice (Dawidoff, 1973). The most usual circumstances for termination of treatment occur when therapist and client mutually agree (1) that the client is "cured" or perhaps has reached desired goals, or will not benefit from further treatment, and (2) that the client will be referred to another professional. When referral is undertaken, the referring therapist has the responsibility for ascertaining the appropriateness of the referral, including the skill of the receiving therapist. Furthermore, he should provide the receiving therapist with information sufficient to enable him to give proper help to the client. The therapist also should follow up on his client's progress in treatment, instead of merely pawning him off on another with a sigh of relief and a fee in his pocket.

In all client contacts, the therapist is expected to exercise due care. Dawidoff (1973) emphasizes the "duty to act skillfully and carefully," meaning that the therapist may be-

come legally vulnerable if he departs too far from standard procedure or if he mishandles the relationship. Later in this chapter, we cite cases illustrating this point.

Privacy and Confidentiality

People who enter therapy often discuss intimate and personal details and concerns. Clients have a right to expect that
these private revelations will be treated confidentially and that
the therapist will not disclose information that might bring
shame or ridicule to the client. *Privacy* refers to the freedom of
clients to determine for themselves the extent and circumstances under which their behavior, beliefs, and opinions are to
be shared with others. *Confidentiality* involves a professional
understanding and a promise that nothing about an individual
will be revealed except under conditions agreed to by the subject. *Privilege,* or privileged communication, is a legal term involving the right to maintain confidentiality in a legal proceeding (Siegel, 1979).

Confidentiality: The Ethical Basis. The issue of confidentiality brings into sharp focus the nature of the therapist's
loyalty to the client, the employing institution, society, the profession, and himself. *The Principles of Medical Ethics,* adopted
by the American Psychiatric Association (1973), deals with
confidentiality as follows: "A physician may not reveal the confidences entrusted to him in the course of medical attendance,
or the deficiencies he may observe in the character of the patients, unless he is required to do so by law or unless it becomes
necessary in order to protect the welfare of the individual or of
the community" (sec. 9). The *Ethical Standards* of the American Association for Counseling and Development (1981) contains several statements pertinent to the issue of confidentiality.
For example, "The counseling relationship and information resulting therefrom shall be kept confidential, consistent with the
obligations of the member as a professional person" (sec. B,
item 2). And "Revelation to others of counseling material must
occur only upon the expressed consent of the client" (sec. B,
item 5).

Codes of ethics provide general guidelines on the therapist's responsibility for dealing with confidential information. They do not, however, indicate priorities when there is a conflict either with values or with law. Parenthetically, we may note that some therapists apparently ignore ethical codes. Thus, in a "rare interview" with a correspondent for a national newsmagazine, a psychiatrist makes the following statement about the emotional condition of Patricia Hearst (the young woman who received much publicity in her kidnaping and role in several terrorist activities): "She is pathetic now. She resembles a person during a war who had just come back from battle" ("A Psychiatrist's Notes," 1976). Public statements describing a client's condition violate the American Psychiatric Association's ethical standards and illustrate a concern expressed in several sections of this book: that therapists and their professional societies have failed to adhere to several ethical principles in the training of therapists and in contacts with clients.

Goldman (1969, p. 88) states that the *privilege* in confidential communication with a therapist belongs to the client: "It is he who is protected by law, not the person to whom he spills the beans. It is he who owns the information and has the right to say who shall have access to it and who shall not." The issue here is not primarily a legal one, in the strict sense; rather, it is a matter of professional duty of the therapist to maintain confidentiality, unless he is required by law to make a disclosure. In the case of a dangerous client, for instance, the therapist may be required to report to appropriate authorities. Furthermore, some states have child protection statutes that require therapists and other professionals to report evidence of battered children.

Ethical codes, statutes, and court decisions have established the principle that people are entitled to keep some things private. Only under proper legal safeguards may they be required to reveal what they would prefer to keep secret. Counselors and psychotherapists have a right to collect information about a client in order to provide proper treatment, but they also have a responsibility to use this information wisely; if they do not, then they must be prepared to be held ethically and legally accountable for abuse of a privilege.

Confidentiality: The Legal Basis. There is a tradition in

this country that an individual has a right to be left alone and to be protected against unwarranted public disclosure of his private affairs. The law recognizes this right and, in some cases, will not permit private communication to be divulged. In the history of privileged communication, the legal tradition allowed for only two relationships in which the privilege against speaking out in court could be applied: husband and wife, and attorney and client. By 1970 this protection had been provided by statute in forty states to the husband-wife relationship and in thirty-eight states to the attorney-client relationship. Over the years the rule has been extended to other relationships. The physician-patient relationship is protected by statute in thirty-six states; seventeen states have such legislation for the psychologist-client relationship (Pardue, Whichard, and Johnson, 1970); and the counselor-client relationship is now protected in nine states (Burgum and Anderson, 1975).

In a legal context, *confidentiality* is the term applied to an exchange of information between two people in a professional-client situation whose confidential relationship has been recognized by statute or case precedent. *Privileged communication* must meet the following conditions (Wigmore, 1961):

1. The communications must originate with the understanding that they will not be disclosed.
2. Confidentiality must be essential to the maintenance of the relationship.
3. The community must accept the need for confidentiality in the relationship.
4. Injury inflicted on the relationship as a result of disclosure or communication must be greater than the benefit gained from proper disposal of litigation.

For many years courts have tended to recognize these criteria in determining which relationships shall be confidential and which shall not. State legislatures, however, have not necessarily followed suit. Thus, as noted, some professions are accorded the privilege in some states but not in others. Unless a state statute deals specifically with a therapist-client relationship, there is no reason to expect that a court will hold it legally privileged.

Several legal experts appear to be most cautious about extending the communications privilege. Wigmore (1961, p. 288) writes: "For more than three centuries, it has been recognized that the public has a right to every man's evidence. When we come to examine the various claims of exemption, we start with the primary assumption that there is a general duty to give what testimony one is capable of giving and that any exemptions which may exist are distinctly exceptional, being so many derogations from a general rule." Burgum and Anderson (1975) have also commented on judicial reluctance to extend the privilege of confidentiality. Courts in Ohio, Indiana, Minnesota, Michigan, Wisconsin, Florida, Virginia, Washington, and California, for example, have indicated that they will not extend this privilege to newly evolving relationships unless it is specifically recognized by state statute. Legally, then, therapists have a confidential relationship with their clients only when such a privilege has been granted by a state legislature. The federal legislature or courts could, of course, extend this privilege, but at this time it seems unlikely that they will do so.

Ethical codes contain prohibitions against revealing information about clients except in certain instances. However, the codes are not legally binding, and, as we have seen, some therapists appear unable to resist the temptation to spread lively or racy information broadside. The professional associations seem to ignore this practice, probably because they lack appropriate means for confronting it or perhaps because they deem it unimportant.

The point here is that counselors and psychotherapists have a clear duty to maintain confidentiality and not to disclose confidential matters unless they are required to do so by law or unless there is some legal justification for doing so. Thus, a therapist may be liable for failure to report that a client is so disturbed as to constitute a danger to others. For example, in *Tarasoff* v. *Regents of the University of California,* 529 P.2d 553 (1975), the California Supreme Court held university psychotherapists liable for "failure to warn" an individual threatened by their client.

In the *Tarasoff* case, Prosenjit Poddar, an outpatient at the University of California hospital, informed his psychotherapist that he planned to kill an unnamed girl, readily identifiable as Tatiana Tarasoff, when she returned home after spending the summer in South America. The therapist advised the university police department of this threat and requested that Poddar be detained. Poddar was taken into custody but soon released when he promised to stay away from Tatiana. Shortly after her return from Brazil, Poddar went to her place of residence and killed her. The parents brought action against the university regents, the police, and doctors in the university hospital, charging that the defendants negligently permitted Poddar to be released from custody without notifying the parents of Tatiana Tarasoff that their daughter was in grave danger. The Alameda County Superior Court found for the defendants, whereupon the parents of Tatiana appealed. The Supreme Court of California reversed the judgment and found the defendants guilty of negligence on a charge of "failure to warn." The court noted that, like a doctor treating physical illness, a psychotherapist treating a dangerous client bears a duty to give threatened persons such warnings as are essential to avert foreseeable danger arising from his patient's condition or treatment. The California court spoke directly to limitations of privileged communications: "Public policy favoring protection of the confidential character of patient-psychotherapist relationship must yield in instances in which disclosure is essential to avert danger to others; the protective privilege ends where the public peril begins."

Siegel (1979) cites a related 1972 case in which a California psychiatrist, George Caesar, refused to testify about a patient he had treated in 1969. Dr. Caesar refused to answer questions about his former patient on the grounds that (1) breaking confidences would be psychologically harmful, (2) he did not have her consent to testify, and (3) the questions might not be relevant to the legal case and would therefore be unnecessary breaches of confidence. The psychiatrist was held in contempt of court; and, after several appeals over the next five years, the U.S. Supreme Court upheld the ruling of the lower court. In 1977 Dr. Caesar served three days in jail.

McIntosh v. *Milano*, 403 A.2d 500 (N.J. 1979), is similar to *Tarasoff* because it also involves a duty to warn on the part

of therapists. In this case Michael Milano, a psychiatrist, had
been treating a young man referred to him by a school psychologist. The initial problem was diagnosed as "adjustment to ado-
lescence." Treatment was provided weekly for a period of two
years. While still in therapy, the young man stole a prescription
pad from Dr. Milano's office and attempted to purchase thirty
Seconal tablets. The pharmacist refused to sell the tablets and
notified Dr. Milano, who tried unsuccessfully to contact his patient. Later that day the patient took a pistol from his parents'
home and killed his next-door neighbor, Kimberly McIntosh.

    Later it was revealed that in the course of therapy the
young patient had discussed several "fantasies," including sexual experiences with Kimberly, who was five years his senior.
He said that he had once shot at Kimberly's car with a BB gun
and that he was jealous of men Kimberly dated and angry when
she moved out of her parents' home and would not give him an
address. He had a possessive attitude toward Kimberly and once
told the psychiatrist that he wished she would "suffer" as he
had.

    Dr. Milano had spoken with the patient's parents on occa-
sions when he felt that the young man might be a danger to
himself or others, but he had made no attempt to contact Kimberly or her parents. After her death Kimberly's mother sued
Dr. Milano, claiming that the doctor had a duty to warn that his
patient posed a threat to her daughter and had breached that
duty.

    The court found for the plaintiff, reasoning that generally
an individual owes no duty to protect a potential victim from
dangers imposed by another but that such a duty does exist
where there is a special relationship between the individual and
the person posing the danger. The court pointed out that such a
duty is not new to the medical profession: "A physician has the
duty to warn third persons against possible exposure to conta-
gious or infectious diseases." This duty, the court noted, "ex-
tends to instances where the physician should have known of
the infectious disease." Although, the court recognized, there
are differences between diagnosing physical illnesses and pre-
dicting dangerousness in the context of psychiatric treatment,

"nevertheless, psychiatrists diagnose, treat, and give opinions based on medical probabilities, particularly relying on a patient's history, without any clear indication of an inability to predict that is here asserted." The court also pointed to the American Psychiatric Association's (1973) *Principles of Medical Ethics,* which recognizes that confidential information must give way where there is a danger to an individual or the community. Thus, the court concluded that, while some relationships entail special responsibilities to patients, these relationships cannot interfere with the therapist's broader responsibility to the community.

These cases illustrate the recurring conflict between ethical codes and legal principles. The issue in such cases is not only confidentiality; it is also whether some precise guidelines can be developed to deal with situations where the therapist's duty to his client may conflict with his duty to other persons or to society.

Duty to Act Skillfully and to Use Due Care

The special relationship between a therapist and his client creates a duty to use special skill and due care in treatment. The therapist represents himself by means of words, by exchanging ideas, and by sharing feelings, and these actions are part of the treatment process. Interpretations are made by the client, actions are taken, and behavior is changed on the basis of a personal encounter. The therapist must guard against confusing or misleading the client; otherwise, he diminishes the effectiveness of treatment and, in some cases, may contribute to damaging actions on the part of the client. The due care principle also includes the duty to act professionally and to adhere to standards acceptable to the community and other professionals.

In *Landau* v. *Werner* (cited in Dawidoff, 1973, pp. 38-41), the inability of an English psychiatrist to resolve a problem of transference in his client, Landau, led to his conviction in a damage suit. When he discovered that Landau was in love with him, he carried out both professional and social relationships, taking her to restaurants and visiting in her apartment. When she discovered that Werner was not in love with her, she returned to her original state of depression and attempted suicide. The court was persuaded that standards of due care had not been exercised and that social contacts between therapist and client are likely to have ill effects. The court concluded that Werner had made a tragic error in his treatment of Landau.

This case illustrates what some tort teachers call the "quality of the touch." "Conservative" judges often feel that a therapist or physician should not obtain pleasure from treating female patients. As Foster (1975, p. 41) states, "His intent and motive become important to the law, and the question may be, Did he sneak a feel or feel a sneak? Whatever the facts, therapists should be warned that monkey business should not be mixed with professional pleasure." The "no-monkey-business" principle is discussed in some detail in Chapter Six, where we deal with unethical practices. It is appropriate here, however, to cite two additional cases to illustrate our point that therapists should be personally honest as well as professionally skillful. In *Zipkin* v. *Freeman,* 436 S.W.2d 753 (Mo. 1968) (see also Foster, 1975; Dawidoff, 1973), suit was brought against a sensuous therapist on a garnishment proceeding. During the period of treatment, the client moved into an apartment over the therapist's office, accompanied him to various social gatherings and taverns, and helped him purchase a farm. These interactions, the plaintiff alleged, constituted an abuse of a relationship and a misapplication of professional services. The court took a negative view of these "beyond-the-couch" relationships and awarded $17,000 in damages against the therapist. In *Roy* v. *Hartogs,* 366 N.Y.S.2d 297 (1975), the client, Julie Roy, brought a malpractice suit against her therapist, Dr. Hartogs, claiming damages as a result of their sexual relations over a period of several months. Hartogs claimed that the relationship was unrelated to professional actions; sex was not part of the therapy, and therefore his actions could not be described as misconduct. The court was not persuaded and ruled for Roy.

The courts seem to be saying to the helping professions that close relationships involving trust and mutual caring between therapist and client are understood and are, in fact, necessary for effective treatment. Such intimacies are permitted as long as the therapist does not use the relationship for personal advantage and as long as he maintains due regard for professional propriety and community conscience. Put another way, there are both ethical and legal boundaries, and the therapist who steps beyond these limits may be taking risks, even when his motives are valid.

Therapy as a Social Force

Psychotherapy has achieved a position of eminence and respectability in American society during the past few decades. Despite recent criticisms, the general public clearly is much influenced by the "therapeutic establishment." As the helping arts have expanded, they are no longer merely "mental health specialties" but have become a profound social force. Essentially, counselors and psychotherapists assert their influence and authority in three ways: (1) as expert witnesses in commitment proceedings and in criminal cases, (2) as definers and interpreters of human behavior, and (3) as paid advice givers.

Therapists as Expert Witnesses. Traditionally, in commitment proceedings and in criminal cases, courts seeking expert testimony on a defendant's behavior or mental health relied primarily on a therapist with a medical degree. More recently, however, psychologists have also become generally recognized as experts who can draw inferences about human behavior that is outside the experiences of the ordinary juror (Pacht and Soloman, 1973). Counselors are not yet widely accepted as expert witnesses, nor have they actively sought much recognition. However, vocational counselors are frequently employed as expert witnesses in cases involving disability claims under the Social Security Act; and in some courts school counselors have been accepted as experts in cases involving child abuse, child custody, and delinquency.

Several questions can be raised about the courts' use of the expert witness. Halleck (1971) notes that it is questionable whether the practice serves either clients or the general public. He believes that one of the major dangers in expert testimony is the mixing of fact and opinion. Halleck is concerned that the medical model for evaluating behavior may lead to inappropriate labeling, that too many people may be deprived of freedom without due process, and that definitions of mental illness are too arbitrary to justify involuntary institutionalization or treatment of patients. Too often, repressive actions are taken against people who are not "mentally ill" but whose behavior may simply be at variance with the social norm.

In his article "The Perils of Wizardry," Bazelon (1974) also raises questions about the role of psychiatrists in the legal process. He voices concern over psychiatric labeling and suggests that such labels are too limited and restrictive when personal rights are involved. Bazelon, a federal appellate court judge, has on several occasions attempted to clarify the role of psychiatrists in legal actions. In 1954, in the influential Durham decision, he extended the M'Naghten Rule, which excuses defendants from the consequences of their actions if they are mentally unable to understand the nature and quality of their actions. According to the Durham Rule, a defendant cannot be held criminally responsible for his acts if he was of diseased and defective mental capacity when he committed the crime charged and if the crime was the product of his mental state. Bazelon specified, however, that psychiatrists must not simply testify that an alleged offense was a product of mental illness. That is the ultimate question and should be answered only by a jury. Psychiatrists were directed to speak clearly and specifically about the defendant's behavior and its consequences. Furthermore, expert witnesses should not be concerned with the legal meanings of diagnosis and should try to separate fact from opinion (Robitscher, 1975).

Bazelon later voiced his disappointment that the purpose of the Durham decision was not fulfilled. Psychiatrists continued to cling adamantly to diagnostic labels without explaining the origin, development, or manifestations of a disease in terms meaningful to a jury. What became more and more apparent was that these terms did not rest on a disciplined investigation of facts. Bazelon noted, "I regret to say that they were used to cover up a lack of relevance, knowledge, and certainty in the practice of institutional psychiatry" (1974, p. 1319). Consequently, the judge became a severe critic of psychiatrists in the courtroom (see Bazelon, 1974, 1975).

The most severe critic of psychiatric abuses in the legal process is Thomas Szasz (1974, 1978). In several books and a score of articles, Szasz has denied the concept of mental illness and stated flatly that labels are used for social control, which he accuses psychiatrists of aiding and abetting. He opposes the use of psychiatric testimony in the courtroom and believes that psychiatrists help deprive people of their personal rights when they classify defendants as "sick." Szasz believes that psychiatrists and other mental health practitioners already have too much authority—that they now want to decide who is sick and who is well, and what behavior is right and what behavior is wrong. Szasz cautions that such practices could lead to a Therapeutic State, in which—as in the Soviet Union—those who disagree with official policy may be labeled mentally sick and sent off to a forced labor camp.

We are not in total agreement with Szasz; however, he has called attention to important moral and legal issues confronting several of the helping professions. Overall, we believe that the issues surrounding the role of the helping professions in the legal process need careful study. In the meantime, responsible people should perhaps devote more attention to their own standards of conduct—their ethics—before they set out to change the world.

Therapists as Interpreters of Behavior. We have previously commented on the growing influence of counseling and psychotherapy over the past decades. Psychotherapy is now firmly rooted in all aspects of our society and is eloquently endorsed by people of authority and influence. The work of counselors and psychotherapists has become more than just a group of services or activities performed by members of the helping crafts. Therapy is a major social force and a primary influencer of our beliefs, attitudes, and values. Counselors in schools and organizations, institutional psychiatrists, social workers, and other helping professionals routinely make interpretations of behavior that influence policy making, standards of conduct, and legislation. All this adds up to authority and control over the lives of people.

The tendency to utilize personal beliefs and value judgments as a basis of therapeutic interpretations permeates the profession. Value judgment not only supplies much of the impetus for activities with individuals but also is a basis for official recommendations and public pronouncements. Therapists rarely acknowledge this fact, and, more seriously, it probably remains relatively unrecognized. As London (1971) has suggested, our efforts have outstripped our knowledge, and we have taken bold steps armed with too few facts and too many opinions. Furthermore, like any militant and persistent social movement, therapy is often regarded as a panacea, not only by its practitioners but by many people in decision-making positions.

Psychotherapy has an important role in society, but it also has a great responsibility, particularly to those people who may not be able to exercise control over their own lives. For example, minors and people with disabling emotional symptoms may often have little freedom of choice. Freedom to choose is a legal concept, quite valid philosophically, but it may be rendered meaningless when one is subjected to dissection of the psyche and has one's every action and thought interpreted and analyzed. Legal actions such as insanity hearings, commitment cases, certain court cases involving minors, and some criminal proceedings all place in jeopardy the freedom of the individual. The dangers of using questionable information, value judgments, and opinions in such cases are obvious.

There is little statute or case law dealing with verbal misdeeds of therapists in legal proceedings such as those mentioned here. There is a scarcity of cases growing out of written and oral statements made by counselors and psychotherapists working in schools and other institutions. Yet almost constant provocation exists, because of the opportunity, and sometimes the necessity, for school and institutional therapists to make derogatory statements about the character and conduct of their clients. However, the usual laws on slander and libel apply equally to all people, including therapists. Defaming and untruthful statements can mean that the therapist may be hauled off to court. Changes are occurring in American society. People are becoming more conscious of their rights and feel more free to attempt to redress a wrong through court action. Therapists are undoubtedly more legally vulnerable today than a decade ago. Professional associations are aware of this problem, and some have cautioned their members that improper statements may result in libel and slander suits.

Therapists as Advice Givers. A high percentage of counselors and psychotherapists work in institutions—schools, colleges, hospitals, youth agencies, and mental health centers. In these settings the therapist must serve two masters: the client and the employing institution. Several dilemmas are inherent under these conditions. First, the therapist's loyalty and responsibility may be divided. He is expected to support and enhance the institution, to adhere to its policies and follow its leadership. These responsibilities may interfere with his commitment to clients. Second, institutions are composed of people with different views, concerns, and ideas about how things are and how things ought to be done. They may pressure the therapist to do things differently from the way he would if he were free to practice in accord with his professional beliefs. Some administrators tend to place major emphasis on maintaining the institution and its reputation, as well as their own. They often expect staff personnel to do likewise. Third, because institutions involve fairly large numbers of people, they tend to collect more information than a single professional person would, to store it in written or electronic records, and to make it more generally available (Ladd, 1971).

Some of the information used by institutions is personal and intimate, and often it is used improperly. Some institutions, schools and colleges in particular, have consistently misused information about students and in the process have invaded the individual's privacy. As Goldman (1969) has noted, they have collected data on students' interests, aptitudes, behaviors, feelings, and families. They have then released this information to other schools, employers, the police, and the FBI without the permission or knowledge of the students or their parents. They have made recommendations that kept people

out of college and out of jobs, and they have provided information that could get people in trouble with the law.

In hospitals, prisons, rehabilitation centers, and mental
health agencies, psychiatrists, psychologists, and social workers
compile extensive records on their clients. This information is
then used in making recommendations and in advising administrators, executive boards, and courts about the proper disposition of a case. The information may have been freely given, and
the client may have understood that it would not, or could not,
be held in confidence. This means little, however, when the
therapist is working with a captive client. Most people serviced
by the institutions named are not there of their own free will,
and many have little understanding of how the information may
be used. It may, in fact, be used to punish, detain, or otherwise
deprive the client of his freedom of choice and freedom of
movement.

The danger to the individual is multiplied by the possibility of inaccuracies in information and by some glaring gaps in
our knowledge about human behavior. Much of the information
used by counselors and psychotherapists is questionable, because it is either subjective or capable of misinterpretations.
Most recommendations bear the imprint of value judgment and
opinion, and the tendency to use psychological labels when describing behavior is often confusing and misleading. The therapist's heart may be pure, but some of his "facts" are often
grossly inaccurate.

The legal implications of the use of information, including oral and written statements about a client, involve matters
of personal rights, possible defamation, libel and slander, and
privileged information. Unfavorable and unsubstantiated statements made about another person can lead to litigation, including the tort of defamation. Slander and libel have been outlawed for hundreds of years. In ancient Rome anyone who
defamed another could be beaten with a club. In modern Turkey a foreigner who slanders or insults a Turkish citizen can
be hauled off to jail. Therapists probably will not be clubbed
(legally, at least) for their statements about a client. But indis-
cretions and inaccuracies in oral and written statements can

lead to lawsuits claiming damages as a result of the statements. Laws of slander and libel influence the therapist's relationship with his clients, the institution where he works, and his obligations to society.

We have already touched on privileged communication as protection for the client. There is, in addition, a second privilege that protects the therapist, acting professionally and properly, from unwarranted damage suits. In this context we are dealing with two types of communication: *absolutely* privileged and *qualifiedly* privileged. Absolute privilege is based on the concept that the public interest in unimpeded communication in certain instances completely outweighs society's concern for an individual's reputation. Qualified privilege exists in situations where society's interest in unhampered communication is conditionally limited by the general mores concerning what is fair and reasonable to given individuals under the practical necessities of daily living. This means that certain individuals have a right to receive confidential information, but society at large does not (Burgum and Anderson, 1975, p. 77). The applicability of the privileged-communication concept to release of information by a counselor or psychotherapist depends on the circumstances of the particular case. General principles often followed in determining therapist privilege include good faith, interests served as a result of release, the purpose of release, and the "right to know." Put another way, courts generally attempt to determine whether the therapist's motives were proper and whether the person receiving the information had a legitimate reason for requesting it. Conversely, the privilege does not exist if information is released improperly, if it is excessively or erroneously published, or if it is released to persons who have no valid reason for receiving it (Burgum and Anderson, 1975).

Therapists and institutions have a right to collect whatever information is specifically and initially necessary to carry out their mission. They also have both a legal and an ethical responsibility to safeguard the rights and privacy of their clients. They must also be able to document what they say with more than opinions, beliefs, and professional hunches.

The professional associations have been strangely silent

on the collection and release of private information. At the same time, therapists around the country continue their efforts to gain privileged-communication rights through legislation. We question whether this privilege should be extended. What is needed, however, is more attention to ethical standards and the development of sensible guidelines to protect the privacy of clients.

Malpractice

Malpractice is generally defined as damage to another person as a result of negligence. The concept is based on several ancient laws which held that a person who injures another person must give him something to compensate for that injury. In the present era, the injured party brings a legal action against the other person or his property, in an effort to set right the injury done to him.

Three conditions must be proved in malpractice litigation: (1) the defendant had a *duty* to the plaintiff; (2) the defendant's conduct constituted *negligence* or improper action; (3) there was a *causal relationship* between that negligence and the damage alleged by the plaintiff (Burgum and Anderson, 1975; see also Schutz, 1982, pp. 2-10). The term "damage" refers to losses suffered in money, body, or mind. "Negligence" is defined as a departure from usual practice; that is, acceptable standards were not followed, and due care was not exercised.

When compared with lawsuits brought against physicians, malpractice actions brought against counselors and psychotherapists are infrequent. Available information suggests that malpractice actions against physicians have more than doubled in the past decade. In 1975 approximately 10,000 suits against physicians were taken to the courts (Barchilon, 1975, p. 11); by 1984 this figure exceeded 20,000 annually. Moreover, the cash awards have almost tripled—from an average of $367,000 in the late 1970s to $954,858 in 1984 (reported in Charlottesville *Daily Progress,* Jan. 17, 1985). As noted, psychiatrists, psychologists, and counselors are sued less often. However, given some current trends, there are valid reasons for believing that more psychiatrists, as well as other counselors and psychotherapists, will have courtroom experiences—as defendants in a lawsuit. Some reasons for this probable increase are suggested by Trent and Muhl (1975, p. 1313): (1) People are becoming more claims conscious and, believing that injuries should be compensated, are more likely to employ lawyers. (2) Helping professionals are engaged in more active and aggressive (we would add "more questionable") therapies, such as encounter groups, primal scream therapy, conditioning techniques, and sexual therapies. Any of these modes of treatment can increase the therapist's exposure to claims. (3) Consumers are more sophisticated; they have information on what constitutes negligence in the psychiatric and psychotherapeutic fields.

The literature reveals that the most frequent causes of malpractice action against therapists are the following:

1. Faulty or negligent rendering of services
2. Wrongful commitment
3. Slander and libel
4. Negligence leading to suicide
5. Birth control and abortion counseling
6. Electroshock therapy
7. Drug therapy
8. Sex therapy
9. Illegal search
10. Nude encounter groups
11. "Sensuous" therapy
12. Failure to supervise a disturbed client

Items 6 and 7 are applicable only to therapists with a medical degree. As for Item 9, we cannot believe that a professional counselor would be so stupid or unethical as to conduct an illegal search; however, the literature cites instances in which institutional "counselors" have searched lockers and clients when looking for drugs.

The American Psychiatric Association, the American Association for Counseling and Development, and other professional associations are currently urging their members to carry liability insurance sufficient to cover dangers of malpractice suits. Articles in their journals, letters to members, and insurance sales brochures call attention to the "shocking" conditions surrounding malpractice. Nowhere do they mention the professionals' responsibility for simultaneously putting their own house in order. We contend that numerous abuses exist in the helping professions, and we believe that a sophisticated public serves a necessary function in calling attention to malpractice. If lawsuits are necessary to this process, then so be it.

Firm legal principles on what might constitute malpractice by nonmedical therapists have not yet been established. The current view, however, is that malpractice actions in counseling and psychotherapy generally follow patterns established in medical malpractice. Several authorities cite a Michigan opinion in which the state's attorney general ruled that the "practice of psychotherapy comes within the practice of medicine found in the statutes" (Huckins, 1968, p. 46). Thus, one can infer that any person performing counseling and psychotherapy, whatever his degree or title, may be liable for malpractice.

Some legal responsibilities accrue to any person presenting himself as able to render services based on special training, expertise, or skill. The *Tarasoff* case, discussed earlier in this chapter, raises some interesting questions regarding the therapist's "duty to warn" a third party or "duty to control" a client who may be a threat to others. The courts have not always agreed on therapists' responsibilities in such cases. The general principle in tort law is that a professional person *may* be liable for controlling a client's conduct to prevent harm to another (1) when a special relationship exists that imposes a duty on the professional or (2) when the relationship includes the other's (client's) right to protection. A recent Colorado District Court case provides an example.

In this case (*Brady, McCarthy, and Delahanty* v. *Hopper*, Civil Action No. 83-JM-451 (D.D.C. Sept. 14, 1983)), James Brady, Timothy McCarthy, and Thomas Delahanty brought a civil action against John J. Hopper, a psychiatrist, charging that he was negligent in examining, diagnosing, and treating John W. Hinckley, Jr. Hopper had treated Hinckley in late 1980 and early 1981. According to the plaintiffs, Hopper had negligently formed the opinion, in spite of Hinckley's suicide attempts, that his patient was not seriously ill. The plaintiffs alleged that Hinckley was a danger to himself and others, that he identified with the assassin in the movie *Taxi Driver,* and that Hopper's treatment was not only ineffective but in fact aggravated Hinckley's mental condition, making him more dangerous. Despite the fact that Hinckley's parents had asked Hopper to hospitalize their son, Hopper continued to treat him on an outpatient basis.

In March 1981 Hinckley left Denver and traveled to Washington, D.C. There, on March 30, 1981, he attempted to assassinate President Reagan and in the process also shot and injured the plaintiffs. Hinckley was tried for these crimes and found not guilty by reason of insanity. He was confined to a mental hospital.

The plaintiffs stated that Hopper had a professional duty to control Hinckley's behavior. They argued that he should have warned the parents of their son's condition and that he should have informed law enforcement officials of his patient's potential for political assassination.

Hopper's defense was that the "duty to control" principle did not apply in this case because Hinckley was an outpatient and that a therapist-outpatient relationship lacks sufficient elements for control. Hopper's attorneys argued that, under Colorado law, the psychiatrist lacked the authority to have his patient committed. Furthermore, they maintained, a warning to others would constitute a breach of confidentiality mandated by Colorado statutes.

The court agreed that Hopper's diagnosis and treatment of Hinckley "fell below the applicable standard of care." However, the court did not agree that the doctor had a "duty to control": "To impose upon those in counseling an ill-defined 'duty to control' would require therapists to be ultimately responsible for the actions of their patients." Under such a rule, "therapists would be potentially liable for all harm inflicted by persons presently or formerly" under their care. The court also rejected the plaintiffs' argument that a special relationship existed between Hopper and Hinckley and ruled for the defendant.

A landmark case involving a college counselor is often used in discussions of negligence in dealing with a potential suicide. In this case (*Bogust* v. *Iverson,* 102 N.W.2d 228 (Wis. 1960)), the parents of a female student who had committed suicide brought suit against a college counselor, charging him with three counts of negligence. Specifically, the parents charged that he had failed (1) to recognize the severity of the client's disturbance and thus did not refer her to a psychiatrist; (2) to warn the parents of their daughter's condition; (3) to provide proper service. The court ruled in favor of the counselor, stating essentially that he lacked proper training and could not be held liable for conditions beyond his knowledge.

In this case ignorance became a defense. It is doubtful whether a counselor would get off this easily today. In today's legal climate, counselors are required to understand their own limitations as well as their skills; and a failure to take some direct precautions with a potential suicide would almost certainly be ruled negligent. As we have already noted, counselors and psychotherapists are now more numerous, more influential, and more visible than in the past. And, along with other professionals, they are now more accountable for their actions. Thus, it can be expected that the public and the courts will take a more critical view of their actions and that negligence actions will increase.

We have dealt with malpractice in counseling and psychotherapy in a fashion somewhat analogous to that of the physician. We have done so in the absence of agreement and because of the lack of statute or case law in this area. There is every reason to believe that general rules and principles on liability apply to all helping professionals, regardless of title, training, or work situation.

The best safeguard against malpractice is professional and personal honesty. Openness in communications with clients and a demonstrated interest in the welfare of those he seeks to help are good defenses against charges of malpractice. An understanding of one's limitations as well as a sense of duty to soci-

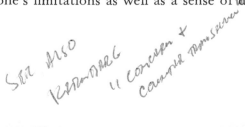

SEE ALSO
REMINDAREC
LL COMCEPN &
CAMPUS MINSERVE

ety should contravene some of the present problems in therapist
liability.

Summary

The legal dimensions of counseling and psychotherapy
are not yet clearly defined. Statute law and case law leave many
questions unanswered and provide few guidelines on the spe-
cifics of therapy and the legal process. The professional associations have given minimal attention to the legal aspects of counseling and psychotherapy. However, there is evidence that
recent events highlighting the legal vulnerability of therapists
and the trend toward accountability may stimulate positive
professional action.

Some general legal principles that can give direction to
the work of professional therapists have been discussed in this
chapter, in the hope that therapists may acquire a better understanding of the legal ramifications of their profession.

4

Professional
and
Legal
Regulation

One criterion of a profession is that it be self-disciplining and self-licensing. Established professionals—whether antique merchants, hairdressers, or therapists—develop standards and policies that, to some degree at least, control entry into the profession, prescribe training standards, and establish procedures and requirements for licensing or certification. Professionals also develop ethical codes, which outline standards of service, describe members' relationships with each other and with the general public, and spell out appropriate and inappropriate behavior of members. It is through such actions that public acceptance and respectability are established. Professionals are also regulated, controlled, held accountable, and sometimes disciplined through legal processes. Statute law in all states controls the practice of such disciplines as medicine and law, and most states exercise some regulatory power, either by statute or case law, over the helping professions. In many instances, laws regulating the helping professions, and other professions for that matter, were enacted at the behest of the professional group concerned.

Professional societies have no legal power per se, and their standards, however appropriate, may be unenforceable without statutes to back them up. Thus, laws may become necessary to prevent practice by unqualified persons, to prevent abuses, to protect the general public and the professions from charlatans and quacks, and to discipline offenders. In the absence of such laws, charlatans and quacks can and do make a comfortable living masquerading as healers, advice givers, and soothers of the psyche. Many of these rogues are in "private practice," but some are also employed by or affiliated with public institutions. The prevalence of incompetents and the abuses in the helping fields and the mental health disciplines provide, in our opinion, the strongest case for the development and implementation of detailed professional standards.

This chapter deals with both professional and legal regulation of several helping professions. Because some description of the characteristics and functions of the profession discussed is necessary to understand the professional and legal aspects, the first half of the chapter provides both a historical and a functional overview of the major specialties in counseling and psychotherapy.

Professional Standards and Regulations

A profession typically assumes responsibility for developing its own standards through its associations. These standards and policy statements generally deal with two major areas of concern. First, standards define and give direction to organizing and implementing programs for training practitioners. Training standards usually stress selection of candidates and recommend content for graduate education, including practicum and internship experiences, supervision, relationships with other professionals, and professional problems and issues. Second, professional standards attempt to specify major functions of the profession and define areas and conditions of practice. Self-regulation based on a code of ethics; social, moral, and legal responsibilities of practitioners; and professional autonomy are traditionally outlined in standards and policy statements. Standards seek to clarify the goals of a profession, enhance its public image, and improve the quality of its service. Counseling and psychotherapy have made considerable progress in developing and implementing standards in recent years.

Two organizations that have developed comprehensive standards for counseling and psychotherapy are the American Association for Counseling and Development and the American Psychological Association. The American Psychiatric Association and the American Medical Association have also given considerable attention to standards for the practice of psychiatry. Since the practice of psychiatry, however, requires a medical license, the regulatory processes are somewhat different from those of counseling and psychology. In the sections that follow, we deal with both self-regulation and legal controls for each major group of helping professionals.

Standards and Regulations for School Counseling. Secondary school counseling developed in response to a need and a demand and grew rapidly during the 1950s and 1960s. In the early years, professional and legal standards were almost nonexistent, and there was little agreement on the proper functions of school counselors. Training programs, in the late 1940s and early 1950s, generally consisted of a few "guidance" courses and placed a heavy emphasis on vocational guidance, testing, and placement. In the absence of professional and legal regulations, schools tended to place teachers in guidance and counseling positions and paid little attention to professional training for such work. Unfortunately, the practice continued until very recent times.

The merger of several professional associations in 1951, which resulted in the birth of the American Personnel and Guidance Association (now American Association for Counseling and Development [AACD]), contributed significantly to the improvement of professionalism in school counseling. The AACD began to define roles of counselors and, through the work of several committees during the 1950s and 1960s, developed the professional standards discussed in this chapter. The first

AACD code of ethics was adopted in 1961 and revised in 1974 and 1981. During that same period, regional accrediting associations set minimum standards for secondary school counselors, and several states passed counselor certification laws. Training programs also improved significantly during that period, particularly following the National Defense Education Act in 1958. By the time elementary school counselors arrived on the scene in the 1960s, the usual standard for school counseling was a master's degree in counseling, and in most states certification was mandated. In many cases, however, individuals employed as counselors prior to the adoption of state certification standards were "grandfathered" or otherwise permitted to continue counseling in schools. The point here is that several current problems in school counseling have a historical base and result from the fact that, in many respects, counseling in educational settings is still in the process of developing.

Many years ago McCully (1962) noted that developing professions encounter numerous problems in their attempts to achieve professional status. He suggested that counseling must achieve several developmental tasks and resolve several professional issues before it could expect to gain the status and acceptance of other helping professions. School counselors still appear to be struggling with many of the problems and issues described by McCully.

Counseling in schools differs from other specialties in several significant ways. The first of these differences is in the training and experience requirement. Most counselors in elementary and secondary schools begin as teachers, and counselor certification standards in most states require teaching experience as a prerequisite. Thus, school counselors have the unique problem of being required to prepare first for some other job in education. They must actually enter their second-choice occupation and achieve experience in it before preparing for a career in counseling.

The skills demanded of teachers are not necessarily those demanded of counselors, and competence in teaching has little bearing on the competence required for effective counseling. In fact, the information-giving and advising techniques of classroom teaching may even inhibit the development of some of the accepting and nonjudgmental techniques of counseling. This circuitous route into the profession has served no useful purpose. The time spent on teacher preparation and teaching experience could be more profitably devoted to additional study in counseling. Supervised internships and practicum experiences could be arranged so that the prospective counselor would gain first-hand experience of counseling in schools. This time-tested practice seems to have served other professions well, and school counseling may profit from their experience. Within recent years, criticism of the teaching requirement has resulted in some modification of this practice.

A second major difference between counselors in schools and those in other settings results from the nature and goals of the educational institution. Schools have specific educational tasks and are required by law to carry out an educational mission. The educational task, by tradition and by legal mandate, is considered the primary task of the school. Counseling tends to be perceived as an activity designed to aid the institution in achieving its primary goal; counselors are viewed as educators first and counselors second. Counselors are not always free to work with clients as they see fit but must adhere to the policies and rules of the institution. School counselors, in most instances, have considerably less professional freedom and autonomy than their colleagues in other settings.

The third major difference between school counseling and counseling or psychotherapy in other settings is the difference in clientele. For the most part, the school counselor's clients are minors who probably have limited freedom in planning and decision making. They are often referred to counselors by teachers, administrators, or parents who have specific concerns about the student and thus may expect direct action and feedback from the counselor. The counselor is expected to work with a large number of students and a variety of concerns and problems, ranging from vocational planning to personal problem solving. The counselor must also develop and maintain close working relationships with teachers, administrators, and parents. He is required to spend time in consultation with these adults and in some instances may provide short-term therapy for them. In addition, school counselors are required to perform such guidance and personnel functions as information giving, advising, testing, and placement. These functions, along with such additional and questionable functions as record keeping and administering tests for the military, often interfere with counseling activities and may leave little time for personal contact with students. These conditions help to create identity problems for school counselors. Perceptions of professional problems and issues can become vague and distorted.

Any discussion of school counseling must acknowledge some of the criticisms leveled against its practitioners, both individually and as a group. The charges are difficult to delineate because they often relate to fundamental attitudes about education and about the needs of those served by the educational establishment. Some criticisms are in reality societal issues that cannot be immediately resolved and may be only indirectly related to counseling. Still others come from related professionals who either fear territorial encroachment by professionals with less training or are genuinely concerned about the quality of mental health services in schools.

Some critics of counseling are philosophically at odds with the notion that such personal and individual help is appropriate. They tend to view counseling as an activity that pampers the weak and believe that people must learn to stand on their own feet and solve their own problems. They may argue that counseling in schools interferes with the educative process and that tax dollars should not be used to support it.

Directly related to these charges is the criticism that counselors in schools are inadequately prepared to perform a counseling function. This issue is confounded by the variety of tasks assigned the school counselor and by the situational demands in the field. As Shertzer and Stone (1975) note, there is little agreement on the role of the school counselor. At the present time, he is many things to many people and, sometimes, nothing to everybody. To level a charge of inadequate preparation without clear agreement regarding job expectancies seems presumptuous.

We maintain that the primary task of any professional using the title of "counselor" is counseling and, furthermore, that the counseling task has been clearly defined. Unfortunately, many jobs and activities described as counseling are at best quasi-administrative or clerical and at worst a fraud and a misrepresentation of the profession. One way out of this dilemma is for school counselors to assume responsibility for delineating their specific roles in the various settings where they are employed. Simultaneously, the profession could develop professional standards guaranteeing minimum preparation for all counselors and specialized preparation for jobs requiring special skill and expertise. Standards designed to improve counselor preparation have been developed by the Association for Counselor Education and Supervision (ACES) (1977). These standards not only recognize the desirability of extending counselor training beyond the traditional one year of graduate study but also point out the necessity of specialized preparation for a variety of work settings. Several universities now follow the ACES recommendations for two-year training programs.

School counselors tend to become defensive in the face of criticism about their practices and often place the blame for shoddy services on administrative interference. Such reactions are understandable; administrators frequently do interfere with the counseling role. Some counselors, however, inadvertently invite role distortion and misuse of their time when they fail to define their jobs and themselves properly. School counselors have not yet been able to deal with such crucial issues as professionalization, nor have they achieved the identity and autonomy necessary for true professional status. Minimum attention has been given to resolving contradictions, validating current practices, and resolving theoretical confusion. There is little evidence that school counselors are fully cognizant of their social and professional responsibilities or that they are much concerned about such influences on their clients as values, value conflicts, parochialism, and ethics.

As noted earlier, some of these deficiencies and problems result from the practices, policies, and peculiarities of the institutions by which counselors are employed. Some school practices militate against effective counseling services, and some teachers and administrators may demand services that conflict with the counseling role. The school counselor almost inevitably undergoes some alienation from his teacher colleagues, and he must deal with the question of what label he will wear in the school. Is he a guidance worker, school counselor, psychological counselor, therapist, generic psychologist, or teacher? To what tasks will he feel committed? Will he have a commitment to institutional goals that reflect his unique training and function, or will he feel alienated from the school? Conversely, will he simply echo the values of the teachers and administrators?

Clearly, then, some of the problems and impediments in school counseling are external; but many are internal. Therefore, if school counselors are to achieve professional status, they will need to increase their obstacle-jumping power and to examine and respond to current criticisms. Most important, counselors must insist on increased autonomy to function within their area of expertise, under their own responsibility, without undue interference from external forces.

Standards in Mental Health Counseling. One of the significant professional developments in counseling during the past decade was the birth of the American Mental Health Counselors Association (AMHCA), now one of thirteen divisions of the AACD. The 8,000 or so AMHCA members appear to feel a need for professional identity separate from mental health workers who serve as counselors in educational settings. Many AMHCA members are in private practice, and in several states this group has led the way for counselor licensure laws. In 1979 leaders of the AMHCA founded the National Academy of Certified Clinical Mental Health Counselors for the purpose of certifying mental health counselors throughout the country.

One of the AMHCA founders believes that as much as 50 percent of all direct counseling is provided by "mental health counselors," but he acknowledges the problem of agreeing on what constitutes counseling. In spite of the fact that the general public and other professionals "recognize and seek out this profession," full legislative recognition continues to elude the counseling profession (Lindenberg, 1984, p. 3). He implies that part of the problem facing the counseling profession lies with the traditional policies and actions of the AACD.

To some degree every profession is subject to analogous professional problems and criticisms. Few professions can function to the satisfaction of everyone, and each has its share of critics and detractors. Such criticism can be useful in encouraging self-examination and essential in stimulating improvement in professional practice.

Professional Standards in Psychology. The profession that most clearly typifies the helping professions is psychology. In fact, both the scientific knowledge that undergirds most therapies and the techniques most commonly used in therapy have their roots in psychology. A sizable percentage of all helping professionals, whether they are psychologists, therapists, educators, or school counselors, identify professionally with psychology, and many are in fact psychologists.

During this century psychology changed from a primarily academic discipline to an applied orientation concerned not only with mental health but also with helping people secure better adjustment and self-expression. Psychology still has a strong academic base, and a large number of psychologists are employed in educational institutions. In 1976, however, more than one-third of the members of the American Psychological Association (APA) surveyed by Dörken were engaged in counseling or psychotherapy; and a 1980 report reveals that almost 50 percent of the members in some APA divisions are employed in providing direct counseling services. Clinical and counseling psychology, two of the specializations within the field, are concerned primarily with the activities of therapy or counseling.

Clinical psychology emerged as a distinct specialization in the middle 1940s. At that time mental health specialists were urgently needed to help meet the needs of World War II veterans with mental and emotional difficulties. The Veterans Administration (VA) employed large numbers of clinical psychologists to staff VA centers throughout the country. During the same period, the VA subsidized university training programs in order to secure highly qualified persons. The VA required a doctoral degree of psychologists in approved VA training programs. This requirement established precedents for quality training, which have greatly influenced the present status of psychology as a helping profession (Jacobs, 1976). Major functions of the clinical psychologist have evolved from evaluation of behavioral problems to providing psychotherapy, conducting psychological consultation, and carrying on research in treatment procedures and other behavioral concerns (Shertzer and Stone, 1975).

Counseling psychology has much in common with clinical psychology. Both use case-study methods, evaluation instruments, and psychotherapeutic interviewing techniques. There are, nevertheless, significant functional distinctions. Brammer and Shostrom (1968) write that counseling psychology is a synthesis of several related trends found in guidance, mental hygiene, psychometrics, social casework, and psychotherapy movements. Counseling psychologists work primarily with normal people and characteristically are employed in educational institutions.

Leaders in APA Division 17 (Counseling Psychology) have attempted on several occasions to define their uniqueness within the fields of counseling and psychology. In the opening article of an issue of the *Counseling Psychologist* devoted to professional certification, Fretz and Mills (1980) made a scholarly attempt to provide perspective on several political issues facing counseling psychologists. In the same journal, Ivey (1981, p. 85) suggests that counseling psychology is the most broadly based specialty in psychology, and Kirk (1980, p. 25) maintains that counseling psychologists should continue their emphasis on development and health. She notes that counseling psychologists have traditionally served an important segment of the population on college campuses and believes that Division 17 members must continue serving this group. Other leaders, responding to Fretz and Mills's carefully researched article, make a case for the counseling psychologist in private practice and in community agencies.

There is some difficulty in demarcating the specialties in professional psychology. Roles and responsibilities tend to overlap, and the breadth and depth of training for clinical and counseling psychology are quite similar. Psychologists recognize that client needs vary and that, therefore, different skills and emphases in therapy are appropriate. In some settings and with some clients, attention to normal functioning and decision making may be emphasized, while other clients may require more extensive diagnosis and long-term treatment.

As noted at the beginning of this chapter, the APA has been influential in advancing psychology as a profession, in providing services, and in setting standards for training and practice. Founded in 1892, the APA now has a membership of approximately 40,000. Beginning in 1953 the APA Committee on a Directory of Psychological Service Centers and the American Board of Psychological Services developed standards for private practitioners and for psychologists in agency settings. The standards recommended that a private practitioner hold a diploma from the American Board of Professional Psychology and that a psychologist in an agency hold a Ph.D. and present at least three years of appropriate supervised experience (Jacobs, 1976, p. 24). These guidelines had considerable impact on certification and licensure laws enacted in several states in the 1950s and 1960s.

These early standards represented important first steps in the direction of professional self-regulation and autonomy. As Jacobs (1976) has noted, however, they were not sufficiently definitive to adequately represent a mature profession. Moreover, they also established double standards in that psychologists working in tax-supported institutions were exempted from the requirements. More work would be necessary in the 1960s and 1970s to establish firm standards and to stabilize the qualifications and functions of the majority of psychologists.

Considerable impetus for more comprehensive and definitive standards emerged from APA Division 17 (Counseling Psychology) and Division 22 (Rehabilitation Psychology) in the 1960s. In 1962 and 1963, a committee from Counseling Psychology prepared a comprehensive outline of standards for rehabilitation counselors. The report emphasized the need for psychological preparation for rehabilitation counselors and pointed out that the counselor should be a professional rather than a technician. Some standard-setting activities of the APA and its divisions were stimulated by such federal legislation as the Vocational Rehabilitation Act of 1965 and the Community Mental Health Centers Act of 1963. At that time professional psychology had not clearly defined the qualifications for psychologists in public institutions. Federal legislation of the 1960s heightened interest in mental health and fostered expansion of psychological services. Various government agencies began to employ "qualified psychologists" but without definitive guidelines on what made one "qualified." In fact, some governmental agencies defined a qualified psychologist as a person with "a master's degree from an accredited university" (Jacobs, 1976, p. 28). Thus, because of their tardiness in setting their own standards, psychologists were faced with the very real possibility that outside agencies would do the job for them.

The APA took steps to prevent this problem when it established the Task Force on Standards for Psychologists in 1970. During the next four years, the task force consulted with several other interested and related professional groups to develop standards for psychological services in all settings and for all people who needed them. Major considerations of the task force were the establishment of the professional identity of psychology and the precise definition of qualifications, functions, and responsibilities of psychologists. The APA Council of Representatives approved the standards in 1974.

The APA standards provide a generic description of psychologists and require that the person offering services hold a doctorate and present evidence of appropriate professional experiences. In his summary of the standards, Jacobs (1976) discusses several of the principles that guided the development of the document. The primary objectives were to improve the quality of psychological services and to determine the acceptable levels for those services. The 1974 document provides for uniform qualifications of practitioners and rejects the concept that psychologists in tax-supported institutions should be permitted to practice with fewer qualifications than other psychologists. Directors of psychological services and chairmen of university training programs are encouraged to urge their staff members to secure licensure or certification and to move toward licensure or certification as a condition of employment. The APA monitors, examines, and accredits university training programs for psychologists.

In 1975 the APA Council of Representatives created a standing Committee on Standards for Providers of Psychological Services. The charge for the committee is to review and revise the standards so that they remain timely and workable.

Standards that describe a profession and define the functions and qualifications of members are essential in self-governance and in helping a profession meet its ethical and social obligations. Mature professions also discharge their responsibilities and maintain the visibility and status of the profession through the activities of special boards, commissions, and standing committees. The APA has several boards with specific responsibilities in such matters as self-governance. In addition, these boards provide a fact-finding and monitoring service for the membership. Illustrative of APA boards is the Board of Social and Ethical Responsibility (BSERP), which has as its area of concern "those aspects of psychology that involve solutions to the fundamental problems of human justice" (American Psychological Association, 1976, p. 9). Created in 1971, the BSERP studies the internal operations of the APA and makes recommendations in areas such as the roles of psychologists in society, human research, research on social problems, and development of public policy actions or statements of the association.

Among the professional societies described in this book, the APA appears to have been most successful in its efforts to define its profession, describe qualifications of its members, and develop stabilizing standards and policies. These activities are essential not only in self-governance but also in providing the public with some measure of the integrity of the profession.

Professional Standards in Psychiatry. Psychiatry is somewhat difficult to distinguish functionally from other psychotherapeutic specialties discussed in this chapter. One obvious distinction lies in training: the psychiatrist has an M.D., and counselors or psychologists generally have a Ph.D. or a master's degree. Therapeutic approaches contribute other fairly clear distinctions. Psychiatric treatment for severe emotional disorders may include chemotherapy (the use of drugs), electro-shock, insulin therapy, hypnosis, psychoanalysis, or individual and group psychotherapy.

Fine distinctions are sometimes made between the types of clients treated by medically trained psychiatrists and psycho-logically trained therapists. In practice such distinctions are often vague and sometimes controversial. Szasz (1974), for example, contends that many emotional disorders are in reality personality problems or disorders of learning and perception rather than illness in a medical sense. While he recognizes that certain brain diseases affect behavior, he objects to the "mental illness concept" that disorders of thought and action are usually related to a neurological defect. He argues that psychiatrists have confused *defects* with *beliefs* and behavior choices. Glasser (1983) also questions psychiatric preoccupation with "sickness" and stresses the role of learning and responsibility assumption in therapy over the focus on pathological difficulties.

We cannot always distinguish "normal" from "deviant," nor is it generally possible to determine whether emotional dif-ficulties result from faulty learning and perception or from neurological defects. As stated earlier, such distinctions tend to be artificial, and labels used to categorize emotional problems may be more indicative of a therapist's orientation than they are useful in diagnosis and treatment.

Psychiatry also differs from psychology in the matter in which it is regulated. It is, in fact, questionable whether self-regulation exists in American psychiatry; certainly, when com-pared to self-regulatory activities in other specialties in therapy, such activities in psychiatry are quite inadequate. Taylor and Torrey (1972), themselves physicians, charge that self-regula-tion in psychiatry has evolved into a form of professional self-protection that fails to ensure competent psychiatric services. Despite an elaborate regulatory facade, the practice of psychi-atry requires nothing more than a medical license. No special skills are required, and no evidence of training in psychiatry is mandated.

Certification of psychiatrists and accreditation of psychi-atric training programs are the two major components of present psychiatric regulation. The regulatory body for certification is the American Board of Psychiatry and Neurology. This twelve-member board includes four persons appointed by the American Psychiatric Association (APA), four by the American Neurological Association, and four by the American Medical Association (AMA). The AMA usually appoints two psychiatrists and two neurologists, with the result that the board is composed of six psychiatrists and six neurologists. The board has been described as an independent agency, but in fact it primarily serves the interests of the parent organizations, the APA and the AMA. It represents a kind of organizational incest (Taylor and Torrey, 1972, p. 34).

The American Board of Psychiatry and Neurology has consistently advocated a policy of voluntary certification. The result of this policy is that almost two-thirds of the psychiatrists in this country practice without board certification. While AMA and APA regulations permit physicians without psychiatric certification to practice, they adhere to strict requirements for entrance to the certifying examination. These requirements limit board eligibility to medical school graduates with three years of training in an accredited psychiatric training program and two years of postresidency experience (American Medical Association, 1969). However, an applicant with two years of training in any medical or surgical specialty may substitute this experience for a year of psychiatric experience. This means that two years of training in colon and rectal surgery may count as a year of experience in psychiatry. This absurdity is designed to protect the medical identity of psychiatry. Two professionals have questioned whether the primary emphasis on a medical background is appropriate in psychiatry: "A Martian newly arrived on this planet might reasonably predict that this professional's practice would consist of performing tonsillectomies, delivering babies, and treating heart failure and epilepsy, while engaging in psychotherapy on the side and organizing the community in the evenings" (Taylor and Torrey, 1972, p. 36).

The second major component of self-regulation in psychiatry deals with the accreditation of training programs. This function is the responsibility of the Joint Residency Review

Committee for Psychiatry and Neurology. Six psychiatrists representing the AMA and the APA serve on this committee, which meets twice annually to review applications for training program accreditation. The committee works from a checklist designed to identify program strengths and weaknesses. Assessment focuses on staff, curriculum, supervised experiences, facilities, and the number of patients seen by a psychiatrist in training. The committee may also complete site visitations and in addition secure supplementary appraisals from field representatives as part of the review process. The committee deliberates in private; thus, the basis for accrediting decisions remains largely unknown.

Standards in Social Work and Marriage and Family Counseling. Many practitioners in related professions also feel that they are doing psychotherapy in the formal sense and are involved in developing and implementing standards for self-governance and professional autonomy. The National Association of Social Workers and the American Association for Marriage and Family Therapy, for example, have attempted to improve the profession by setting standards for the training, licensure, and conduct of members.

Social workers, who often perform a clinical or therapeutic role, generally complete a two-year graduate program leading to a master's degree in social work. The social worker often functions as a member of a team that may include a psychologist, a psychiatrist, and other mental health specialists. Social workers also are found in welfare, corrections, education, and community agency activities. The National Association of Social Workers has not yet established standards for approving members who provide counseling services, either privately or in a public institution. However, in some states—Virginia, for example—licensure for the private practice of counseling encompasses social workers as well as psychologists and counselors.

The American Association for Marriage and Family Therapy (1982b) has developed comprehensive standards for persons in this counseling specialty. It requires a master's degree in an appropriate behavioral science, mental health discipline, or recognized helping profession. Supervised clinical experience and demonstrated preparation for the practice of marriage and family counseling are also required for membership. A state license can qualify an individual for membership if the state's licensing standards meet the clinical standards of the association.

Professional Ethics

Ethical standards or codes represent yet another way that professionals attempt to govern and discipline themselves. Ethical standards deal with proper professional conduct and serve as guidelines for the therapist's work with clients. In addition, ethical standards help the therapist deal with such questions as "What modes of conduct are favorable or unfavorable to service for this client?" and "What conduct is requisite in this situation?"

These standards arise and are necessary because therapists individually and collectively have assumed public obligations that dictate ethical responsibility. Therapists claim special skills and competence not generally possessed by others; and public sanctions, acceptance, and support are in large measure based on the faith that therapeutic assistance is both helpful and professional. The client who seeks help from the therapist or from the institution that employs a counselor or psychologist has the right to expect competent and responsible services. The client has a right to judge the adequacy of the intervention on his behalf and to hold the therapist accountable for the results. Ethical responsibility encompasses not only what therapists do in face-to-face encounters with clients but also other acts and statements that pertain to or affect that service.

If the practitioner's professional obligation is in fact a source of professional prestige, his prestige is also a source of professional obligation. Therapy and therapists are not uniformly prestigious, and either or both may be held in low repute in some circles. Nevertheless, the perceptions and expectations of clients and the general public are factors in ethical responsibility. The more indiscriminating the client's view of the therapist is, the more scrupulous he must be in his actions with the client. The more hostile or suspicious the client is, the more cautious the therapist must be in his interventions (Levy, 1972, p. 99).

In other chapters of this book, we discuss ethical conflicts and dilemmas inherent in the practice of psychotherapy.
Often these dilemmas have their basis in our traditional beliefs
in the dignity and worth of the human being. How, for example, can one intervene in the lives of some clients without rob-
bing them of this dignity? In institutional work the therapist is
often faced with overlapping loyalties and responsibilities. How
does he resolve conflicts between the client, the institution, and
society? We have argued that a therapist is primarily responsible
to his client, but ultimately he is also responsible to society.
Hogan (1974) has identified two sets of ethical ideas that therapists employ in making judgments: the ethics of conscience
and the ethics of social responsibility. To elaborate on Hogan's
beliefs, the therapist's ethical decisions will be based on the
values to which he and his colleagues subscribe, the responsibility he feels for his profession's reputation, and his desire for
continued public sanction of his work.

The adoption of ethical standards and the knowledge of
ethical principles do not in themselves solve ethical problems of
therapists. Furthermore, ethical codes alone cannot solve the
professional problem of incompetent and unethical therapists.
Ethical standards of a professional group are primarily directed
at its members and thus may have little influence on those who
choose to practice counseling or psychotherapy without benefit
of professional affiliation or colleague support. In fact, it is
doubtful whether many popular "healers" could qualify for
membership in some of the prestigious professions discussed in
this book.

Ethical standards generally discourage the practice of
therapy by unqualified persons; however, some professions accept members mainly on the basis of their interest and willingness to pay dues. Furthermore, while some professions have
ethics committees, they have no machinery for dealing with unethical conduct. This failure highlights some of the concerns
and criticisms raised throughout this book. Professional associations that fail to establish reasonable qualifications for members or procedures for monitoring member activities have no
basis for a claim to professionalization.

The American Psychological Association provides a good example of a professional group willing to accept its ethical and social responsibilities. Reference has already been made to the APA standards for training and approval of training programs. The APA has also developed distinct standards for membership. Psychologists regarded as qualified are those who either are approved by the American Board of Professional Psychology or are licensed or certified by state examining boards. The first two principles in the APA's *Ethical Principles of Psychologists* emphasize the social responsibilities of psychologists. As noted in Principle 2, "The maintenance of high standards of competence is a responsibility shared by all psychologists, in the interest of the public and the profession as a whole" (American Psychological Association, 1981).

The APA has established procedures to monitor the behavior of its members and has prescribed penalties for ethical violations. Under the bylaws of the association, a Committee on Scientific and Professional Ethics and Conduct (CSPEC) is set up to receive and investigate complaints of unethical conduct of members and to recommend action on cases investigated. For violation of the *Ethical Principles,* the APA may expel a member or administer a lesser penalty, such as a reprimand or supervision (American Psychological Association, 1974, p. 703).

In addition to its monitoring functions for the national association, the CSPEC has adopted a set of procedures as a guide for state association ethics committees. These committees are responsible for investigating and resolving cases of unethical professional misconduct of members of state associations; at the request of the CSPEC, the committee also may deal with ethical violations by APA members. The CSPEC emphasizes that its primary function is to protect the association and the public against unethical practices by psychologists (American Psychological Association, 1981).

There is a connection between ethical responsibilities and legal principles that is applicable to therapy. As noted in Chapter Three, one who, by reason of special skill and training, undertakes a service to another is legally obligated to perform that service properly. Thus, both ethical and legal considera-

tions may be important in shaping the therapist's professional
ethical conduct.

Licensure and Certification

The most widely used legal methods for regulating the
practice of counseling and psychotherapy are state laws that
license or certify practitioners. Although a license or certificate
does not ensure competence or ethically proper behavior, it
does inform the public that the therapist has at least minimum
qualifications for the service he offers. Although some certification and licensure standards are so minimal as to be farcical, the
fact that they exist at all provides a measure of protection to
the public. Standards or laws also offer some protection for the
profession and have the added effect of providing legal recognition of counseling and psychotherapy. Although distinctions between licensure and certification are not always clear, some
slight differences can be noted.

Professional licensure laws define the practice of a profession and restrict functions to those who meet specified qualifications. A licensing law usually forbids use of a title—psychologist, for example—by an unqualified person. Certification laws
may or may not include a definition of practice; but they, too,
generally limit use of the title to those qualified to practice.
Each of the fifty states has statutes regulating the practice of
psychology. Of these, twenty-six have licensure laws, and the
remainder have certification.

All state boards of education maintain credentialing programs for school counselors, school psychologists, school social
workers, and other mental health specialists employed in education. Certificates are issued to qualified applicants, usually on
the basis of a master's degree in their area of specialization. Additionally, some professional groups award certificates or diplomas based on the competency and expertise of applicant
members. An example is the postdoctoral diploma granted by
the American Board of Professional Psychology. Diplomas are
issued by the board in clinical, counseling, and industrial psychology and are based on a written and oral examination of the
applicant's professional knowledge.

Licensure or certification for the private practice of counseling, by counselors not credentialed as psychologists or psychiatrists, has emerged recently as a major professional issue. Several complex problems and intense arguments surround this issue. Many counselors maintain that counseling is a unique mental health profession. They contend that, although some functions of counselors and other therapists overlap, the practice of counseling cannot be likened to the practice of psychology. They cite philosophical orientation, the developmental focus of counseling, and the work setting as major differences between themselves and other therapists. Other counselors hold that the differences between the practice of psychology and the practice of counseling are so minuscule as to render legal differentiation impossible. They point out that counselor training is primarily psychological, even though the training may have been in schools of education, not psychology. They object to psychology licensure laws that exclude counselors, contending that such laws deprive them of their constitutional right to practice their profession. In many instances the courts have been asked to resolve these arguments.

Weldon v. *Virginia State Board of Psychologist Examiners* (Corporation Ct., Newport News, Va. 1974) was one of the first cases to test psychology licensure laws. In this case the plaintiff, a counselor engaged in private practice, argued that he was exempt from the state psychology licensure laws, since counseling is an activity separate from psychology. The State Board of Psychologist Examiners disagreed and secured a court order restraining Weldon from practice. Weldon appealed, and the court upheld his contention that counseling is a separate activity: "[We disagree] with the Virginia State Board of Psychologist Examiners in holding that appellant is practicing psychology, thus requiring him to be licensed under the laws of the State of Virginia. . . . The profession of personnel and guidance counseling is a separate profession and should be so recognized." Nonetheless, according to the court, "This profession does utilize the tools of the psychologist as [do] many other professions; therefore, it would be necessary for him [Weldon] to be licensed under existing laws [for psychologists]." In support of this somewhat contradictory opinion, the court cited a

Virginia statute, which "appears to say" that, in the absence of a regulatory body governing "guidance and personnel counseling," a counselor in private practice who uses the tools of psychology is subject to the laws governing the practice of psychology.

An Ohio case provides further illustration of the confusion and conflict surrounding the licensure and practice of psychology and counseling. In *City of Cleveland* v. *Cook,* 75-CRB 11478 (Mun. Ct. 1975), the court rendered a definitive verdict supporting counseling as a separate profession. In the Ohio case, Culbreth Cook, holder of a Ph.D. in counseling, was charged in a criminal warrant with practicing psychology without a license. Cook's attorney argued that Cook was in fact engaged in the practice of counseling, not psychology, and that he was eminently qualified to counsel and had a right to earn a living in his profession: "It's either totally unconstitutional or something is radically wrong" when someone who is capable is not permitted to provide services to persons who request them. Primarily on the basis of this argument, the court dismissed the charge against Cook.

The courts spoke again in *Mississippi Board of Psychological Examiners* v. *Coxe,* 355 So. 2d 669 (Miss. 1978). In this case the State Board of Psychological Examiners refused to license Ray Coxe as a psychologist because his major area of doctoral study was "counseling psychology," not psychology. Coxe took legal action, and the Harrison County court ordered that he be licensed. The Board of Psychological Examiners appealed to the Mississippi Supreme Court, which again ruled for Coxe.

The private practice of counseling and legal recognition of counseling as separate from psychology are related issues that have generated considerable conflict between psychologists and counselors in some localities. Alexander (1982) points out that state APA groups have generally opposed licensure or certification for counselors and have attempted to prevent counselors from practicing for a fee. He notes that state boards of psychological examiners are controlled by psychologists and that it is difficult for a counselor to gain permission to take the psychology licensure examination even when he has met the stated requirements.

Two examples provided by Fretz and Mills (1980) illustrate the point: (1) A graduate of a counseling and guidance program with many graduates practicing as professional psychologists is declared ineligible to take the licensing exam because his training is "not primarily psychological in nature." (2) A graduate of an APA-approved counseling psychology program is declared ineligible for employment in a mental health center, since the center relies on third-party payments, payments available only to clinical psychologists in that state. These and similar events led counselors to conclude that they were being denied the right to practice their profession in the public sector. The main obstacle was psychology licensure legislation, but other conditions also threatened to make counselors second-class citizens in the mental health field.

In 1977 the Department of Health, Education, and Welfare issued a report calling for national certification of all health professionals and the establishment of national training standards. Federal reimbursement (including Medicaid) would be limited to personnel licensed by state boards meeting national standards. Counselors saw in this proposal the possibility of their being excluded from many employment opportunities (Cottingham and Warner, 1978). The need for counselors to have some type of legal credential was therefore clear.

Virginia had led the way by enacting a law providing for licensure for the private practice of counseling in 1975. This law defined the activities of counselors and required a master's degree in counseling, guidance, and personnel work plus four years' experience as a prerequisite for certification. At the request of the state branch of the American Personnel and Guidance Association, the 1976 Virginia General Assembly amended and expanded the 1975 statute. The current law provides for the licensure of counselors in private practice and the creation of a behavioral science board to regulate licensing of counselors, psychologists, and social workers.

To be licensed in Virginia, counselors must have completed at least sixty semester hours of graduate work and must hold a master's degree in counseling or personnel services. The sixty hours must include a minimum of six hours of practicum or internship. Two years of postdegree supervised experience are also required. Candidates for licensure must also pass an examination and have their applications reviewed by a board of professional counselors.

During the past decade, ten states have enacted licensure laws for counselors. In a few instances, serious efforts have been made to deal with counselor competence, professionalism, and service to the public. In most cases, however, the major incentive for counselor licensure appears to have been monopolistic control of private practice, third-party payments, and counselor identity. Minimal attention has been given to counselor skills, public responsibility, and periodic performance review. In some states Boards of Professional Counselors not only control the licensing process but deal with ethical violations as well. Such a system raises serious questions about the willingness of counselors to regulate the professional behavior of practitioners.

As previously suggested, licensure and certification laws will not solve all the problems confronting the helping professions, and some leaders in the field have questioned the wisdom of the current emphasis on legal regulation of counseling and psychotherapy. Rogers (1973) believes that licensure laws have the effect of freezing a profession in a past image, since licensure examination questions are often drawn from materials used ten to twenty years earlier and examiners tend to have been trained fifteen to twenty years earlier. Rogers also feels that the desire to professionalize can lead to a rigid bureaucracy in which inflexible rules replace sound professional judgment and ignore such factors as quality of work and the effectiveness of the therapist.

Cottingham (1980) has summarized some of the results—or lack of results—of licensure laws in counseling and psychology in American society:

1. There is no evidence that licensure directly affects the competence or honesty of helping agents, or that licensure of counselors and psychologists protects the public, or that abolition of licensure laws would result in danger or harm to the public.
2. Many qualified practitioners are excluded from the licensure process.

3.   Many competent counselors and psychologists believe that
     licensure serves more to protect the self-interests of help-
     ing professionals than to protect the public from incompe-
     tent practitioners and quacks. Licensure may be more po-
     litical than professional.
4.   Some state legislatures appear to be disenchanted with oc-
     cupational regulation in general and with psychology in
     particular.

     Clearly, the advocates of strong licensure laws for coun-
selors and psychotherapists have advanced several good and
sufficient reasons for the legislation. At the same time, such
statutes do represent external controls of the profession, and
the original reasons for the legislation may one day be replaced
by quite different reasons. Once a precedent is established, a
legislature, for example, could establish the maximum fee for
therapeutic services, and the profession would be powerless to
prevent it. We regard such legislative interference as highly im-
probable in the immediate future, but the example does illustrate the possible problems faced by professions when they
turn to law for regulation of their activities.
     Dworkin (1971), in his essay on legal "paternalism," ob-
jects to laws requiring licensure for certain professions, claiming
that such laws interfere unnecessarily with a large number of
people and protect only a few. He places licensure laws in a cat-
egory with other paternalistic laws, which, for example, require
motorcyclists to wear safety helmets and make suicide a criminal offense. Dworkin concedes that some paternalistic laws may
be legitimate, but he argues that other methods of accomplishing the desired end should be substituted for legal regulation,
even if they involve delay and inconvenience.

Summary

     This chapter has described issues, problems, and trends
related to the professionalization of counseling and psychotherapy. Each of the professional groups discussed has made progress during the past three decades in refining its practices and in
developing procedures for self-regulation. Such professional as-

sociations as the American Psychological Association and the American Association for Counseling and Development have played major roles in the advancement of counseling and psychology and appear to be even more active and influential in this decade.

We believe that it is necessary and desirable for professions to develop methods for self-regulation and self-discipline —not only for the preservation of professional autonomy and identity but also for the maintenance of relationships with clients and the general public. At the present time, control of the helping professions is divided among the training institutions, the states handling licensure and certification, and professional associations. The trend toward more external controls through licensure laws, federal statutes, and court decisions has been noted. We view this trend with mixed feelings and with considerable concern about possible consequences of legal regulation. Some legal methods for controlling the professional activities of therapists, particularly if these methods weed out the incompetents, are probably legitimate. Professionals, however, should not rely solely on legislatures and courts to solve their problems unless they are prepared to give up some freedom and professional autonomy.

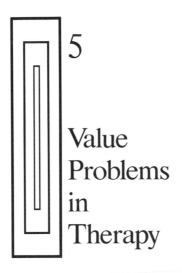

5

Value
Problems
in
Therapy

Human interaction is guided by the values and personal philosophy of the parties involved. Values and philosophy determine how we react to experiences in life, how we plan our life goals, and the manner in which we attempt to achieve these goals. Few people act independently of their values, even when those values are unclear and vaguely defined. Personal values, as they apply to the work of the counselor, have been the focus of considerable attention for several years. Bergin (1980) believes that a good understanding of cultural and individual values is integral to understanding a client's feelings and behavior. He states that there is no such thing as value-free therapy; the counselor constantly confronts values that come from many sources, operate at many levels, and frequently are permeated with ambiguity.

Our clients grow, learn, and have numerous and continuing experiences, which they interpret in a unique way. These experiences and perceptions tend to influence attitudes, which in turn provide guides to behavior. These guides may be generally described as values. Our values are reflected in the way we spend our time, express our interests and concerns, and view others and ourselves. Values, then, are long-range attitudes, convictions, wishes, hopes, and faith. Values are the principles we live by.

Since the major source of values is found in experiences, we would expect that different experiences would give rise to different values and that values would change as a result of experiences. A shepherd in Turkey would not be expected to subscribe to the same values as an automobile worker in Detroit, nor would a teenager in San Francisco be expected to have the same values as a retired Georgia farmer. Moreover, since a person's experiences are not static, his values are not expected to remain static. As guides to individual behavior, values evolve, mature, and change as the person and his life change.

The value theory of Raths, Hamrin, and Simon (1978) has considerable relevance for mental health professions. In their view values are part of a person's identity and operate in complex circumstances, which usually involve more than simple extremes of right or wrong, good or bad, true or false. The conditions under which behavior is guided, in which values operate, typically involve conflicting demands, a weighing, a balancing, and finally an action that reflects a multitude of forces. Thus, values seldom function in a pure and abstract form. Complicated judgments and decisions are involved, and the person's values are reflected in the choices he finally makes.

Perry (1974) describes values as attitudes that influence the way people respond to ideas, events, and objects they encounter. He believes that values have no objective status: "It is not a quality of the world we experience; rather, value exists only in the eye of the beholder. The silence of the desert is without value until some wanderer finds it lonely and terrifying; the cataract, until some human finds it sublime, or until it is harnessed to satisfy human needs" (p. 396). Perry quotes Spinoza, who wrote that we do not strive for, long for, or desire anything because we deem it to be good, but on the other hand we deem a thing to be good because we wish for it or strive for it. Perry describes such terms as "good" and "value" in empirical terms. For him, saying that something is good or valuable is equivalent to saying that someone takes an interest in it.

The therapist must develop an awareness not only of his own values but also of the value structure of others. All people have beliefs about how things ought to be or how they would like them to be. We are *for* some things and *against* others; we hold some things to be *good* and others *bad,* some *true* and some *false.* This polarity, however, is not reducible to that between *yes* and *no* in the logical sense, because a thing or an action can be partially good and partially bad or at one time right and at another time wrong. And one can equivocate on "yes" or respond "no" with finality. The disposition to favor some things and to disfavor others leads, however, to choices and decisions or, to put it more directly, significantly influences the behavior of both client and therapist.

Values lie largely in the realm of ethics and ethical behavior. They have to do with real and fancied choices. They are primarily social in scope and application. Their sphere is all human conduct, in which significant alternatives are available. A choice must exist, and we choose one mode of behavior as preferable or better when compared with other alternatives. Values are always hierarchically integrated; that is, they are related in respect to a greater or lesser degree of desirability. Without choice there would be no occasion for value judgments and decisions. These conditions provide further evidence of the influence of values in counseling and psychotherapy.

Effects of Social Change on Values

Social changes of the past few decades have dramatically altered all aspects of American life: private lives, education, marriage, work, and life in the community (Bell, 1976). In analyzing the forces that are changing the modern world, Toffler (1980) concludes that we are now in a third "tidal wave" of change in world history. In this period of recurring social upheaval, change is virtually the sole constant. Today it is impossible to predict the future and difficult to comprehend the present. Toffler believes that the constant struggle to deal with change is psychologically stressful for the individual. Social standards shift so rapidly that people have trouble finding personal identity and meaning in life. When life's tasks change too fast to allow for easy mastery, people may find development difficult or even blocked. Similarly, in their study of adult life, Lowenthal, Thurnher, Chiriboga, and Associates (1975) discovered that lifestyles, self-perceptions, and personal values are all influenced by societal factors and that complex social change creates stress and conflict in people of all ages.

These conditions point to several implications for counselors and therapists. Sociocultural changes have a major impact on many clients, and the effective counselor must be aware of these factors. Generalized knowledge about social forces is insufficient; assumptions made from generalized information may lead to misconceptions and inappropriate services.

Some of the most dramatic changes of this century have occurred in rules for personal conduct. Social values have changed markedly; traditional rules have been discarded and new ones adopted. The new rules are more tolerant, encourage greater individual freedom, and place more emphasis on personal enjoyment. Yankelovich (1981) believes that the new rules for personal conduct have encouraged people to become seekers of self-fulfillment and personal pleasure. The greater acceptance of sex outside of marriage, emphasis on the body and physical fitness, and above all the search for personal enjoyment are examples of the striking changes in values and in rules of personal behavior.

Several religious leaders and fundamentalist Christian groups around the country are uneasy about these changes. Fundamentalist minister Jerry Falwell clearly believes that the "moral cancer" on the face of the nation includes abortion, homosexuality, Hollywood, nudity, drugs, and sex outside of marriage. He attributes the "moral decadence of the country" to the "godless humanists" and "liberal Democrats," who have distorted our "traditional American values" (Falwell, 1984). To deal with the evils of these "leftist" thinkers and politicians,

Falwell formed the conservative political action group Moral Majority.

Billy Graham, who is not in the same league with Falwell, takes a similar conservative position on some of the same issues. For example, in his newspaper column for March 7, 1984, he advises a young homosexual to seek a counselor who would make it clear that a "homosexual lifestyle is wrong." Graham leaves no doubt that homosexuality is deviant and "contrary to the Bible."

In spite of this dismal picture of a decaying society, both Falwell and Graham believe that the "great ideals on which this nation was founded" can be restored. To that end Falwell has accepted the challenge to carry his message "to the halls of Congress, to the White House, and across this great land" (Goodman and Price, 1981).

Clearly, the fundamentalist philosophy is solidly conservative, both politically and socially. Its proponents are generally opposed to the welfare system and to many human/social service programs, particularly those supported by the federal government. They claim to be for human rights, but they are opposed to the Equal Rights Amendment, and many support such 1960s segregationists as Jesse Helms and George Wallace. They are strong law-and-order people and vocal in their support for a strong defense establishment. Although often vague on their meaning of the term "values," they are fond of such events as "I Love America" rallies and have long advocated prayer in public schools. They speak of "Bible-believing" Christians and clearly see the United States as a Christian nation.

Therapists may not agree with Falwell (1984) that "two thirds of the young people are recommiting themselves to traditional values." Nevertheless, there is evidence of a shift to the right in this country, and therein lies an issue that the helping professions cannot ignore.

If it is acknowledged that there is no such thing as a value-free therapy, then the value contrasts between therapists and society at large may become more marked. Evidence presented by Gross and Kahn (1983) suggests that the philosophy of therapists is markedly different from that of the fundamentalists. Values ranked highest by therapists in the Gross and Kahn study included inner harmony, love, self-respect, wisdom, and friendship. Religious values of therapists in this study differed from those espoused by the Christian right. In fact, Gross and Kahn found that 30 percent of one group of professionals had no religious beliefs and described their views as agnostic or atheist.

It has long been assumed that the personal philosophy of therapists may be at variance with that of the society in which they operate. Counselors and psychologists by and large claim to value individual freedom, open-mindedness, personal pleasure, and loving relationships. Therapists tend to be accepting, non-judgmental, and objective in their attitudes about the human condition. Many embrace a philosophy described as humanistic —emphasizing the ability of humans to develop creatively and positively. If, as expected, the general population is shifting away from these views toward a more judgmental, punitive, law-and-order posture, what are the implications for therapists?

Characteristic Contemporary Values

One of the most prominent beliefs about contemporary society is that it is geared to mass production and sweeping technology. Economic motives and increased profits are viewed as driving forces in human conduct. Kemp (1967), in his discussion of the "marketplace orientation," notes that the individual is constantly reminded that he is valued most for what he produces and not for what he thinks or what he knows. Children learn quite early that they are loved more if they conform to standards based on success and productivity. Thus, young people have no basis for self-respect; their significance is unrelated to their beliefs, their values, or even the fact that they are people. Kemp argues that, as societies become saturated with technology, people lose their individuality: "They become depersonalized, products on the market like the machines they have helped to produce. It is not wisdom or understanding of persons that is considered significant, but the impersonal knowledge of mechanistic naturalism" (p. 69).

Many years ago Williams (1956) drew up an interesting list of dominant American values. His list included the following values, or modes of organizing human conduct: achievement and success; economic prosperity, bigness, and rewards; activity and work, primarily a legacy from our Puritan past; moral orientation, humanitarianism, material comfort, equality, and freedom. Snygg (1972) questions some of these values, pointing to the "fiction" of economic man and the error of viewing competition as a motive for human behavior. He notes that economic gain is not the only motive for work and productivity; equally important are prestige, peer approval, and personal satisfaction. Although, in Snygg's view, competition is a method frequently used to "get more work out of people" or to get students to work harder, it is a relatively ineffective way of getting people to produce more; therefore, such methods are being abandoned. Snygg believes that our attempts to link values to individual behavior leave many questions unanswered.

In a provocative article dealing with high technology, Aubrey and D'Andrea (1984) theorize that technology possesses the power of a great hurricane that will dominate our lives in the twenty-first century. They describe some of the pitfalls in romanticized and inordinately optimistic promises of technology. They see increased stress and worker displacement followed by psychological problems, interpersonal conflict, and value changes as the other inevitable and unpleasant side of "high tech."

A high-tech future is characterized by both hopefulness and gloom. The sense of hopefulness is rooted in an awareness of the qualitative changes currently in motion. The feeling is reinforced by the possibility that these changes can result in a more progressive social order as the manifestations of a post-industrial era are unveiled. Theoretically, the greater efficiency of high technology should lead to a reduction in human labor. Work should become less monotonous, and most people should have more leisure time. But high technology is just as likely to present a myriad of forces antithetical to the welfare of mankind. For example, it may result in permanent unemployment or underemployment for a large number of persons and in a deterioration in America's traditional work ethic (Aubrey and D'Andrea, 1984, pp. 5-7).

   Although the studies cited are interesting and provocative, it remains difficult to analyze contemporary values, partly because of the complexity of contemporary society and the changing nature of the Western culture. A casual consideration of the great diversity in the country, ranging from trappers in Alaska to oil tycoons in Texas, suggests the tentativeness of any generalizations. Furthermore, within the same region and time span, various groups might hold different views on lifestyles and on such topics as individual freedom, honesty, and morality. Philosophers, social psychologists, and popular writers do not always agree on the essential characteristics of contemporary values. Consider, for example, the various reactions and interpretations of commentators and political scientists to the underlying causes of Watergate, government snooping, and FBI scandals. Some social analysts view dishonesty in high places and abuse of power as a manifestation of general moral deterioration, while others maintain that the crimes of a few scoundrels have only loose relevance to the moral fiber of the nation.

   Still, we are persuaded that some characteristics stand out. We are a production-oriented society, we idealize technology, and we value achievement and success. We admire those who can "get things done," and we respect a diligent worker or a "high charger." We covet material comforts, we like money, and, as Katona (1951) has concluded, "The more we get, the more we want." But there are other value orientations that cannot be overlooked and should not be minimized. The ideas on which the country's political and social structure was built— freedom, equality, democracy, and justice—are also visible, particularly during periods of political upheaval or economic stress. Consider, with Cooper (1969), changes in attitudes resulting from the civil rights struggle of the 1950s and 1960s and the student protest movement of the 1960s. Or observe the moral tightrope on which politicians now cautiously tread as a result of public outrage over political chicanery and immorality. One can argue, of course, that politicians are no more ethical than they were before Watergate or "Abscam," only more afraid of being exposed. But these examples do illustrate that a concern for basic ethical principles is present in much of our society.

Many of the values described do not necessarily complement others, and some are in conflict. Not surprisingly, some modes are more adequate for one group than for another. Some individuals use a conforming mode to achieve success; others may use illegal means to attain wealth or power. Others may reject cultural goals or values and, in effect, become dropouts (Grossack and Gardner, 1972).

Some Dilemmas

There was a time when a therapist was not supposed to deal with values, and any suggestion that values should be imposed on clients was considered not only coercive but antitherapeutic. Nonetheless, both clients and therapists have values, and there are prevailing values in communities and in families. These value attitudes may not be in harmony; in fact, the client's problem may be directly related to conflicts between his values and those of the community or family. One of the questions for the therapist, then, is the degree of disequilibrium resulting from this divergence of values. But even more important is the question of how the therapist helps his client experience a value system without an authoritarian imposition of his own values. We do not believe that therapists should have only mild values or that expressions of beliefs or attitudes are prima facie wrong. On the contrary, often a therapist must take a consistent and firm position during the process of ministering to his clients.

The individual who seeks help from a therapist is often in desperate circumstances. He is uncertain about his future, he may be unable to make decisions, and he may regard his situation as hopeless. He is in counseling because everything else has failed. Here he hopes to find assistance in meeting his needs and in planning a course of action. He can still take responsibility for his life, and he is still capable of making some decisions, as demonstrated by his act of seeking help. Ethically, the therapist cannot assume decision-making responsibility for the client but must facilitate client self-understanding and self-direction. This condition presents us with a further dilemma. Suppose, for example, that the behavior of the client seems certain to lead to greater suffering for the client or for others. Can value-free therapy be done under these conditions? And what are the therapist's responsibilities to society?

London (1964, p. 13) writes that "so-called moral neutrality" in therapy is, from the therapist's point of view, a libertarian position regardless of how the client sees it; and in fact some clients may see it as insidious. Some of the concepts that serve to legitimize moral neutrality are "freedom," "democracy," "self-realization," and "self-actualization." All these concepts are oriented toward people's freedom to do as they please. But even the most democratic theories recognize some limitations on individual behavior and are generous with such terms as "social responsibility" and "productivity." This latter concept seems to suggest that therapists regard themselves as a genuine social force. If so, then to what extent are therapists obligated to represent themselves to the public and their clients as a committed social agency? Is it possible that desperate clients may be required to give up some freedom as payment for being helped?

We turn now to a related, equally troublesome, and perhaps insoluble value paradox. For several decades the helping professions have made the judgment that a large number of people are unhappy, maladjusted, confused, deviant, and mentally ill. Furthermore, the public has been advised that such people can be helped by "counseling," "psychotherapy," or similar activities from several experts—that is, counselors, psychologists, and psychiatrists. And, as noted elsewhere in this book, the public believes that therapy is a worthwhile endeavor. Public faith is based partly on information about the benefits of therapy but mainly on trust of people believed to be experts. Professional judgment about who is deviant or sick is based either on the conclusions resulting from our own knowledge and diagnostic acumen or from the judgment of society in the form of legal adjudications or commitment procedures. In the former instance, the *Diagnostic and Statistical Manual of Mental Disorders* (American Psychiatric Association, 1980) may provide the basis for deciding that an individual is deviant and requires therapy. In the latter case, we may simply agree with the judgment of society, or one of its agents, that an individual's behavior is maladaptive or unacceptable and simultaneously accept the charge to provide a remedy agreeable to society. In either event therapists have taken the stance that they have the expertise to make judgments about other human beings and, furthermore, that therapy is a vehicle for correcting socially undesirable behavior.

Therapists also, perhaps unconsciously, have imposed their values on those who may be unable to refuse services. This condition poses several difficult questions. How do we reconcile our proclaimed faith in the dignity and worth of man with the widespread practice of supporting standards, practices, and values of society and its institutions? Do therapists simply accept the standards of society and help people "adjust" or conform? Is there a measure that can be used to determine the adequacy of value systems in various societies, and is there a method of measuring positive and negative values?

We have some confidence in the capacity of the helping professions to diagnose and treat a limited number of personal and social problems. Counselors and psychotherapists have a major role, for example, in dealing with such problems as crime and punishment, drug addiction, and alcoholism. We are somewhat uncertain, however, about whether therapists should make political and social judgments and decisions about who is normal or deviant. We suspect that such questions had best be left to philosophers and legal experts.

Implications for Counseling

We are reminded of a former client, a college student, who revealed during counseling that he stood in violation of the honor code in that he had prior information on a final examination. He rationalized his behavior by explaining his need to achieve high marks, primarily because his parents expected it. On the surface, at least, his concerns centered not on the "right" or "wrong" of his act but, rather, on the concern that he would

be exposed as a cheat and perhaps dismissed. Yet counseling
did involve the value system of this young client because he had
acted on values—success and achievement—introjected by his
parents.

It seems clear that many problems and conflicts revealed
in therapy involve the values of the client or those of the family
and cultural group. Consider, for example, the following client
statements and the values that are operating in each situation.

"I should not be having sex before I am married."
(My church and parents think it is wrong.)

"I should try to be a better parent."
(Society expects it.)

"I need to make more money so we can have some of the
extras."
(I value material goods, and my family desires them.)

"We need to get people on jobs and off the welfare rolls."
(People should work and take care of themselves.)

"I must graduate from college."
(I must be a success.)

The client may realize that he is trying to live by introjected values that may be inconsistent with his own desires or
needs. Therapy can help resolve some of the conflict and confusion resulting from attempts to answer questions about what is
right or wrong or good or bad. However, it is not the business of
therapy to answer ethical questions for clients, nor is it appropriate for the therapist to provide absolution for sins committed
or contemplated. Such matters are best left to the clergy. Furthermore, we question, with Frankel (1967), the assumption of
some therapists that neurotic behavior is blameless. On the contrary, we believe that therapy must help the client understand
that he makes choices and decisions and that he alone is responsible for his decisions.

Earlier we noted that therapy can assist clients in understanding and experiencing a value system. Helping clients dis-

cover and analyze not only their beliefs but also their needs, desires, and concerns is an essential part of this process. Individuals can thereby discover their capacity for making choices and for assuming responsibility for their own lives. Finally, they can learn that values are not fixed but are easily alterable, and that sometimes a change in values may be a wise decision.

Summary

We are living in a time when technical advancements and computerized thinking have a pervasive influence on the individual. The sense of *being* has to some extent succumbed to depersonalization of all forms of human relationships. It is thus relatively easy for a person to lose his sense of identity and well-being. His values are often confused and contradictory.

We are not altogether certain about the role of the therapist in the values area, but we are certain that he cannot ignore it. Several questions have been raised in relation to therapists' obligations to both the client and society. At what point should the therapist involve himself in the value system of his clients? How is this to be done? Is a therapist obligated to challenge the values of a client when he believes that those values are bad or wrong? What kind of behavior can a therapist permit? What are his obligations to society?

It seems clear that therapists must become well acquainted with the topography of modern values. The therapist must also have some understanding of social change and be sufficiently expert at identifying the relationship between social change and changes in value systems. It is only from this perspective that he can understand something of the value system of those he seeks to help.

6

Ethical
Conflicts
in
Therapeutic
Practice

In previous chapters we have emphasized that practitioners, in order to maintain acceptable standards of ethical practice in serving their clients and profession, must continually monitor their own behavior, upgrade their skills, increase their knowledge, and perfect a personal theory of ethics with which to make decisions. Unfortunately, there are some individuals in all professions who behave unethically. These persons, whether operating out of ignorance of the ethical consequences of their acts or out of conscious manipulation to attain personal goals, are dangerous to the welfare of their clients, the effectiveness of their institutions, the integrity and reputation of their colleagues, and the stability of their profession.

In our democratic society, people are, of course, free to act in any way they choose as long as they do not overstep legal bounds or irritate someone in a position of power. But, in addition, individuals—especially professionals—are expected to exercise this freedom in a responsible manner. Although laws are established and ethical codes are standardized to help regulate acceptable behavior, the enforcement of these rules is virtually impossible. As it should be in a democratic society, where individual freedom and rights are sacred, responsibility is left to the individual.

Unethical and Incompetent Practice

An unethical therapist may be defined as one who lacks sufficient integrity, moral commitment, and sound judgment to maintain standards of right and wrong actions in his professional practice. He may be unaware of or unconcerned about the ethical standards of his profession and ignorant of the possible negative effects of his behavior. When the therapist acts out of ignorance, inadequate training, self-interest, or faulty judgment, he may be following unethical practices (Schwebel, 1955).

Incompetent therapist behavior, although an integral part of unethical practices, is somewhat different. For the purpose of this book, an incompetent therapist is defined as one who lacks the skill, ability, or qualifications to carry out a therapeutic task responsibly and effectively. Failure to recognize one's fallibilities and limitations as a professional and as a person is also an element of incompetence. It now can be seen that ethics has to do with the philosophical realm while competence has to do with acquired knowledge and skill.

Most of the members of the helping professions are competent, honest, ethical, and dedicated. A few, however, do not feel compelled to live up to any external standard except the accumulation of financial resources and personal gain. They feel no responsibility to anyone but themselves and seemingly have no ethical conscience. Still worse, some of those who are engaging in unethical practices are not even aware of the damage they may be inflicting. These individuals are sometimes protected by other professionals, who may be reluctant to interfere or to admit that there are incompetent practitioners in their own ranks. A sense of loyalty to the profession may outweigh the commitment to effective service for clients. It is, of course, often diffi-

cult to substantiate a charge of incompetence or unethical practice. This fact undoubtedly discourages some individuals who
may be appalled by the acts of their colleagues—the colleagues
who are having sex with their clients, abusing them verbally, or
prescribing craziness that is worse than the presenting complaints.

Viscott (1972) explains from his own perspective why he
believes incompetence is perpetuated in psychiatry. He uses as
an example the case of a respected clinician, whom he refers to
as Dr. Delwin. Because Dr. Delwin supports many internists,
radiologists, psychiatrists, and hospital staff members who
would attest to his capabilities, any attempt to petition the
medical society with claims of incompetence would be fruitless.
Although he is getting rich by administering electroshock therapy as a cure-all to anyone who will sit still long enough to have
electrodes attached, Delwin has solid protection from the many
doctors who depend on him for referrals. Viscott hypothesizes
that therapists stick together to hide incompetents because of a
fear that tomorrow someone might question *their* competence.

Haley (1980, p. 388) also notes that incompetent therapists can comfortably operate by following a few basic rules:
(1) Conceal ignorance from colleagues by working only with
long-term cases; thus, referral sources will forget whom they
sent over and will not discover that few clients ever improved.
(2) Soundproof all doors and windows and never record sessions; thus, supervisors will be unable to learn what you really
do, only what you tell them you do. (3) Conceal ignorance from
clients by saying nothing and letting them talk and talk and
talk. (4) If clients do not improve, insist that they are resisting
and blame *them* for not trying hard enough or (5) insist that
the client really has changed but is not yet aware of the de-
layed effects. (6) Avoid details of cases, preferring instead to
use case summaries with lots of jargon and fancy diagnoses.
"For example, a clinician can say about a woman who has the
problem of compulsive counting, 'The patient was encouraged
to explore the origins of the counting compulsion, and the roots
of psychopathology were discovered in childhood experiences.'
This will sound better than a verbatim transcript, which might

read, 'Therapist: When you were a child, did you refer to different ways of going to the bathroom as number one and number two?' "

Incompetent therapists who must resort to such disguises and professional games are fortunately relatively few compared to the large number of ethical and effective professionals. But ignoring them for fear of increased malpractice insurance premiums does not make the problem vanish. Unethical and incompetent behavior will continue as long as it is tolerated. The helping professions will achieve greater respectability when more attention is given to higher standards of practice and when members devote more attention to policing their own ranks.

Historical Perspective

Incompetence and unethical behavior are nothing new to the helping professions. They have permeated human history since the first "psychotherapists" in 10,000 B.C. drilled holes in the skulls of the mentally afflicted to let the demons escape. Whether it is admitted or not, those in the helping professions have inherited—along with the many significant contributions of medicine, philosophy, and the newer sciences of psychology and sociology—some of the many atrocities, mistakes, and errors indicative of unethical behavior. We often hear of the successful attempts to improve our bank of knowledge, but we rarely hear of the errors, bumbling mistakes, misjudgments, and scientific disasters that have inflicted much pain on the poor souls who inadvertently served as subjects for the experimentations of physicians, clinicians, and scientists. To put our heritage in perspective, it is appropriate to examine not only the contributions to the field but also the injustices and immoral clinical actions.

Unfortunately, it often takes several decades to understand the differences between truly therapeutic practices and those that are deleterious to the client's welfare. Historians may look back one hundred years from now and shudder at the thought of undergoing some of our "primitive" treatment techniques. It was not long ago—just a few hundred years—that bloodletting, witch burning, and flagellation were the accepted forms of treating people with behavioral disorders. Consider, for example, the physician in Charles II's court who was called into consultation to aid the recovery of his ailing Royal Majesty. The "tested" medications and therapeutic methodologies provided by this doctor included lizard's blood, crocodile dung, hoof of ass, putrid meat, frog sperm, goat gallstones, powdered Egyptian mummy, eunuch fat, fox urine, sneezing powder, human skull extract, and forty-four other substances. After the solution was administered, a pint of blood was then extracted from the king's arms and legs, followed by an enema comprising fifteen substances, a blister raised on the top of his shaved head, a plaster of pitch and pigeon dung on his feet, and the application of a bezoar stone—after which His Majesty, King Charles II, expired (Ullmann and Krasner, 1975).

Even the great Greek physician Galen, who is revered as one of the great thinkers of the world, had unusual notions about what was helpful to his patients. With much confidence and the enthusiastic support of his colleagues, Galen proclaimed that body moisture induces foolishness in a patient, dryness produces wisdom, and the ratio between these two variables indicates the state of a person's relative sanity. Galenic medicine was further expanded by his successors, who hypothesized that epilepsy is caused by the simultaneous occurrence of phlegm and the first quarter of the moon.

In 1100 the physician Arcimatheus of Salerno was having incredible results with his prognoses for recovery. Arcimatheus employed a parallel strategy before administering any treatment. He first convinced the patient that recovery would come very quickly, and he then explained to the patient's relatives that the illness was severely critical. If the patient recovered, the doctor's reputation was enhanced. If he died, the outcome was just as had been predicted.

Further refinement of assessment procedures culminated in a fifteenth-century "handbook of psychotherapy" researched by two Dominican monks, who titled their masterpiece *Hammer of the Witches*. This "handbook" recommended as a diagnostic device for abnormality "trial by swimming." The patient's right thumb was tied to the left toe, and the left thumb tied to the right toe; then she was submerged in a deep lake. If the patient sank, she was innocent, but very dead; if she floated, she was diagnosed as "abnormal" and burned at the stake as a witch.

We may shudder with disgust at these accepted medical practices of the past and wonder how any intelligent person could have possibly believed in these witch doctors. Techniques employed hundreds of years ago, deemed appropriate then, have not stood the test of time and have proved to be not only neutral but disastrous, and sometimes fatal. It is thus important to examine the procedures that we use every day in order to be confident that they have been thoroughly researched and tested and are therefore helpful. Universal truths, postulates, and theories allegedly passed down from the gods may turn out to be as foolish as the practices of our predecessors. With our humility once again restored, we begin to realize the tenuous ground on which we stand.

Little White Lies and Big Black Ones

There is no profession more potentially useful or devastating than psychotherapy. Its effects and outcomes are subtle, disguised, and often invisible, even to the client. Unlike a person with a broken arm who visits his physician to get it repaired, the person with behavioral concerns cannot visit his local therapist, tell him where it hurts, and expect total recovery after swallowing a few pills or wearing a cast. Not only are the client's concerns sometimes unspecified, unobservable, and variable, but the professional he goes to for help does not possess an array of methods and reliable electronic equipment to diagnose the difficulty, treat the disorder, and promote a cure. The therapist does not have at his disposal a thermometer or an X ray to measure the extent or intensity of the difficulty, nor does he have a chemical antidote or mechanical apparatus to make the symptoms disappear and restore tranquil and effective functioning to the client. He must rely on his skill, knowledge, and commitment to helping. In short, he must use the self as an instrument of treatment.

Each day the therapist is faced with ethical conflicts, whether he is aware of them or not. Issues of privacy and confidentiality, for example, are imposed on unsuspecting practitioners by administrators, clients, or families who wish to know certain classified information. In addition, there are those unethical acts that all therapists commit and pretend that they do not. In spite of our best efforts to act responsibly in all things that we do, it is inevitable that we will slip occasionally. Kottler (1983) has reviewed a sampling of these "slightly" unethical behaviors. Such a summary helps us rid ourselves of the attitude that unethical conduct is an abstract condition that applies only to other people. A common "little white lie" takes the form of deceiving clients for their own good. Since we are experts, after all, we know what is best. So we twist the truth a bit by telling clients "I *know* I can help you" (when I only *hope* so), "I don't really have a strong opinion about you" (when I like or dislike you quite a bit), "Everything will be kept strictly confidential" (unless I slip up, or you tell me something against the law, or I talk to my colleagues about the case). And then, of course, we have our manipulative games—for example, giving clients paradoxical directives, using deception like a master magician—all for the purest of motives. We delude ourselves by saying that none of these maneuvers are all *that* bad. We are not benefiting ourselves, only trying to do our jobs better. And if we have to use a little deceit here and there, what is the harm?

The questionable practices discussed in the following paragraphs often prove harmful to clients. Some, of course, are less detrimental than others. The practice of focusing on oneself in the interview or telling a story that is not really for the client's own good is a representative example. Whenever a therapist says anything in an interview that is not intended to help the client, he may be acting unethically. Therapists are paid to deliver a professional service. When they are not delivering that service, for even two minutes while talking about something important in their own lives, they are acting unethically. In its seriousness and consequences, however, this unethical behavior is not comparable to that of the individual who, through insensitivity or incompetence, is unaware that he has been pushing a client too hard and that the client has reached the breaking point. If this client were driven to suicide, it would be as if the therapist had pulled the trigger. The failure to exercise responsible clinical judgment is considerably more serious, and hence more unethical, than the failure to keep the entire interview focused on the client.

It is important to look at ethical practices from the perspective of effects on the client. The goal, then, is not to become a perfect, fully functioning human being who always acts ethically and responsibly but an individual willing to refine techniques, to grow professionally and personally, and, more often than not, to act in an ethical and competent manner.

Beyond-the-Couch Relationships. Becoming personally involved with clients beyond appropriate limits is an ethical conflict that therapists frequently encounter. Client attempts at sexual seductions, transference and countertransference dynamics, and interactions with clients in social encounters are all experiences that practitioners must deal with on a regular basis. Unfortunately, dealing with the impulses and emotions aroused by an attractive client is not a skill that is learned in graduate school. Hard work is involved in restraining the honest and spontaneous desire to love another person who is attractive.

This belief that it is unethical and counterproductive to engage in a sexual affair or emotional involvement with a client is not universal. There are therapists who genuinely believe and practice the notion that sexual involvement with a client may be beneficial. They may reason that only an actual demonstration can truly teach clients how to love or to be sexually responsive. Freud's colleague Sandor Ferenczi helped his clients express their physical affections toward him as a way of compensating for their childhood deprivations, and Wilheim Reich felt that repression could best be released through sexual liberation (Serban, 1981). A more contemporary practitioner, a psychiatrist who has received much notoriety through the publication of his books, practices an approach to therapy that includes group therapy orgies and regular sex with his clients. In promoting the book *Inside a Psychiatrist's Head* (Shepard, 1972), the publishers inscribe on the back cover the following sketch of the author and his conceptions of how to help people:

> Martin Shepard, M.D., is a psychiatrist who believes that a couch is for something better than talking. His championship of sexual encounter groups and individual sexual freedom has made him one of the most controversial members of his profession.
>
> In this remarkably candid and graphic book, Martin Shepard vividly demonstrates that he personally practices what he preaches as he describes his own erotic encounters with his wife, girl friends, other men, and even his own patients.

Regardless of any conceivable benefits from sexual encounters, it is incomprehensible that the possible side effects, problems, and complications could ever justify this activity. Certainly, the therapist would lose the needed sense of objectivity and neutrality necessary to be helpful, not to mention the exploitive, oppressive, and manipulative implications. Sex with clients only further confuses a relationship that is already unequal in power and control (Dujovne, 1983).

Yet therapists are human beings. We all become sexually and emotionally aroused and have desires to act on such feelings. In the therapeutic relationship, where so much emotional intensity evolves in the client's head and where the therapist acts as a model of effectiveness, it is easy to see how transference and countertransference relationships might develop and grow beyond manageable limits. Not only could such unethical transgressions occur, but they do. It has been conservatively estimated that 5 percent of practicing therapists have engaged in intercourse with their clients (Holroyd and Brodsky, 1977). These therapists risk dangers to their clients' psychological health; lawsuits alleging rape, breach of fiduciary trust, or malpractice; and loss of their professional licenses (Knapp, 1980).

However much it might be denied, therapists like some clients more than others, just as parents feel differently about each of their children (in spite of the guilt that this notion evokes). There are those clients who are personally attractive and others whom we would never care to be around in anything other than a professional encounter. It is crucial for therapists to exercise restraint and sound judgment, and to honor moral obligations toward the persons with whom they are entrusted.

The purpose here is not to deny that therapists have feelings for their clients but to suggest that they should hold inappropriate impulses in check for the duration of the professional relationship. Sexual or emotional involvement with a client is unethical as well as legally risky. Consider the following example:

You have been seeing a client in therapy for four months. You know virtually everything about the person. You know her sex life, her love life, her needs, wants, desires, strengths, and weaknesses. She has made evident to you that she is attracted to you and loves you very much. You also regard the client as an attractive person with characteristics that you prize and search for in a mate. And you are torn between expressing your feelings and making sexual advances, which you know she would respond to, or stifling your affections. What do you do?

You can continue just as you are, denying that you feel anything, pretending that the problem does not exist or believing that it will magically resolve itself, taking a chance that your feelings will not get in the way of the therapy. But suppose this client tells you that she has met a man whom she really likes. As a professional, the most effective thing you can express is support, but you may not want to do that because of feelings of jealousy or wanting to hold her back so that you can continue to fantasize about her.

A second possibility is to continue seeing the client, attempt to deliver professional services, and initiate a personal relationship after hours. This is probably the most unethical thing a practitioner could do. As we well know, it is extremely difficult to help someone psychologically when one has a vested interest in that person.

The third possible approach, and the one that we sanction, is to accept the fact that you feel strongly for this client but realize that, as a professional, you cannot indulge your emotions. An ethical therapist realizes that clients are unusually susceptible to feelings of adoration for their therapists, and that affection can be translated into sexual desire. They are growing and getting better as a direct result of the treatment, so they feel gratitude to the person whom they consider responsible for their new-found freedom. When asked by a client how he really feels, the ethical therapist has no problem communicating honestly and straightforwardly: "I think you are a very attractive person. In any other circumstances, I might allow myself to become involved with you. But since I am a professional whose priority is to help you, that relationship is impossible." Such feedback is honest, does not deny feelings, and yet models to the client how an individual can reach a state of emotional control.

If the therapist does genuinely believe that he is in love with his client or wishes to act on sexual impulses, he has an ethical responsibility to terminate the therapy and refer the client to a colleague who can more appropriately be of service. Getting supervision may also be helpful to work through unresolved issues (Dujovne, 1983) as well as obtaining written release from liability for malpractice from the client to prevent legal problems in the future (Serban, 1981).

Promoting Dependencies in Clients. Therapists are often unaware that they may be developing dependencies in their clients. Instead of providing opportunities for clients to make decisions in their own lives, therapists may continually give advice and offer what they believe to be solutions to problems. These therapists may even perpetuate the notion that clients cannot make it on their own and need continued professional services to survive. The therapist, knowing that the clients do not have the power to leave the nest, is thereby guaranteed a source of income and security.

A key issue is for therapists to critically assess whether they are promoting such dependencies in clients by failing to help them become independent or by seeing them longer than necessary. If the client could be effectively helped in eight sessions, and the therapist keeps him coming back for three years, some dependency clearly has been fostered. It is difficult to rely on a person as a mentor and guru for three years and *not* develop a dependency in the relationship.

Our ultimate goal must be to promote independence in clients. The most important way to promote such independence is to be aware of every reference he makes to the therapist's role in helping him get better. In such instances the therapist can immediately point out and reinforce the idea that the client has done all the work. The therapist was essentially a sounding board, a resource person, someone objective who could listen and give the client valuable feedback and support. It is the client who changes and takes the risks. He is the one who accrues the benefits and experiences the disappointments. He is the one ultimately responsible for his growth. When the sessions have ended, the client can then say to himself that, since he has done the work and is responsible for his own growth, he is perfectly capable of continuing such productive behaviors without the help of a therapist.

The following is an example of a dependency conflict and how it might be handled.

Over the course of a forty-five-minute therapy session with your client, you have been focusing on the client's inability to confront certain significant individuals. Because the sessions themselves occupy less than one hour per week in the client's life, you realize that, to promote lasting change, the client will have to work outside of the sessions. As part of your *modus operandi,* you suggest that the client engage in psychological homework assignments between sessions. You then ask him what he would like to work on. The client, either out of misunderstanding, resistance to changing, or just plain inability to come up with the answer, says that he cannot think of anything to work on. You then erroneously conclude that you as the therapist must tell him what to do: "When your mother comes home at four o'clock tomorrow, I want you to take her aside, sit her down, and explain to her how unfair it is that she requires these things of you."

In such a message, you effectively communicate to the client that you know what is best, that this is what he has to do to get better, and that things will be fine if he does what you tell him to do. What this approach implies is that the client does not have any responsibility for coming up with the assignment. As a result, he may feel resentment toward you and will not be as committed to accomplishing the assignment, since it was your idea. He is also more likely to become discouraged and fail than if he had suggested the task.

Although it is more time consuming and entails more patience and hard work on your part, you will promote independence by helping the client discover things for himself. When he says that he cannot think of anything to work on, you can concentrate on helping him to understand why. You can help him come up with examples of the kinds of things he can do. You can prod him along. If he mentions something that does not quite fall in line with what you think would be more effective, you might say: "That's a great idea. But can you think of modifying it in any way?" With this approach the client feels responsible for setting his own goals and structuring his own course of action. He will therefore be much more committed to accomplishing his goals. When the sessions eventually are terminated, he will have the training and skills to continue his own therapy and promote his own further growth.

Deceiving the Client for Therapeutic Purposes. The whole issue of therapeutic deception has come to the forefront as structural family therapy (Minuchin and Fishman, 1981), strategic family therapy (Madanes, 1981), tactical therapy (Fisch, Weakland, and Segal, 1982), and other offshoots of the Milton Erickson school have become widely and effectively used. Haley (1976), spokesman for the directive therapy cause, argues that manipulation and deception are unavoidable, since in our influencing capabilities the primary mission is to maneuver the client to change—often against his will. Haley therefore believes that lying or deceit for tactical reasons—giving false information or concealing true information for the client's own good—"is not quite a lie."

Certainly, no matter how we justify or rationalize our actions, we are lying whenever we trick clients out of their symptoms, whenever we take on pretend roles, whenever we operate paradoxically. "The question in this situation is not so much a question of whether the therapist is telling a lie but whether he is behaving unethically" (Haley, 1976, p. 203). According to the therapeutic pragmatists, the lofty goal of being totally honest with clients at all costs is hardly practical or productive. A physician wrestles with this ethical dilemma each time he prescribes a drug. Should he explain, completely and honestly, all the possible side effects of a medication (including symptoms such as impotence, skin discolorations, nausea, or tremors), knowing that the patient may not comply with necessary treatment and therefore suffer even worse physical consequences? Or should the physician avoid mentioning information likely to sabotage medical intervention?

Haley's (1976, p. 208) rebuttal of his critics who claim that honesty is always the best policy is certainly thought provoking:

> Disagreeing with such a view is rather like attacking home and mother. Yet several questions can be raised. First, we must accept the fact that the therapeutic situation is not an honest human experience; it is a *paid* relationship. The therapist is receiving money to be human with a patient, which is rather inhuman. Second, it can be argued that no therapist of any school can share with a patient all of his observations and understanding. Third, it is doubtful that a patient can actually achieve autonomy when exposed to the understanding therapeutic approach. Finally, and most important, it is unlikely that an honest sharing of understanding within a paid relationship solves the problem the patient is paying his money to recover from.

Secrecy, mystery, and selective disclosure are a great part of the methodologies preferred by faith healers. While psychologists, psychiatrists, social workers, and counselors are hardly faith healers (although some would disagree), there are similarities in the techniques used. Kottler (1983), in his investigation of witch doctors in the Peruvian Andes, found that, like contemporary therapists, witch doctors enhance their reputations and influencing capabilities by capitalizing on their clients' expectations. In place of tweed suits, white lab coats, and horn-rimmed glasses, the witch doctor wears a formal poncho displaying his expertise. A stuffed condor on his wall replaces the framed certificate that proclaims specialized expertise. In fact, much of what the witch doctor does is deliberately intended to encourage an atmosphere of secrecy. Like the best Freudian, he is ambiguous and elusive in his metaphors. He is aloof and deliberately creates an aura of mystery—rarely explaining what he does and why he does it. He capitalizes on the placebo effects of any healing encounter (whether it is hypnosis, sorcery, or psychotherapy), which has certain necessary conditions defined by O'Connell (1975):

1. An unequal relationship exists between the healer and the recipient.
2. There are certain contextual rules that the client will obey (for example, the therapist gets the more comfortable chair).
3. Information (interventions, gestures, medications, chants, or rituals) is transmitted to the recipient.
4. Both participants agree to share common beliefs, language, symbolic systems.
5. The recipient trusts the healer and believes in his power.
6. The healer demonstrates confidence in his methods, communicates enthusiasm for the rituals, and has a high expectancy of success.
7. The procedure, intervention, operation, ritual, or ceremony culminates in some prescriptive activity.

On the whole, we believe, it is probably advantageous (if not more personally comfortable) to resort to deception only after all other approaches have been exhausted—and, of course, only for the benefit of the client. It is not that trickery, paradoxical directions, and deceit do not work, because they *are* quite efficient and effective ways to break destructive patterns, but that they are considerably less elegant than those strategies that squarely place the responsibility for change on the client's shoulders.

Putting the Focus on Oneself. In a therapeutic relationship, a therapist's self-disclosures can effectively promote the therapeutic relationship, illustrate a principle, model how effectively a human being can act in a certain situation, and show that the therapist is a person, not just a role. These are all examples of helpful self-disclosures. There is, though, a fine line between an effective self-disclosure and that used just because the therapist likes to hear himself talk, wants the client's approval, or attempts to use therapy time to meet his own needs.

Whenever a therapist takes the focus off the client and puts it on himself—either in his role as an expert or out of a desire to get help for himself—he is shortchanging the client. Whenever a therapist directs the course of discussion to something he feels is pressing rather than what is evident in the client's data, he is ignoring his obligation to deliver a professional service. Whenever the therapist engages in long-winded stories or anecdotes irrelevant to the client's presenting concern, he is keeping the focus on himself and acting unethically. Each and every time the therapist focuses primarily on himself, he is wasting time in the interview and negating the client's importance.

In a review of the ways in which therapists satisfy their own needs during sessions with their clients, Watkins (1983) initially mentions attentional failures, or those times when the therapist tunes a client out and retreats into fantasy. Boredom, impatience, negative countertransference, perceived threat, and fatigue are all listed as possible contributing factors for putting the internal focus on ourselves. A more direct method of client abuse is the use of overt aggressive acts. These may involve sarcasm, teasing, hurtful remarks, or inappropriate language that stuns the client into submission or withdrawal. The "silent treatment" can be dished out as a punitive measure for uncooperative clients—clients who, in spite of our best efforts to be helpful, make our lives difficult by playing games and not doing their homework. We forget that it is essentially the client's job to resist; if he knew how to be cooperative and how to change, he would not be in our offices to begin with. Yet it is difficult for us not to take rejection personally, and we respond by pouting or punishing. It is always helpful to remind ourselves that the client's pace and readiness level, rather than our own agenda, are of primary importance. Such a realization helps us to be more patient and to avoid putting the focus on ourselves in the interview.

Exceeding Personal Competence Levels. A therapist often finds himself operating out of his area of expertise. Every client that a therapist encounters has a distinctly different concern and therefore requires specialized treatment. Each time a therapist is confronted with a problem for which he is ill prepared, untrained, or inexperienced, he faces an ethical dilemma: Should he attempt to deal with the problem and see whether he can help without the preferred skills, or should he refer the client to someone more capable? Certainly, the therapist would much prefer to deal with the problem himself if that is at all possible. One of the ways in which therapists continue to grow and learn is by encountering and mastering new difficulties. Workshop training, specialized texts, and consulting are often designed for just such a purpose: to enable the practitioner to learn new skills and therapeutic strategies. The ethical conflict arises, however, when one realizes that his attempts to experiment with competencies in which he is not yet proficient, or will never truly master, can jeopardize a client's well-being.

The psychological helping profession comprises an array of specialists who are trained to meet a variety of needs competently and expertly. Resources available include psychiatrists, nurses, psychologists, social workers, marriage counselors, neurologists, internists, pastoral counselors, psychometricians, lawyers, vocational guidance counselors, and other personnel who are trained to deal with specific behavioral, emotional, and physical problems. The effective clinician is aware of the available resources and is prepared to make referrals when he does not feel competent or prepared to help.

The therapist needs to recognize his own limitations and strengths in order to serve his client population most competently. When a particular area of weakness is diagnosed, the therapist can then work on educating himself and gaining expertise in that area. He can thereby grow with the times, advance with technological society, and meet the changing needs of his clients. In the meantime, *before* he reaches appropriate skill levels, he can refer clients with particular problems to others with specialized expertise in areas where he is not thoroughly prepared.

Imposing Personal Values on the Client. Imposing one's own values and beliefs on a client is another unethical behavior that is commonly engaged in but rarely questioned (Ajzen, 1973). Do therapists have the right to train their clients into duplicate selves? Admittedly, therapy is an influencing interaction between a trained expert and a recipient of professional services; but who should decide what behaviors need to be changed and in what direction? If the client is to be the expert in declaring goals, is the therapist then the expert in how to reach them?

Some approaches to helping, such as rational-emotive therapy (Ellis, 1974), contend that, indeed, the key to a desirable outcome lies in changing a client's irrational beliefs and substituting the therapist's more sensible beliefs through a systematic indoctrination. Even such nondirective therapists as Rogers (1951) inadvertently but systematically influence their clients in directions they think desirable. Using such nonverbal cues as smiles, nods, and verbal rewards, the therapist reinforces his client for being open, genuine, revealing, or for working hard at growth.

Is it therefore necessary and desirable to withhold our values from clients? Values are the components of our personal code of action. They allow us to select therapeutic options based on a schema of what is basically good or bad for people. Values give our life meaning, which, in turn, gives us new values to guide us and tell us how to live (Yalom, 1980). According to most of the existentialists (Yalom, May, Victor Frankl), the principal task of the therapy profession is to work with values to create new meaning, to touch clients with our moral philosophy, thereby giving birth to a new order that is more self-enhancing than the old.

In all that we do, deliberately and subtly, we constantly influence clients with our values (even if we alter those values for a particular client's goals). That is our job. We are paid to be influential. Although our texts, speeches, ethical codes, and responses on comprehensive exams reflect our *desire* to be neutral and value free, we constantly model our personal value system and inadvertently or consciously seduce clients to follow a similar path. We hold values that are impossible (and perhaps undesirable) to hide: that living is better than dying, that truth is superior to deceit, that action is preferable to stagnation, that freedom beats feeling trapped. We selectively and conditionally give positive regard (in spite of Rogers's idealistic notions) when clients do their homework, share their feelings, make progress; in contrast, we give clients the cold shoulder (which we call neutrality) when they play games, act destructively or aggressively, and sabotage or resist our best efforts to be helpful.

Although it is desirable, and indeed ethical, to avoid imposing our values on clients, such a mission is practically impossible. In his classic book *Persuasion and Healing,* Frank (1974) warns that therapists might as well accept the fact that they exert strong influence on their clients. It is better, however, to exert this influence on a conscious and controlled, rather than an unconscious, level. Awareness of the potential power and influence that a therapist can wield as a model to the clients is the first step toward realizing the awesome responsibility involved. If it is decided that systematic influence, control, or manipulation is ethically justified and desirable, who is to do the manipulating, under what circumstances, with which clients, and with what rationale in mind? Who is to say that the therapist's values are more right than the client's or that homogeneous, rather than diverse, value systems are more desirable? Just as there is no therapy approach suited to all therapists and clients, there is probably no value system that is so universal and inflexible that it needs to be imprinted in everyone's brain.

The therapist has a primary responsibility to help the client meet mutually established goals. His secondary responsibility is to help the client lead a productive and satisfying life. He should never have a vested interest in converting the client into a disciple of his own value system but should instead concentrate on helping the client develop his own useful value system. However, since we cannot avoid displaying our values, we had better be clear on what they are, admit them when they slip out, and train and warn our clients to identify them so that they make their *own* choices unpressured by the tendency to imitate ours.

Denying Responsibility for Errors. We are now assuming that damage has been done, that the therapist has made an error, that he did not use his best judgment, or that things did not work out the way they were supposed to. Therapists are human beings, and they do make mistakes. Unless the mistake resulted from incompetent behavior, it is not in itself unethical. Often, however, the therapist, after making an error, denies responsibility for it and for its consequences. That *is* unethical. When errors are made or when interventions turn out to be ineffective, it is useful to note these experiences so that they will not be repeated.

For instance, a therapist working in a mental health center has seen a client for three sessions. After careful consideration he decides to gamble on confronting the client about his denial, believing that this will be an effective way of dealing with client resistance. The therapist consults his supervisor, who agrees with the strategy. When the therapist acts on his decision, the client breaks into tears. In fact, the client was not ready to handle the confrontation at the time. A major setback occurred in the therapy relationship, and the client failed to return for the next session. The therapist must now decide what he will note in the case file. There is a temptation to blame the result on the supervisor, since she advised the therapist to act. There is also a temptation to state that the client's reason for leaving had nothing to do with the ineffective confrontation. However, the therapist has an ethical responsibility to state that he made a mistake, that he judged that this would be an appropriate course of action to take, given the data available. Accepting responsibility for one's actions is one of the most difficult things to do, but it is crucial to every other ethical behavior.

Personal and Professional Rigidity. Is it unethical to restrict ourselves to only one theoretical approach—to force clients to comply with *our* systems, learn *our* language, conform to *our* methodologies? Are we justified in exclusively identifying ourselves as Adlerians, Gestaltists, psychoanalysts, rational-emotive therapists, or client-centered therapists when valuable techniques, knowledge, and research from other competing schools of thought could help us operate more efficiently and effectively? Naturally, there is quite a difference of opinion regarding this issue, since some practitioners find mastering a single therapeutic approach enough for a life's work while critics contend that this constitutes terminal rigidity and dogmatism. Yet many eclectics and pragmatists can be equally dogmatic and certainly ineffective by spreading themselves too thin.

Fisch, Weakland, and Segal (1982) believe that we should view a theory as a conceptual map—neither taking it too seriously, so that it hampers objective observation, nor discounting its value in organizing our premises concerning how people grow and how best to facilitate productive change. "Like any map, it is basically a tool to help someone find his way from one place to another—in this case from the therapist's encountering a client's problem to its successful resolution. As a tool, a map is never the actuality. It is always provisional and is to be judged primarily by the results of its use" (p. 7).

Even if we should prefer to affiliate ourselves with a specific theory because of its particular suitability to our personality, philosophy, training, collegial relationships, type of practice, or client population, we do ourselves and our clients little justice when we have a vested interest in the status quo or exhibit rigidity and resistance to learning new therapeutic strategies even if they were spawned by a rival camp. It is unethical for us to do any less than all we are capable of to help those who have given their trust, indifferent to which theories we use as long as the results are successful.

Confidentiality

Confidentiality is both a legal and an ethical problem for helping professionals. Current professional literature deals at length with such matters as privacy, privileged communication, confidentiality, records, and use of test information. In Chapter Three we reviewed the legal ramifications of these issues. Here, however, let us consider confidentiality and its ethical implications, something the therapist faces each day. Each time a therapist leaves a session, he is faced with the perplexing problem of storing away information and remembering what he can and cannot talk about to others. The conflict is compounded when the therapist is employed in a school or small agency where everyone knows everyone else's business.

Intentional breaches of confidentiality can occur for a number of reasons: to meet the therapist's own needs, to protect the client's welfare, or to protect an endangered party who may be threatened by a potentially dangerous client. A client, for example, may confide in a therapy interview that he has committed a violent crime and has vowed to continue such activities, which may endanger the welfare of others. Although the therapist has morally obligated himself to remain silent, he may choose to nullify that contract and go to the police with his information. The therapist has then made a moral decision that human life takes priority over a vow of confidentiality. He has put himself into a "no-win" conflict, because whatever action he takes he is likely to break a moral obligation or a law. It is possible, however, to protect oneself against such conflicts by explicitly defining confidentiality and explaining that it will *not* be honored in certain specified instances. Clients should know exactly what they are getting themselves into and when they become vulnerable. From the very outset, the issues can be explained.

All clients wonder what is expected of them the first time they come for an interview. They wonder whether the therapist is trustworthy and what he will do with the private information that he is privileged to hear. Clients even question whether they should waste their time disclosing anything until they are certain that the therapist is capable of understanding and helping. Consequently, initial interviews are often tentative. The client is testing the therapist, surveying the situation, and deciding whether it is a safe environment in which to let down his defenses.

Therapists, then, had better address themselves to the client's fears and hesitancy, and take sufficient time to explain the intricacies of confidentiality: "You are probably wondering whether this is a safe place to open up and whether I can be trusted. I can assure you that everything we talk about in this interview will be held in strictest confidence. Nobody will know what goes on in here unless *you* tell them. I don't expect you to believe what I am saying. You have no reason to; I am a perfect stranger. I hope to demonstrate to you that I am honest and worthy of earning your trust. I can assure you and give my solemn promise that nothing you say to me in confidence will leave these sessions unless you tell somebody, or give me specific permission to do so, or under the following conditions." With a bit of diplomacy and sensitivity, the therapist can then present the specific circumstances under which confidentiality can no longer apply.

Corey, Corey, and Callanan (1984) define these instances under which information must be provided by therapists: (1) when the therapist is appointed by the court, (2) when there is a risk of suicide, (3) when a malpractice suit is initiated against the therapist, (4) when a client's mental health is in question as part of a civil action, (5) when a child is the victim of a crime, (6) when the client is a danger to himself or to others, (7) when the client is in need of hospitalization, or (8) when the client expresses an intent to commit a crime that is considered dangerous to society or other persons. The problem of confidentiality, as an ethical or a legal issue, or as a dangerous area for unethical or incompetent conduct, comes to the surface only when we do not find the balance between protecting client rights and ensuring the safety of others.

Problems of Diagnosis and Assessment

One of the main tasks of psychological helpers is to initiate an assessment process with clients. After obtaining information on the client's cognitive capacity, his attitudes and values, his habits and goals, the therapist attempts to formulate a diagnostic impression of the nature of the presenting problem, its characteristics and symptoms, and the way in which these are manifested in the client. Diagnosis helps both therapist and client identify problem areas in need of attention and provides guidelines on problem resolution. To counsel without some attention to assessment and diagnosis is as hazardous as negotiating a winding road in total darkness. However, although the assessment process is of value in helping to organize treatment plans and summarize the client's problem, it also raises definite ethical issues related to stigmatization.

Historically, society has a basic intolerance of deviance. Individual differences and abnormality have rigid boundaries that are not to be violated under penalty of isolation or punishment. To be labeled a criminal, psychotic, or deviant, one need only commit a single act. While the behavior may never be repeated and the consequences of the act soon may be forgotten, the label may remain eternally in the offender's records and in the minds of others. Therapists are frequently labelers. Many of us spend our lives searching out and identifying pathology, diagnosing mental illness, and inflicting labels on all who come our way. The labels themselves not only create additional conflicts but can actually sabotage progress through their influencing powers to shape the perceptions of the therapist, the client, and all the significant others who become aware that the label exists (Reich, 1981).

Labels are most often ascribed to persons rather than to their behavior. Labels are disabling. They categorize, stigmatize, and reduce the totality of a human being to a single word. Labels teach their victims to resign themselves to the fact that they are what they are and that nothing can be done about it. "Alcoholics," "schizophrenics," "homosexuals," and "slow readers" are all people who are labeled and thereby reduced to only a small portion of their behavior.

The ethical problems of labeling, its categorizing and denigrating nature, can be overcome if we look at it as a way of identifying goals. Behavioral labels do not remain forever. Unlike the terms "brain damaged," "neurotic," "obese," or "dull," which label a person and imply that he can never change, such terms as "drinking-beer behaviors," "being-embarrassed-in-English-class behaviors," and "worrying-in-airport behaviors" imply that the person is irreducible and that only his acts can be classified. Labeling can be behavioristic in method yet humanistic in orientation. An individual's uniqueness is preserved intact, although his self-defeating behaviors are labeled for the purpose of changing them.

In the process of functional behavioral labeling, a client's specific behaviors are described in meaningful, illustrative, individualized language, not only so that the counselor can understand clearly which concerns are to be addressed but so that the client can understand how, when, where, and with whom the self-defeating patterns are exhibited. There are, thus, therapeutic advantages to functional behavioral labeling:

1. Clients learn the methods of identifying and describing complex, abstract, ambiguous processes in specific, useful terms.
   Before: "Uh, I don't know exactly, I just can't seem to concentrate anymore."
   After: "I have difficulty structuring my study time on the weekends I spend at home, particularly when I allow the distractions of my brother and girl friend to interfere."
2. Clients understand that they are unique individuals with characteristically different concerns.
   Before: "I've been told that I'm a drug addict."
   After: "I'm a person who tends to overindulge in cocaine and marijuana when I feel school pressures building up."
3. Clients describe their behavior in such a way that it can be changed. Whereas a *personality* characteristic is stable, invariant, and permanent, a *behavior* can be changed.
   Before: "I'm shy. That's the way I've always been."
   After: "I sometimes *act* shy when I meet a new guy who is attractive to me."
4. Clients label their behavior in the specific situations where they have difficulty.
   Before: "I'm depressed."
   After: "I feel depressed in situations like my job and marriage in which I feel powerless to do anything to change."

5. Clients accept responsibility for their destructive behaviors rather than blaming them on something external, such as bad genes.

    Before: "I'm passive. Everyone in my family is. What do you expect?"

    After: "I act passively in some novel situations because I have learned to let others take charge. But in situations where I feel comfortable, I don't act passively at all."

There is, and will continue to be, great pressure on all psychological helpers to test, diagnose, and label. In some multi-disciplinary institutions, psychologists or counselors may find that their chief responsibility is to assume the role of a diagnostician, assessor, or tester. To ensure that he remains ethically responsible and guards against committing some of the abuses described, the practitioner should be aware of the consequences of his actions—the aftereffects, short range and long range, of labeling—and should use assessment procedures as they are intended: to help both the therapist and the client organize and sort out what is going on and determine how best to treat it.

Summary

Several conditions contribute to incompetent and unethical behavior. Faulty or inadequate training, lack of skill, poor judgment, laziness, and lack of commitment to acceptable professional practices all lead to incompetent services. Unethical behavior may arise from ignorance or lack of a philosophical base for understanding ethical problems and for making ethical decisions. Other unethical practices result from external pressures and from a desire for personal gain and professional enhancement. Furthermore, it is sometimes difficult to adhere to principles when they are in conflict with an employing institution and when it is simply easier to ignore a problem or dilemma. We also recognize that general principles, ethical codes, and conventional wisdom are not always easy to apply to specific situations.

We do not pretend that therapists can be ethically correct or professionally competent in all their professional endeavors. We have contended throughout this book that most helping professionals are competent, ethical, and socially conscious individuals. However, the profession also has its share of conscious rogues—incompetents who are abusing clients, damaging the profession, and deceiving the public. We all have a responsibility to confront injustice, incompetence, and unethical conduct —in ourselves and in our colleagues.

7

Special
Therapeutic
Strategies

Certain therapeutic procedures—such as hypnosis, paradoxical directives, behavior modification, biofeedback, sex therapy, psychopharmacology, group work, and several applications of therapy in the media—involve additional ethical principles to govern their use. All these specialized treatment modalities have recently gained new popularity because of innovations in research, theory, and technique. Ethical and legal issues implicit in these strategies will undoubtedly become more complex as a result of the use of new technologies, such as the microcomputer, cable television, and biofeedback; clinical specialties that involve work with the addicted, the disabled, the very young, or the very old; and the greater attention being paid to client rights and truly *informed* consent. Especially with regard to confidentiality and privacy concerns, many of the profession's specialists who work with families or groups are experiencing complex ethical and legal dilemmas. Similar moral conflicts arise, as well, for those medically trained therapists who rely on chemical agents as adjuncts to their talking cures.

Psychopharmacology

Most psychiatric journals are littered with advertisements from the pharmaceutical industry which proclaim the latest cure for mental illness. Legions of sales representatives appeal to psychiatrists as well as internists and gynecologists to try out their latest antidepressants, tranquilizers, or sleeping potions. While certainly this aggressive marketing campaign helps physicians keep up with recent discoveries and refinements in psychopharmacology, the advertisements seem to dwarf the few scholarly articles that report actual tests of the efficacy of the drugs. It is not uncommon for full-sized ads to dominate over half the space in a psychiatric journal. Headlines proclaim in thick letters (with the precautions, contraindications, and adverse reactions in minuscule print):

THE BASIC TOOL OF WESTERN PSYCHIATRY
—THORAZINE

To bring your elderly patient out of his apathetic/withdrawn senile behavior—RITALIN

NORPRAMIN: Lightens and brightens the days of your depressed patients.

Now initial therapy for many patients can be as simple as ONE TABLET, ONCE DAILY . . . ELAVIL

Admittedly, psychopharmacology is helpful and even crucial to the treatment of many psychotic, depressed, and anxious clients. However, some medications (such as the billions of Valium tablets prescribed annually) are overpromoted as the cure-all for any psychological discomfort. Many people are taught to believe that only their pills are keeping them together; therapy sessions are scheduled as mere formalities to justify needed monitoring of blood levels. Clients thus learn that they are not responsible for their problems; and many physicians in general practice get insurance reimbursements, since they are paid not for talking but for *doing* something, such as writing prescriptions.

For medically trained therapists, or those who routinely work with psychopharmacological treatments, there are special problems concerning the way in which the drugs are presented. If clients were to be fully informed of all the side effects that could conceivably appear after the ingestion of medication, they would probably never take any of it. What person who claims sanity would voluntarily take a medication that promises the possibility of impaired mobility, fatigue, muscle tremors, weight gain, dizziness, blurred vision, restlessness, constipation, and an assortment of allergic side effects, including convulsions or death? In addition to the physical side effects of such drugs, there are also dangers of sabotaging needed treatment for the underlying causes because the warning symptoms have been temporarily obliterated. On the other hand, for clients who are suicidal and endogenously depressed, or for those with major sleep disruptions or with active hallucinations, it is probably unethical *not* to prescribe medication (or make appropriate referrals for an evaluation). When antidepressant, antianxiety, and antipsychotic medications are realistically introduced—that is, when the client is told what they can probably do and given sufficient information regarding the consequences of their use—clients can truly give their *informed* consent to participate in treatment. In short, if the client (whenever possible) is (1) involved in a discussion of the benefits and side effects of the medication, (2) fully informed about the likely physical and psychological results, (3) made a partner in the decision-making process, and (4) helped to work through concerns as part of therapy, treatment efforts will be more responsible and, ultimately, more successful.

Behavior Modification

In the 1960s and early 1970s, a new approach to therapy received widespread attention. Based on learning theory and strongly influenced by data from laboratory experimentation with animals, behavior therapy had its share of proponents as well as detractors. Some techniques used by behaviorists—for example, aversion therapy and the use of cattle prods to produce electric shock in unruly mental patients—soon brought charges of unethical practices from several individuals. Many professionals as well as legislators and laypersons were repulsed by some of these techniques. The major issues were not whether behavior therapy, appropriately used, is effective (the fact is that behavioral techniques are among some of the most reliable options) but, rather, how, when, and by whom this form of therapy should be applied.

The Association for the Advancement of Behavior Therapy has addressed many of the ethical problems in the application of these helping techniques. It has therefore attempted to establish standards for acceptable professional behavior, including the following guidelines (Azrin and others, 1977):

1. Therapeutic goals should be specific, realistic, and mutually determined, so that clients understand all the implications of treatment and give informed consent to proceed.
2. Scientific methods should be used to select the most safe, appropriate, and effective treatment strategy from among several viable options.
3. Controversial and experimental treatments that are not consistent with generally accepted practices should be avoided.
4. All participants in treatment should be motivated volunteers who are free from coercion.
5. Behavior therapists should work toward the best interests of their clients rather than the agendas of public agencies or other parties.
6. Before any treatment is attempted, harmful side effects and consequences should be ruled out.
7. Written permission should be obtained from clients and information given about who will have access to treatment results.
8. Behavior therapists should have appropriate qualifications, training, experience, and supervision before they attempt any work with the public.

In this age of increasing concern about authority and violations of individual freedom and human rights, behaviorists and, for that matter, mental health practitioners of all persuasions may find their work restricted by legal and quasi-legal external controls. This is unfortunate, because controls tend to increase in time and eventually become excessively restrictive and authoritarian. While most of us agree that some restrictions on experimentation with human subjects and on questionable therapeutic practices are necessary, these restrictions should be imposed by responsible professions and not by external forces. As London (1971, p. 252) has stated: "All good people who have power over others, even just a little power and even for a little while, need access to an ethic that can guide their use of it."

Biofeedback

Although the operation of psychophysiological feedback equipment is usually considered a component of the larger behavior therapies, there are additional ethical concerns related to the marketing of these therapeutic treatments. Although essentially an instrument of information for learning, which is also particularly helpful with psychosomatic complaints, tension, and anxiety, biofeedback equipment has enjoyed a brisk mail-order business for years and has been marketed for applications ranging from altering the autonomic nervous system to improving powers of ESP.

Onoda (1978) comments on the number of "weekend practitioners" who have studied their equipment owner's manuals but have no practical understanding of either physiology or electronics. Often the capability of the biofeedback devices or the competence of the operator is misrepresented in such a way as to imply expertise where none exists. Derner (1982) recommends that biofeedback hardware be used *only* in conjunction with structured therapy experiences. The Biofeedback Society of America has attempted to regulate this fledgling discipline by establishing minimum training standards for certification. Nevertheless, especially with experimental treatment modalities, ethical marketing efforts should be cautious, conservative, and *understated.*

Group Therapy

Group work is the only therapeutic activity in which other clients, who are themselves in need of help, help serve as cotherapists (Gazda, Duncan, and Sisson, 1971). Clients have no therapeutic training and are not guided by any professional code of ethics or obligated to honor privileged communication; yet they regularly engage in confronting their peers, interpreting their behavior, and providing a form of counseling. It is just these factors that also lend group therapy its effectiveness. Nowhere else can so many clients be reached so efficiently or can one individual learn within the controlled safety of a "minisociety" how to alter his behavior and receive continual support and feedback from peers under the direction of a trained professional. Besides the inherent pleasure and satisfaction of interacting intimately with others, clients often feel increased responsibility to change when they face others each week. Whether one is learning to be assertive, to rid one's body of foreign substances (food, drugs, smoking, alcohol), to learn skills of interacting with others, or to eliminate needless guilt or worry, the group setting can be a viable and effective means by which to promote lasting change.

Concurrent learning occurs through observation, fantasy involvement, and active participation. Role-playing techniques, psychodrama, expression of feelings, and confrontations all lend themselves particularly well to group settings and heighten the impact of therapeutic interventions. In what better setting than a therapy group could an individual learn to increase interpersonal effectiveness? The process of experimental living with peers mirrors the real world in that typical daily encounters require individuals to function in a group (Cohn and others, 1973). A sense of belongingness and communality develops out of being a member of a group. These feelings are often soothing to clients, particularly when they realize that they are not alone, that others have similar problems.

"Though kinship is the most basic and widespread bond between human beings, the bond of reciprocity is almost as universal" (Singer, 1981, p. 37). When people are together in

groups, there is an instinctual and universal urge to help one another, to act altruistically in the best interests of community
welfare. While much of this behavior is part of reciprocal exchange networks that are part of all species' survival mechanisms, people generally want to help other people because *it
feels good.* Any number of previously described philosophical
positions, such as the sociobiological and utilitarian theories,
can adequately explain why people act ethically in group situations—even at personal risk. However, the fact remains that
therapeutic groups, even with their special problems, provide in-
credibly potent environments for change.

Group counseling also can be seen as an oppressive influence—for example, when it deradicalizes children to conform
to the status quo (Jeffries, 1973). Children are socialized into
roles that take away their individuality and mold them into obe-
dient citizens who follow rules without question. "The successful five-year-old, upon entering school in a democratic society,
learns quickly that he may speak only when he is given permission to do so by the representative of social order. Further,
when he does speak, he must use the socially approved words,
subdued intonation, and the approved sexual mannerisms in
order to increase his success ratio" (Jeffries, 1973, pp. 113-
114). Oppressive counselors, Jeffries reasons, through their own
strict conformance to rules and as an instrument of society,
gently lure children to adjust to a system that does not respond
to their needs. She uses as an example the case of Eric, an eight-
year-old black child who plotted to alter the system in his classroom to make things more interesting and relevant. After physical punishment, reprimands, and tranquilizers proved ineffective
in controlling his maladaptive behavior, Eric was referred to
group counseling. The well-intended, though untrained and inexperienced, counselor then attempted to create powerful dynamics for producing social change by placing the radical Eric in
a group of warm, friendly, and well-adjusted peers. As a result,
Eric was provided only with a place to "blow off steam" and
soon joined the silent majority, who accepted things as they
were.

Rowe and Winborn (1973) systematically searched the

popular and professional literature to identify the criticisms and fears related to group work. In order of frequency of appearance, such issues as the following emerged: concern about leader competence, lack of professional and ethical standards, possible psychological damage, postgroup adjustment problems, lack of screening procedures, lack of explicit goals, danger of commercial abuse, problems of confidentiality, and lack of legal restraints and licenses.

In addition to these justified criticisms, many irrational fears also were verbalized that equated group work with drug experiences; called it part of a conspiracy; and focused on its gimmickry, moral indoctrination, and potential to produce dependence. Each objection raised represents another hurdle in the way of the respectability and professionalization of group work. Whether these criticisms are valid or merely are the personal fears of a few individuals is an issue that has not been substantially researched. The fact remains that these fears *do* exist and, perhaps justifiably, inhibit the progress of the group movement.

Group practitioners experience other ethical difficulties in their role. While they are influential and powerful, they have less control over the proceedings than in individual sessions (Kottler, 1983). Confidentiality cannot be enforced (Davis and Meara, 1982), verbal abuse is more likely (Corey and others, 1982), and leaders sometimes have little training and few qualifications to deal with critical incidents that occur (Gumaer, 1982). Furthermore, dependency effects are prevalent in groups, screening of participants is often haphazard, and there is no licensure or certification to regulate professional practice (Kottler, 1982).

Possible undesirable effects, as a direct result of the group experience, are compounded when close associates or peers are grouped together. Estranged work relationships, loss of prestige, embarrassment, and other negative outcomes can be monitored and controlled in the group sessions, but leader responsibility often ceases when the members leave the artificial safety of therapy. Although the therapist will attempt to do all in his power to promote effective functioning in his clients while they interact within his domain, he should also accept a reasonable degree of responsibility and encourage client accountability for actions in the outside world (Zimpfer, 1971).

The therapist's power to influence is necessarily reduced in a group situation where others also accept responsibility for control. In fact, group members fall into the role of assistants or cocounselors when they attempt to help and give feedback to peers. Since the therapist is the professional, he is the one who must assume ultimate responsibility for what goes on in the sessions—a situation difficult enough in individual therapy and much more so in a group setting where control is delegated to others.

Protecting the individuality and right to privacy of each group member can be equally difficult. The usual pressures to conform and produce, which are evident in other groups, are not exempt in therapy. If the group leader plays a passive role, unconditionally accepting all behavior without intervention, individuals who treasure silence, who do not feel like responding, or who feel vulnerable may be violated and their defenses mercilessly attacked. Even if the silent client does bend to the overwhelming social pressure of his peers to produce appropriate responses, he may attribute any of his progress to these external influences rather than to himself. The therapist needs to remain sensitive to the individual rights of his clients and to intervene when they are compromised.

Much of the controversy surrounding group work has centered on encounter groups. The encounter movement began in the 1950s and reached widespread prominence in the middle 1960s. "Our culture has a propensity for corrupting a good idea through overexposure" (Lakin, 1970, p. 68). Appealing to lonely hearts, the passive, inhibited, and social misfits, these treatment groups enthusiastically advertise themselves as capable of bestowing self-actualization on anyone (psychopaths, "normals," and psychotics alike) for a modest fee and the willingness to express a few emotions. Encounter groups promise belongingness, growth, intimacy, and authenticity. "They are designed to provide, albeit through artificial means—and most frequently in an illusory fashion—the indiscriminate confluence that souls who have lost their character of individual self-affirmation so desperately crave" (Denes, 1975, p. 15).

The group leaders, who represent themselves as "educational consultants," are not required to have any skills or training or to meet the criteria that apply to professional practitioners. Even hairdressers and barbers need a license to work with the human head, yet encounter group leaders are exempt from regulation when dealing with what is *in* the human head (Peters, 1973).

In their now classic study of encounter group casualties, Lieberman, Yalom, and Miles (1973) found that two-thirds of the group participants surveyed found the experience unrewarding. Even when dropouts were excluded from the analysis, 8 percent of the 210 subjects reported a negative impact six months after the experience. The researchers concluded that encounter groups do not appear to be a potent agent of change and contain a significant risk of psychological damage (Yalom, 1975). In addition, leaders with an aggressive, challenging style are most likely to cause casualties.

In spite of the lack of systematic regulation of encounter group leaders, most adhere to ethical practices as well as might be expected for their level of training and expertise. The accounts of many zealous encounter "graduates" attest to the worthiness of the experience. "The fact that we know little about the enduring effects of training does not diminish the conviction that we are dealing with significant and potent group processes" (Lakin, 1970, p. 69).

Encounter groups are only as effective and safe as their leaders make them. In a comprehensive study of therapy outcomes, in which he found that 5 percent of the patients studied deteriorated as a direct result of the treatment, Bergin (1975) concluded that the critical factor was the therapist's personality, not the type of treatment. Encounter groups can be a useful and effective means to help promote growth *if* adequate screening of participants is done and *if* the leader is competent and ethical.

Hartley, Roback, and Abramowitz (1976) recommend ways to reduce or eliminate the deleterious effects of encounter groups. Predictions can be made about the type of person most likely to be harmed (for example, individuals who have a low self-concept or who manifest psychopathology or who are in the midst of a crisis), and these persons can be screened and excluded. Every effort should be made on the part of the group leader to ensure that only stable individuals are included. Brief case histories, intake interviews, and psychological testing are often helpful. Positive experiences can best be assured through a democratic and safe atmosphere, a well-trained leader, and protection of clients from coercion and abuse.

Caution should also be exercised, Zimpfer (1971) warns, in situations where there is a destructive group member, experimentation with dangerous methods (drugs, sex, marathons), or concurrent individual counseling with group members (which could induce favoritism or jealousy) or where the clients are forced to participate. In addition, Zimpfer recommends the following minimum guidelines for ethical behavior in groups:

1. A theoretical base and rationale for group work should be developed and should include knowledge of interpersonal relationships. A therapist should know what motivates people and how they characteristically act in group settings.
2. The employing institution should approve and be aware of the group activities.
3. The therapist's work should be restricted to those client populations that he can handle competently; for example, school counselors should not be working with psychotic groups.
4. The leader should be aware of the limitations and dangers as well as the advantages of group work and have the capacity to control the process when appropriate.
5. The leader should assess a potential participant's willingness to cooperate in a group and the likelihood that it is the most appropriate form of treatment for the client's individual concern. Care must be exercised not to cajole individual clients to join the group for the therapist's convenience rather than their own best interests.
6. A leader should use only those techniques and process in-

terventions in which he has been trained and is competent.
Nothing is more potentially detrimental than an ineffective
confrontation.
7. The leader should be aware of referral and consultation
    sources and have adequate backup support and supervision
    when he needs help.

The Association for Specialists in Group Work has developed a comprehensive and detailed set of ethical guidelines to
aid practitioners in their decision making as well as to establish
standards of practice (Roberts, 1982). Group therapists are
mandated to provide accurate information to participants regarding confidentiality, personal risks, and leader qualifications;
to be responsible for member safety jeopardized by threats, in-
timidation, prejudices, or questionable techniques; and to safeguard ethical conduct by confronting colleagues who are abusing client rights.

Family Therapy

All the ethical concerns of group work are compounded
in the treatment of multiple family members who go home together after the session. Some clinicians believe that therapy inevitably changes family relationships, whether others attend
sessions or not. Other practitioners believe that marital and family therapy is, by its very nature, unethical, since the clinician
cannot avoid taking sides. These potentially divided loyalties
are viewed by many family therapists, such as Jay Haley and
Salvador Minuchin, as desirable, since deliberate alignments of
the therapist with one family member or another help to break
up destructive power hierarchies. Nevertheless, there is the
problem of defining who is the "identified patient" in dysfunc-
tional families.

Still other ethical issues make the marketing and practice
of family therapy especially difficult. Because the therapist is
ordinarily more active and directive in sessions, there is a greater
risk of imposing personal values on client belief systems. And in
any systems-oriented approach to treatment, the importance of

the individual is always reduced. "Once people decide to pool their resources and work toward a common purpose, individual needs are necessarily shelved in favor of what is good for the majority. This compromise ensures that none of us gets exactly what we want, although most people get a little bit of what they are willing to accept" (Kottler, 1983, p. 288).

Confidentiality issues are certainly more complex as well, especially with regard to handling family secrets. Piercy and Sprenkle (1983, p. 395) present the following case to their students as an illustration of possible conflicting interests: "You have been providing marital therapy to a couple for three months. During one session in which the wife is late, the husband tells you in confidence that when the wife's physical problems are stabilized he will probably divorce her. What would you do?"

Sex Therapy

This subspecialty of marital therapy has received increased media exposure because of greater freedom in discussing human sexuality and because of favorable success rates in alleviating presenting symptoms. In fact, there are probably very few other therapeutic treatment modalities that have been more consistently effective in reaching their stated objectives. Most of the problems associated with the ethical promotion of sex therapy have to do with the controversial nature of openly discussing such sensitive issues in public. One would expect professionals to be especially cautious and conservative in their approaches, considering the possibilities of misinterpretations, distortion, and exaggeration. Yet even a seemingly elementary principle—such as the avoidance of any physical contact between a sex therapist and client—is not universally accepted by all in the profession. Hartman and Fithian (1972) have advocated the use of sexological examinations, in which the cotherapists take turns stimulating the genitals of clients to stimulate feelings (among other things), assess sexual responsiveness, and teach methods of arousal and foreplay. Apart from any therapeutic benefits of such an approach in helping partners become more sensitive and skilled, certain ethical hazards place the clinician in a rather vulnerable position, not to mention the possible negative effects on the therapeutic relationship. Bancroft (1981) mentions, in this regard, that physical contact can lead to sexual confusion and can aggravate problems in some clients.

Other ethical issues are raised when the therapist, hoping to minimize the complications of direct physical involvement, uses surrogates to act as "player/coaches" in the educational process. Are we justified in acting as "pimps" to find skilled partners for our clients, who are desperately in need of learned, sensitive instruction? Even though such strategies have been found effective by Masters, Johnson, and Kolodny (1977), they ceased using surrogates because of the confusion regarding their status, roles, and professional identity.

The American Association of Sex Educators, Counselors, and Therapists (AASECT) has attempted to address many of these issues by specifically prohibiting any nudity or sexual activity by the client or therapist, as participant or observer, since they "go beyond the boundaries of established therapeutic practice" (AASECT, 1979, p. 7). Yet, in its *Code of Ethics* the sentence containing this prohibition continues with the escape clause that "nudity" or "observation of client sexual activity" may be used "only when there is good evidence that they serve the best interests of the client." What exactly constitutes "good evidence" and "best interests of clients" is apparently left open to individual interpretation.

While admitting that the use of surrogates is highly controversial, AASECT does, however, find such methods ethically permissible if (1) the surrogate's role is clarified and does not include the functions of a therapist; (2) the surrogate protects the dignity, welfare, and confidentiality of the client; (3) all possible social, psychological, physical, and legal issues are discussed; and (4) consent is obtained from the spouses of client and surrogate if either party is married.

Additionally, there are other ethical issues that complicate the work of sex therapists—the special value problems inherent in the treatment of homosexual, transsexual, and other elective varieties of sexual behavior. Unless the therapist has sufficiently clarified and worked through his own values and biases with regard to sexuality, even more damage can be inflicted on clients because of the extra shame, insecurity, and discomfort many people experience while exploring taboo subjects. The sex therapist needs even more than the usual dose of sensitivity, responsibility, and caution that is common to our profession because of the extra vulnerability for clients *and* therapists.

Hypnosis and Other Directives

The Milton Erickson school of therapy has spawned a whole new generation of practitioners. These practitioners—of methods such as strategic therapy (Madanes, 1981; Haley, 1976), neurolinguistic programming (Bandler and Grinder, 1979), and tactical therapy (Fisch, Weakland, and Segal, 1982) —have had great success in using hypnotic induction procedures, paradoxical directives, and other forms of treatment that involve explicit control, deceit, and lies. According to Fisch, Weakland, and Segal (p. 87), "It may seem cold and calculating to talk about ways of controlling the process of treatment, but we believe it is evident, on a little reflection, that the client is not in a position to know how his problem should best be approached. If he did, why would he be seeking professional help?" They would further argue that, since the main goal of therapy is to get people to behave and think differently, directive interventions make such changes occur more efficiently. Everything a therapist does is directive; every gesture or movement is a directive to do or not do something. And when Jay Haley, the father (or at least uncle) of modern directive therapy, was asked how he could get people to comply with his sometimes bizarre instructions, he replied: "I mean, if you can get somebody to lie on his back and talk to the ceiling while a psychoanalyst sits behind him, for seven or eight years and pay money to do that, people will do anything" (Haley, 1980, p. 386).

Hypnosis is a more subtle form of directive therapy but one in which the clinician intensifies the influencing process by facilitating a hypersuggestable state of consciousness. The presentation of the procedure to the client is actually the first stage of induction; therefore, particular care is usually employed to describe precisely and accurately what will occur. Most of the misconceptions and myths are perpetrated by stage and entertainment hypnotists rather than professional therapists: (1) that the client is "put to sleep"; (2) that hypnosis can "make" people stop smoking and/or lose weight; (3) that the hypnotist has special powers; and (4) that the client's conscious mind will melt away, revealing a closet full of hidden secrets. In addition, some people fallaciously believe that hypnosis will weaken the mind or is a form of brainwashing, that it will perpetuate nervous breakdowns, that clients will lose their free will, or that the subject may never reawaken. In fact, most skilled hypnotists will emphasize the client's total control of the situation, thereby allaying fears and placing the responsibility for cooperation where it belongs: "You can open your eyes any time you want to, though you will probably wish to keep them closed so that you may remain peacefully relaxed."

Fromm (1980) explains that it is relatively simple to use hypnosis but difficult to use it judiciously and appropriately. Ethical practitioners avoid sensationalizing hypnosis and restrict its use to only those areas that are defined by the standards of the various professional organizations, such as the International Society of Hypnosis, the Society for Clinical and Experimental Hypnosis, the American Society of Clinical Hypnosis, and Division 30 (Hypnosis) of the American Psychological Association. Furthermore, as in most areas of therapeutic practice, members of these professional societies are admonished to be discreet and scientific in their presentations and to avoid advertising themselves in the media.

Therapy in the Media

In the past ten years—particularly with the books of Albert Ellis and Wayne Dyer—a new genre of self-therapy has been created. By means of various self-help books, "clients" can try to rid themselves of irrational beliefs or "erroneous zones," within the privacy of their own homes after a few hours of study. Other psychologists, psychiatrists, social workers, and educators have since jumped on the bandwagon, publishing their techniques for curing shyness, lovesickness, depression, boredom, or the heebie-jeebies. While certainly the authors and book publishers make fantastic claims for the efficacy of their books' advice, many consumers also report that they gained valuable insight and suggestions from their reading. They may also appreciate the perceived advantages of economy, brevity, privacy, and convenience of books that simulate therapeutic experiences.

Most of the problems associated with the self-help literature are the result of deceitful advertising and unvalidated claims on the book jackets (Fisher, 1984). Other ethical issues concern professionals who are fearful of turning loose powerful psychological principles on the public without any support or supervision. If the persuasive advertising that promises emotional release, behavioral control, or intellectual nirvana is accurate, there is even more reason to fear the power of these tools without professional assistance.

Once the authors hit the talk-show circuit to promote their self-help books, they may reach millions of viewers during a single fifteen-minute session of capsulized advice. The public has responded with such enthusiasm to these new heroes of the media that television game-show producers clamor to fill airwaves with articulate therapists. Every large city now has its resident experts who will take calls on the radio, provide three minutes of therapy, and then advise about what to do next.

Several professional groups are now attempting to establish standards of validity and good taste for self-help therapy. These standards require authors to provide accurate marketing information, to be experts in the field, and to warn readers about the limitations of their programs. Much of the potential harm of media therapy might be avoided if therapists do not "exploit personal intimacy and pain for the sake of commercialized entertainment" (Rice, 1981, p. 91).

Summary

In this chapter we have explored several specialized strategies used within the context of therapeutic practice. Each specific technology, whether the use of drugs, hardware, or innovative treatment modalities, has unique ethical problems for the practitioner. In all cases we urge therapists to receive adequate training, supervision, and certification before using clients as guinea pigs. Whereas certainly caution and restraint are appropriate guiding principles for the use of any specialized therapeutic strategy, failure to educate ourselves about these methodologies cheats our clients of some extremely effective means to help rid them of debilitating symptoms.

8

Marketing
Therapeutic
Services

So many bewildering claims are made to the client shopping for
a therapist that he is perplexed and does not know where to
turn. Quacks, witch doctors, and healers can label themselves
as counselors or therapists in many states. How is a client to
separate the competent from the incompetent when the marketing of professional services is so muddled?

Truth in Marketing

Strupp (1975) implies that the lack of truth in marketing professional services is responsible for criticisms leveled at
therapists: their elitism, the expense of treatment, and the lack
of any authoritative statement indicating what therapists actually do. He contends that "the client has a right to know
what he is buying, and the therapist, like the manufacturer of
a product or the seller of a service, has a responsibility to be explicit on this subject" (p. 39). The helping professional can at-

tain ethical respectability, Strupp suggests, by being open, specific, and honest about the nature of therapeutic services, the goals of treatment, and what is likely to happen in the sessions.

Therapists who engage in professional services without specifying what the client is likely to get for his money are asking persons to follow a mysterious open-ended journey without any notion of where they are going, how they will get there, and how long it will take. Frequently therapists fend off the questions of inquisitive clients by responding, "It all depends on how hard you work" or "You will get better when you are ready to," as if some fairy with a magic wand hovers above their shoulder waiting for the appropriate time to heal them.

The mass media contribute to and exaggerate the myth of therapist omnipotence. Wahl (1976), for instance, describes how television promotes this myth. As portrayed on television, psychotherapists are readily able to help solve crimes by specifying the age, sex, and unconscious motivations of the criminal. One popular detective series featured a psychiatrist, brought in to help in the police investigation of a murder. After a cursory examination of the evidence, the consulting psychiatrist promptly concluded: "He is young, probably a college dropout from a broken home who, for some reason, harbors great hostility toward his mother, which he has never resolved. Perhaps she deserted him or his father when he was young and he has never forgiven her. Now, when he kills these women, he is really killing his mother, the application of makeup being the messiness of a rebellious child. He is probably impotent and drinks a good deal, mostly Bloody Marys, and wears suspenders to bolster his failing masculine self-image" (p. 4).

Somewhat less sensationally, Eber and O'Brien (1982) conclude, from their study of therapists as portrayed in movies, that a standard formula markets the members of our profession as "god-hero-doctor" who can repair the damage inflicted by a single traumatic event in but a few sessions: "The notion of the psychotherapeutic sleuth and the single traumatic incident persists because it apparently resonates with a need in all of us for an answer, one that is comprehensible and one that offers help. It responds also to the need to perceive the therapist, the idealized hero, as omniscient and omnipotent" (p. 120).

It is no wonder that the public believes in the power of therapists. They are consistently portrayed as masters of insight who have the ability to peer into people's minds, read their thoughts, and know exactly what they will do. Certainly the media are partially responsible for perpetuating the myths, but therapists themselves are just as guilty of deceit when they fail to be truthful about what they can and cannot deliver. And occasionally the media even attempt to debunk the myths, as an article in *Playboy* magazine demonstrates: "Psychology. The great pseudo science. A few phenomena explained, a few theories advanced. But no predictions. Because nobody really knows. The tool has not yet been invented that enables scientists to peer into the mind, the personality, the brain, the soul, or whatever it is that makes us tick. Until the microscope was invented, man could only speculate about the nature of disease. Until the telescope, we knew nothing of the universe. And until their fantastic gadget does come along, psychologists will remain, in effect, witch doctors" (Pearce, 1975, p. 161). In another journalistic satire, Theroux (1975) paints the following portrait:

> The psychiatrist—you begin with a sigh and end with a *triste*—what exactly does he do? He studies monkeys, examines criminals, administers drugs, testifies in legal proceedings, signs commitment papers, occasionally fools around with biochemical research, but best of all loves just to sit around on his buns. . . . But he's a great figure, Magellan, Vasco da Gama, and the Cabots, father and son, combined. . . .
>
> Psychiatrists are the new monks, their offices the secular monasteries against whose walls come to wait, while seeking to be shriven, the guilt-ridden, the sinner, the troubled-in-mind. Officially, there are about 25,000 registered psychiatrists in this country. It may disturb you to know that only about one fourth of the people practicing the craft in the United States have been certified; the rest of them, shingling out, for all I know, under such titles as mediums, mesmerizers, head counselors, kludds, or Wizards of Oz, are nothing more than a lot of horoscopical busy bodies, clini-

cal psychologists, and social adjusters with a pas-
sion for tampering and who, just for kicks, decide
to have a passing shy at the brain to test their own
oblique theories as to why people honk out, are a
bit voom-voomed, have guests in their attic (p.
161).

The confusion and resentment expressed by the public
and the media only reflect our own battles of uncertainty in the
profession. There are many therapists who contradict one another, who deliver promises they cannot keep, or who argue
passionately in the public forum for their favorite pathways to
truth. Yet as the Russian novelist Turgenev once reminded his
colleague Tolstoy: "The people who bind themselves to systems are those who are unable to encompass the whole truth
and try to catch it by the tail; a system is like the tail of truth,
but truth is like a lizard; it leaves its tail in your fingers and
runs away knowing full well that it will grow a new one in a
twinkling" (Boorstein, 1983, p. 81).

Elusive as truth may be, therapists have an obligation to
market their services as objectively, realistically, and professionally as possible. As a client's belief in the power of therapy
increases, so does his impatience for a quick cure (Widiger and
Rorer, 1984). Hence, truth in marketing therapy has become
more important as prospective consumers have become more
sophisticated and demanding.

Consumer Protection

Restrictions on advertising and public promotion rest on
the historical conception that professionals are devoted to public service rather than to making money and that overt marketing tarnishes the profession's image and undermines public
confidence (Bayles, 1981). However, these restrictions—although
they may prevent boastfulness and a deterioration of the profession's image—also undermine fair trade, freedom of speech,
competitive market pricing, and the availability of services to
the disadvantaged who are unaware of what help might be useful. A compromise position has evolved in which restrictions

have been placed on the style or content of information provided to the public. Contracting, professional directories, agency forms, or explicit descriptions of qualifications and services performed are common examples of disclosures to consumers (Gill, 1982).

The American Association for Marriage and Family Therapy speaks directly and specifically about the responsibility of its clinical members to avoid misrepresentation of services provided to prospective clients. In its *Standards on Public Information and Advertising,* it recommends the following marketing guidelines:

1. Advertisements should provide only sufficient information to help the public make informed choices regarding appropriate professionals.
2. Information could include but not be limited to (a) names and addresses, (b) languages spoken, (c) office hours, (d) earned degrees, licenses, state certification, (e) specialties, and (f) appropriate fee information.
3. Extravagant, brash, emotional, persuasive, or self-praising statements are considered improper.

The American Psychological Association and the National Academy of Certified Clinical Mental Health Counselors share the concern for marketing therapeutic services in an ethical, accurate, and professional manner. In their view information should be restricted to verifiable statements that are based on acceptable empirical findings. The APA statement on public statements and announcements of services (Principle 4) recommends that an advertisement for professional services include name, degrees, licensure or certification, specialization, and type of service offered. Other information can be offered provided it does not mislead the consumer, create unjustified expectations, appeal to fears or anxieties, solicit clients, include testimonials, or imply unique abilities.

It is doubtful whether the following advertisement meets professional standards. The announcement was distributed in a Sunday supplement of a daily newspaper.

Mrs. Williams: Spiritual Healer. Are you worried, unhappy, or having trouble with loved ones? See Mrs. Williams. She succeeds where others have failed. $5 off with this coupon. . . .

Mrs. Williams does not mention her professional background or professional training, or even whether she has either. Perhaps she was trained in Palm Beach. If she read a popular magazine five years ago, she may have found the following advertisement:

Palm Beach Psychotherapy Training Center Inc. Any licensed practitioner of the healing arts can earn a diploma, certificate, and license. Method A: 10 written lessons and examination. Method B: Advanced course, 20 hours in residence. $300. Graduates will be awarded D-C-L promptly and qualified to practice as a clinical psychotherapist. Send an outline of your academic and occupational status to P.B.P.T.C. . . .

A more appropriate and objective announcement of counseling services is provided in the following announcement:

Counseling Associates of Virginia
John W. Doe, Ph.D., Licensed Professional Coun-
      selor
Individual and Group
Hours by Appointment

Practitioners can best protect the welfare of consumers by providing factual information devoid of sensationalism, exaggeration, direct solicitation, and superficiality. In other words, we ought not to come across as ambulance chasers out to make a fast buck but, rather, as highly competent professionals with restraint and dignity.

The Client's Bill of Rights

In an attempt to delineate for practitioners as well as for prospective consumers the criteria for evaluating and marketing productive therapy experiences, we have created a list of client

rights, integrating the views of authors such as Kottler and
Vriend (1975), Haley (1976), Koch and Koch (1976), Parloff
(1976), Berger (1982), and Corey, Corey, and Callanan (1984).
Before such a document is tacked on the walls of any individual's office, however, it would have to undergo revisions in
order to reflect that individual's unique style of practice. Such a
Bill of Rights can be useful for the therapist in preventing negligence and self-serving motives. It also helps the client understand the criteria by which to make informed choices regarding
participation in therapy.

According to Goldberg (1977), the client's rights can best
be preserved by attention to the concepts of equity and balance
in the therapeutic relationship. Roles, goals, and responsibilities
should be clarified. He even suggests that therapists specifically
and explicitly negotiate a contract with clients. Such a contract
would stipulate the therapist's expectations, the demands of the
relationship, costs, services provided, length of sessions and
treatment, provisions for cancellation and termination, protection against no-shows by the client, and guarantees of confidentiality and good faith. Hare-Mustin and others (1979) also mention the importance of periodic renegotiation of the contract
as treatment progresses and goals change.

Whether or not a formalized contractual arrangement is
made, the therapist will find it helpful to explore with the client
most of the following items before undertaking treatment.

The client has a right:

1. To indicate what he or she believes will occur in treatment and to have misconceptions corrected.
2. To receive help, regardless of socioeconomic status, physical attractiveness, presenting problem, race, religion, or sex.
3. To hear a clear and concise definition of what therapy is,
   how and why it works, and what expected roles will be.
4. To know that therapy involves hard work, personal risks,
   discomfort, and pain and that progress is unlikely without
   concerted effort.
5. To understand the meaning of confidentiality—how data
   will be handled, who else has access to the privileged communication, and in what circumstances it may be violated.

6. To work with a therapist who is a trained and competent expert in the profession; who has appropriate degrees, licenses, and certifications; and who has maintained a high quality of continuing education after graduation.

7. To the assurance that he will become more independent as a result of treatment and *not* dependent on the therapist for continued guidance and solutions in the future.

8. To a businesslike contractual arrangement, with fees and conditions clearly spelled out, adjusted rates on a sliding scale, and reasonable efforts made to review the agreement periodically.

9. To therapeutic sessions where the content is focused directly on the client's welfare or interest and not on self-indulgent small talk and irrelevant and inappropriate disclosures by the therapist.

10. To an honest, straightforward relationship in which the therapist regularly and sensitively provides constructive feedback.

11. To the assurance that *everything* a therapist does or says is intended only to facilitate further growth in sessions, that no conflicts of interest, hidden agendas, or self-indulgent gratifications are being promoted.

12. To have help in setting short- and long-term goals that are specific, realistic, and attainable.

13. To have carry-over and follow-up from session to session, including regular monitoring of life events between appointments.

14. To ask, at any time, before, during, or after treatment, for a description of the plan of action individually designed for the particular case, including the specific rationale for any intervention attempted.

15. To review, revise, and have an active part in the design of treatment, including an understanding of how such a blueprint was constructed, so that similar strategies may be recreated, independently, in the future.

16. To work with a therapist who is a model of personal effectiveness, who is constantly striving for greater mastery in his or her own life, and who has attained a high degree

of skill in any area where the client may be experiencing difficulty.

17. To know the limitations, dangers, and risks of treatment.

18. To structured practice of issues currently being worked on: role-playing exercises in sessions and psychological homework outside of sessions.

19. To have presenting symptoms regarded as important and worthy of therapeutic work, not discarded in favor of what the therapist believes is the *real* problem.

20. To work with a professional who is flexible and pragmatic in his approach, adapting treatment strategies to each individual rather than forcing compliance to a rigid, established routine.

21. To efficient and cost-effective treatment requiring the minimum amount of time to reach mutually agreed goals.

22. To share in the decision to terminate therapy.

23. To have assurance that, upon termination, efforts will be made to facilitate a smooth transition and that follow-up checks will be made to ensure that continued progress is maintained.

24. To redress grievances in the event that a therapist acts unethically, irresponsibly, or incompetently.

Summary

It is the therapist's responsibility not only to deliver expert therapeutic help but also to describe accurately what he can and cannot do for the public. At the very minimum, prospective clients have a right to know about the therapist's training, qualifications, fees, specialties, and limitations, as well as his conceptions of how therapy will help. It is through the honest and precise labeling of their services that therapists establish true credibility with their clients, their colleagues, and themselves.

9

Ethical
Principles
and
Individual
Conduct

In his entertaining description of the mythical island called Utopia, Sir Thomas More explains that in ethics the Utopians are much concerned with such matters as good and virtue and pain and pleasure. According to More, the members of this perfectly organized society maintain that there are certain natural laws and that one of these is a high regard for all members of the group. This being a major principle to live by, it then follows that one person does not pursue his own interests at the expense of other people's.

Unlike the Utopians, our society has been unable to reach such common agreements on right principles of conduct in human intercourse. We are capable of rational thought, however; and we have some understanding of ethically valid rules that give direction to our behavior. The rules, which are in reality guidelines, are often flexible and subject to modification, particularly in a free society. Books on ethics, ethical standards, and to some extent legal codes are based on commonly accepted principles of right and wrong and are attempts to describe in a general way how we should or must behave. Most people, for much of the time, attempt to adhere to the behavior standards of their culture. But there are lapses because, being human, we are not always willing to obey ethical codes, legal mandates, or moral principles. We may also insist on living by our own principles or obeying our own consciences, and such actions may conflict with group standards or requirements. In order to prevent too much deviation from the accepted standard, social institutions, churches, legislative bodies, and the courts attempt to provide specific directions and to influence people to adhere to *right* principles. Professional societies, out of concern for the welfare of the profession and in their desire to avoid external control, also develop standards of practice and ethical codes that they hope members will follow in making ethical decisions.

Most therapists, philosophically at least, subscribe to the basic ethical standards and principles of their profession. In a like manner, most of us support and obey the law, and we generally accept the need for societal rules to govern human conduct. But we do not do so blindly or without question. Quite frequently we assert our personal independence; we choose to ignore a rule, disobey a law, or violate a principle because it seems to us—at that moment at least—that the matter has nothing to do with us, and that it is not significant anyway. Or we may disobey a law or a rule because we believe that it is wrong. In other words, we make a free choice, for or against a law or a principle and for or against ethical behavior. This choice is an individual matter and beyond the reach of any person, group, or power.

Dunham (1971) believes that an individual begins to make free decisions when he first realizes that other people may be as important as he is. If he decides that they are, he freely embraces ethics; if not, he ignores ethics and behaves as he chooses. We suggest that one also is required to make an ethical choice when he is confronted with the realization that living free requires living by a set of moral principles. Living free, in preference to existing in defeat, frequently requires acting on behalf of those principles even when such actions may be painful.

We assume that most therapists entered the profession voluntarily. They chose to be a counselor or psychotherapist rather than a haberdasher or car salesman. Put another way, they indicated a preference for selling a service rather than goods or products. Having chosen to enter a profession, and upon being admitted to it, the individual becomes a recipient of some of the privileges as well as some of the status and prestige that the profession affords. Likewise, he assumes a duty and a responsibility to the profession. This responsibility is ethical in nature, and it is in one sense more acute than the responsibility incurred by one who sells a product, since what a therapist sells cannot be touched, weighed, or measured. It is the therapist's obligation to render a useful service and to do so within the guidelines established by his profession. Therapists and other professionals can probably get away with many unethical and even illegal practices if they choose to do so. In spite of such publicized scandals as Medicaid frauds and storefront clinics designed to exploit the helpless and defraud the government, the risks of being caught and prosecuted are quite minimal.

Moreover, it is unlikely that unethical and illegal practices will be greatly curtailed through more external controls. While refined licensure and certification laws will help to weed out many untrained "counselors" and "advisers," statutory controls will not eliminate the scoundrels who hold proper professional credentials and meet all the legal qualifications for licensure or certification. What will discourage unethical practitioners are consumer education programs and monitoring procedures that lead to public disclosure. The American Psychological Association has developed elaborate and formal procedures for expelling violators of its ethical code. The prospect of having one's name printed on a sheet of paper and mailed to all APA members with a note that the individual named has been ejected from the club for an ethical violation ought to discourage unethical behavior. Even powerful politicians caught with secretaries who cannot type have trouble explaining such blunders to their colleagues.

In the preceding pages of this book, we have presented a basic introduction to the principles of ethics applicable to the helping professions. Several legal principles that have relevance for the practice of therapy have been presented, and some landmark court cases have been reviewed. Several statutes and court rulings undoubtedly soon will be replaced by more current statutes and refined court decisions. These actions will result in changes that will require therapists and their professional associations to remain alert to legal circumscriptions within which they work.

It has been one hundred years since Freud called attention to mental therapy as a method of treating emotional disorders and seventy-five years since Clifford Beers described the sufferings of the mentally ill. It has taken a comparatively lengthy period of time for counseling and psychotherapy to develop effective methods of treating people with debilitating emotional problems. Only during the past four decades have mental therapists gained acceptance as legitimate professionals. This acceptance included public trust and faith in the usefulness of therapy. Therapists, while primarily clinicians and not researchers, have been motivated to conduct considerable research in an effort to validate their techniques and to develop new approaches to treatment. Theories and techniques are becoming more precise and more useful in explaining behavior and in treating people who need mental health services. These developments have contributed, in part, to the wide acceptance and profound influence of counseling and psychotherapy in modern society. The power to influence not only individual clients but also, and more pervasively, public attitudes and policies in matters pertaining to "mental health," "deviance," and "right" behavior carries with it grave responsibilities. At the present time, therapists have not agreed on the characteristics of these responsibilities.

Hare-Mustin and her colleagues (1979) present several cogent arguments on the responsibilities of therapists for incorporating ethical standards into their work. Hare-Mustin suggests that we may need to rethink our images of clients and retool our training programs if our practice of counseling and psychotherapy is to be consistent with the ethical principles we espouse. For example, some therapies place the client in a dependent, relatively helpless position vis-à-vis the therapist while simultaneously endorsing independence, freedom, and self-determination as major goals of helping. If we are truly sensitive to the concept of self-determination and freedom, then our training programs should foster an image of clients as strong, responsible people, and we should practice these principles in the client-therapist relationship (pp. 4–5).

Hare-Mustin argues that therapists are responsible for ensuring that clients make informed choices about entering and continuing in therapy. Knowledge of three areas provides the background for such choices: (1) procedures, goals, and possible side effects of therapy; (2) qualifications, policies, and practices of the therapist; and (3) available sources of help other than therapy (p. 5). She believes that many clients have questions about the competence of their therapist and may develop serious questions about the value of therapy. No psychotherapist enjoys having his competence questioned, and it is not easy to accept criticism. However, therapists need to recognize that some questions are inevitable and that some criticisms may be valid.

Reamer (1982, p. 34) also makes a strong case regarding the responsibilities of therapists for protecting client rights to freedom in choice making: "An individual's right to freedom takes precedence over his or her right to basic well-being." Thus, according to Reamer, a therapist may have to interfere with the freedom of a client who has threatened to harm another person; but he cannot interfere with a client who chooses to engage in apparently self-destructive behavior unless the client has been coerced or is so disturbed that he has no knowledge of the likely consequences of his behavior and is therefore unable to make a rational choice. Likewise, one cannot interfere with an alcoholic who has made an informed choice to continue drinking unless the drinking behavior threatens the welfare of others; and one cannot interfere with a client who chooses to remain in an unhappy marriage or one who chooses to live in a dirty, unattractive room, if the choice is rational and informed.

Several experts describe the therapist's responsibility for establishing contracts with clients; that is, written or verbal

deals spelling out the goals of therapy and the expectations, requirements, and boundaries of the helping activity. In Chapter
Six we provide more specificity on this agreement.

A few authorities have described the therapist's ethical responsibilities within the perspective of role behavior and legal
liability. Hart (1979) and Widiger and Rorer (1984) define *role,
causal, capacity,* and *liability* responsibility. *Role responsibility*
refers to the fulfillment of duties, tasks, or obligations inherent
in a title, job, or office. Responsible people take their duties
seriously; they work to improve their services or skills, and they
are sensitive to the people they serve. *Causal responsibility* refers to a result, consequence, or outcome. By their actions
therapists cause events or consequences in the lives of their clients. They are required to assume some degree of responsibility
for the results of their service, good or bad. *Capacity responsibility* refers to the possession of certain necessary qualities or
abilities to govern one's actions. In this society therapists are
expected to possess several carefully defined capacities—skills
and understandings necessary to function as a professional.
They may be ethically and legally culpable if they are found
lacking in those skills—assuming of course that they claim professional skill and expertise. *Liability responsibility* means that
a person can be held accountable for the results of his actions.
A therapist, then, may be held responsible by a professional association's ethics committee or in a court of law. As noted in
Chapter Three, one can be sued for malpractice if certain conditions are present.

Critical Issues Facing Therapists

In the first edition of this book, 1977, we identified and
discussed five issues facing the psychological helping professions: (1) improper and casual methods of selecting students for
graduate preparation, (2) lack of practicality and utility of some
aspects of preparation programs, (3) use of outmoded training
models, (4) inadequate attention to professional standards and
professionalization, and (5) lack of role models.

These issues remain, and other equally critical issues must

be confronted. Among these are *inappropriate credentialing procedures*. Credentialing, as used here, refers to three activities: program accreditation, licensure of individual practitioners, and certification. As noted in Chapter Four, the American Psychological Association has for years accredited doctoral-level preparation programs in clinical, counseling, and school psychology. More recently it has begun accrediting programs described as combined professional-scientific psychology. All fifty states and the District of Columbia now license psychologists. Zemlick (1980) has raised several questions regarding the reluctance or inability of the APA to enforce its credentialing standards. He cites several examples of both ethical and legal violations in such critical areas as credentialing and licensing. He charges that psychology "covers up" many of its questionable and unethical practices.

Counselors have their own problems with credentialing, and ethical questions surrounding program accreditation, licensure, and certification are simply too numerous to discuss here. However, some issues must be identified.

The American Association for Counseling and Development, through its accreditation unit, has approved 28 of 424 counselor education programs since the inception of this unit in 1981. Minimal requirements for accreditation are that programs train counselors at a two-year master's level. Ten states now license counselors—some at the master's level. The major arguments for program accreditation and individual practitioner licensure are program improvement and protection for the public. But given the fact of hundreds of programs training counselors at the master's level, and thousands of licensed professional counselors now ready to engage in private practice, it is doubtful whether the AACD's efforts have yet been productive of greater professionalization or public protection.

These conditions become even more critical when a second issue, *lack of attention to ethical issues,* is considered. The American Psychological Association has an active ethics committee that does not seem hesitant to discipline members for questionable conduct. Professional associations for counselors (AACD and several divisions) have adopted ethical standards or guidelines, but these standards are generally ignored. The AACD has made no serious effort to monitor the professional behavior of members, even those in private practice. An attempt to discover whether state branches have procedures for disciplining members for ethical violations produced one set of guidelines for state ethics committees, patterned after the APA's but never enforced. In fact, that state branch of the AACD feels no need for an ethics committee because ethical complaints are referred to the same board that administers the licensure law. Members of that board refer cases to the attorney general before acting on ethics cases and deny any conflict of interests resulting from their actions.

Numerous additional charges of failure to develop viable standards and monitor their activities could be leveled at helping professionals. Those issues identified here are merely illustrative of the issues that must be dealt with as the helping professions attempt to keep pace with changing morality and a society that relies heavily on counseling. One of the major challenges to the helping professions is to develop and maintain high standards and to make certain that counselors and psychotherapists are held accountable for their actions.

A Final Note

Ethical codes or standards provide helpful guidelines for the professional behavior of counselors and psychotherapists. These codes, while sometimes imprecise and often debatable, represent the consensus of a large number of reputable professionals and thus deserve the close attention of all mental health practitioners. By the same logic, laws enacted by democratically elected legislators or legal decisions issued by the courts represent an essential social arrangement and cannot be violated with impunity. Society in general and those who pay for therapeutic services in particular have a right to expect that those who minister to psychological needs adhere to some general rules of professional conduct. One can believe that a law is immoral and seek to have it repealed, or he can disagree with an ethical code and work to have it revised. All rules or laws are subject to criticism, review, and revision when they are deemed wrong or un-necessary. But this does not mean that they can be ignored or subjected to individual validation. If they were, then most rules, customs, or laws would be meaningless.

Rules governing the professional behavior of therapists are necessary to the continued existence of the profession. Moreover, as we have argued throughout this book, therapists who accept the status provided by a profession have a responsibility for adhering to the principles set forth in the profession's code of ethics. We may question the specific meanings of a code and debate its application; but if fundamental principles are ignored, then we are lost, because we have no basis for making judgments and no way of knowing whether we have behaved properly or improperly.

Ultimately, each person is responsible for his own ethical behavior. Ethical decisions at any given time represent a blend of feelings, beliefs, prejudices, and experiences. We have repeatedly urged adherence to the ethical codes of the mental health professions. At the same time, we maintain that each person's primary obligation is to do at all times what he believes to be right. Dunham's (1971) rule on ethical behavior is that each person must be treated as an end; no person should be treated merely as a means. This rule, consistently applied, will shape ethical decisions, influence consequences, and help to create a proper climate for ethical decision making.

Appendix A

American Psychological Association: Ethical Principles of Psychologists

Preamble

Psychologists respect the dignity and worth of the individual and strive for the preservation and protection of fundamental human rights. They are committed to increasing knowledge of human behavior and of people's understanding of themselves

These revised *Ethical Principles* apply to psychologists, to students

and others and to the utilization of such knowledge for the pro-
motion of human welfare. While pursuing these objectives, they
make every effort to protect the welfare of those who seek their
services and of the research participants that may be the object
of study. They use their skills only for purposes consistent with
these values and do not knowingly permit their misuse by oth-
ers. While demanding for themselves freedom of inquiry and
communication, psychologists accept the responsibility this
freedom requires: competence, objectivity in the application of
skills, and concern for the best interests of clients, colleagues,
students, research participants, and society. In the pursuit of
these ideals, psychologists subscribe to principles in the follow-
ing areas: (1) Responsibility, (2) Competence, (3) Moral and
Legal Standards, (4) Public Statements, (5) Confidentiality, (6)
Welfare of the Consumer, (7) Professional Relationships, (8) As-
sessment Techniques, (9) Research with Human Participants,
and (10) Care and Use of Animals.

Acceptance of membership in the American Psychologi-
cal Association commits the member to adherence to these prin-
ciples.

Psychologists cooperate with duly constituted commit-
tees of the American Psychological Association, in particular,
the Committee on Scientific and Professional Ethics and Con-
duct, by responding to inquiries promptly and completely.
Members also respond promptly and completely to inquiries
from duly constituted state association ethics committees and
professional standards review committees.

---

of psychology, and to others who do work of a psychological nature under
the supervision of a psychologist. They are also intended for the guidance
of nonmembers of the Association who are engaged in psychological research or practice.

Any complaints of unethical conduct filed after January 24, 1981,
shall be governed by this 1981 revision. However, conduct (a) complained
about after January 24, 1981, but which occurred prior to that date, and
(b) not considered unethical under prior versions of the principles but considered unethical under the 1981 revision, shall not be deemed a violation
of ethical principles. Any complaints pending as of January 24, 1981, shall
be governed either by the 1979 or by the 1981 version of the *Ethical Princi-*
ples, at the sound discretion of the Committee on Scientific and Professional Ethics and Conduct.

Principle 1
Responsibility

In providing services, psychologists maintain the highest standards of their profession. They accept responsibility for the consequences of their acts and make every effort to ensure that their services are used appropriately.

a. As scientists, psychologists accept responsibility for the selection of their research topics and the methods used in investigation, analysis, and reporting. They plan their research in ways to minimize the possibility that their findings will be misleading. They provide thorough discussion of the limitations of their data, especially where their work touches on social policy or might be construed to the detriment of persons in specific age, sex, ethnic, socioeconomic, or other social groups. In publishing reports of their work, they never suppress disconfirming data, and they acknowledge the existence of alternative hypotheses and explanations of their findings. Psychologists take credit only for work they have actually done.

b. Psychologists clarify in advance with all appropriate persons and agencies the expectations for sharing and utilizing research data. They avoid relationships that may limit their objectivity or create a conflict of interest. Interference with the milieu in which data are collected is kept to a minimum.

c. Psychologists have the responsibility to attempt to prevent distortion, misuse, or suppression of psychological findings by the institution or agency of which they are employees.

d. As members of governmental or other organizational bodies, psychologists remain accountable as individuals to the highest standards of their profession.

e. As teachers, psychologists recognize their primary obligation to help others acquire knowledge and skill. They maintain high standards of scholarship by presenting psychological information objectively, fully, and accurately.

f. As practitioners, psychologists know that they bear a heavy social responsibility because their recommendations and professional actions may alter the lives of others. They are alert to personal, social, organizational, financial, or political situations and pressures that might lead to misuse of their influence.

Principle 2
Competence

The maintenance of high standards of competence is a responsibility shared by all psychologists, in the interest of the public and the profession as a whole. Psychologists recognize the boundaries of their competence and the limitations of their techniques. They only provide services and only use techniques for which they are qualified by training and experience. In those areas in which recognized standards do not yet exist, psychologists take whatever precautions are necessary to protect the welfare of their clients. They maintain knowledge of current scientific and professional information related to the services they render.

a. Psychologists accurately represent their competence, education, training, and experience. They claim as evidence of educational qualifications only those degrees obtained from institutions acceptable under the Bylaws and Rules of Council of the American Psychological Association.

b. As teachers, psychologists perform their duties on the basis of careful preparation so that their instruction is accurate, current, and scholarly.

c. Psychologists recognize the need for continuing education and are open to new procedures and changes in expectations and values over time.

d. Psychologists recognize differences among people, such as those that may be associated with age, sex, socioeconomic, and ethnic backgrounds. When necessary, they obtain training, experience, or counsel to assure competent service or research relating to such persons.

e. Psychologists responsible for decisions involving individuals or policies based on test results have an understanding of psychological or educational measurement, validation problems, and test research.

f. Psychologists recognize that personal problems and conflicts may interfere with professional effectiveness. Accordingly, they refrain from undertaking any activity in which their personal problems are likely to lead to inadequate performance or harm to a client, colleague, student, or research participant. If engaged in such activity when they become aware of their personal problems, they seek competent professional assistance to determine whether they should suspend, terminate, or limit the scope of their professional and/or scientific activities.

Principle 3
Moral and Legal Standards

Psychologists' moral and ethical standards of behavior are a personal matter to the same degree as they are for any other citizen, except as these may compromise the fulfillment of their professional responsibilities or reduce the public trust in psychology and psychologists. Regarding their own behavior, psychologists are sensitive to prevailing community standards and to the possible impact that conformity to or deviation from these standards may have upon the quality of their performance as psychologists. Psychologists are also aware of the possible impact of their public behavior upon the ability of colleagues to perform their professional duties.

a. As teachers, psychologists are aware of the fact that their personal values may affect the selection and presentation of instructional materials. When dealing with topics that may give offense, they recognize and respect the diverse attitudes that students may have toward such materials.

b. As employees or employers, psychologists do not engage in or condone practices that are inhumane or that result in illegal or unjustifiable actions. Such practices include, but are not limited to, those based on considerations of race, handicap, age, gender, sexual preference, religion, or national origin in hiring, promotion, or training.

c. In their professional roles, psychologists avoid any action that will violate or diminish the legal and civil rights of clients or of others who may be affected by their actions.

d. As practitioners and researchers, psychologists act in accord with Association standards and guidelines related to practice and to the conduct of research with human beings and animals. In the ordinary course of events, psychologists adhere to relevant governmental laws and institutional regulations. When federal, state, provincial, organizational, or institutional laws, regulations, or practices are in conflict with Association standards and guidelines, psychologists make known their commitment to Association standards and guidelines and, wherever possible, work toward a resolution of the conflict. Both practitioners and researchers are concerned with the development of such legal and quasi-legal regulations as best serve the public interest, and they work toward changing existing regulations that are not beneficial to the public interest.

Principle 4
Public Statements

Public statements, announcements of services, advertising, and promotional activities of psychologists serve the purpose of helping the public make informed judgments and choices. Psychologists represent accurately and objectively their professional qualifications, affiliations, and functions, as well as those of the institutions or organizations with which they or the statements may be associated. In public statements providing psychological information or professional opinions or providing information about the availability of psychological products, publications, and services, psychologists base their statements on scientifically acceptable psychological findings and techniques with full recognition of the limits and uncertainties of such evidence.

a. When announcing or advertising professional services, psychologists may list the following information to describe the provider and services provided: name, highest relevant academic degree earned from a regionally accredited institution, date, type, and level of certification or licensure, diplomate status, APA membership status, address, telephone number, office hours, a brief listing of the type of psychological services offered, an appropriate presentation of fee information, foreign languages spoken, and policy with regard to third-party payments. Additional relevant or important consumer information may be included if not prohibited by other sections of these Ethical Principles.

b. In announcing or advertising the availability of psychological products, publications, or services, psychologists do not present their affiliation with any organization in a manner that falsely implies sponsorship or certification by that organization. In particular and for example, psychologists do not state APA membership or fellow status in a way to suggest that such status implies specialized professional competence or qualifications. Public statements include, but are not limited to, communication by means of periodical, book, list, directory, television, radio, or motion picture. They do not contain (i) a false, fraudulent, misleading, deceptive, or unfair statement; (ii) a misinterpretation of fact or a statement likely to mislead or deceive because in context it makes only a partial disclosure of relevant facts; (iii) a testimonial from a patient regarding the quality of a psychologist's services or products; (iv) a statement intended or likely to create false or unjustified expectations of favorable results; (v) a statement implying unusual, unique, or one-of-a-kind abilities; (vi) a statement intended or likely to appeal to a client's fears, anxieties, or emotions concerning the possible results of failure to obtain the offered services; (vii) a statement concerning the comparative desirability of offered services; (viii) a statement of direct solicitation of individual clients.

c. Psychologists do not compensate or give anything of value to a representative of the press, radio, television, or other communication medium in anticipation of or in return for professional publicity in a news item. A paid advertisement must be identified as such, unless it is apparent from the context that it is a paid advertisement. If communicated to the public by use of radio or television, an advertisement is prerecorded and approved for broadcast by the psychologist, and a recording of the actual transmission is retained by the psychologist.

d. Announcements or advertisements of "personal growth groups," clinics, and agencies give a clear statement of purpose and a clear description of the experiences to be provided. The education, training, and experience of the staff members are appropriately specified.

e. Psychologists associated with the development or promotion of psychological devices, books, or other products offered for commercial sale make reasonable efforts to ensure that announcements and advertisements are presented in a professional, scientifically acceptable, and factually informative manner.

f. Psychologists do not participate for personal gain in commercial announcements or advertisements recommending to the public the purchase or use of proprietary or single-source products or services when that participation is based solely upon their identification as psychologists.

g. Psychologists present the science of psychology and offer their services, products, and publications fairly and accurately, avoiding misrepresentation through sensationalism, exaggeration, or superficiality. Psychologists are guided by the primary obligation to aid the public in developing informed judgments, opinions, and choices.

h. As teachers, psychologists ensure that statements in catalogs and course outlines are accurate and not misleading, particularly in terms of subject matter to be covered, bases for evaluating progress, and the nature of course experiences. Announcements, brochures, or advertisements describing workshops, seminars, or other educational programs accurately describe the audience for which the program is intended, as well as eligibility requirements, educational objectives, and nature of the materials to be covered. These announcements also accurately represent the education, training, and experience of the psychologists presenting the programs and any fees involved.

i. Public announcements or advertisements soliciting research participants in which clinical services or other professional services are offered as an inducement make clear the nature of the services as well as the costs and other obligations to be accepted by participants in the research.

j. A psychologist accepts the obligation to correct others who represent the psychologist's professional qualifications, or associations with products or services, in a manner incompatible with these guidelines.

k. Individual diagnostic and therapeutic services are provided only in the context of a professional psychological relationship. When personal advice is given by means of public lectures or demonstrations, newspaper or magazine articles, radio or television programs, mail, or similar media, the psychologist utilizes the most current relevant data and exercises the highest level of professional judgment.

l. Products that are described or presented by means of public lectures or demonstrations, newspaper or magazine articles, radio or television programs, or similar media meet the same recognized standards as exist for products used in the context of a professional relationship.

Principle 5
Confidentiality

Psychologists have a primary obligation to respect the confidentiality of information obtained from persons in the course of their work as psychologists. They reveal such information to others only with the consent of the person or the person's legal representative, except in those unusual circumstances in which not to do so would result in clear danger to the person or to others. Where appropriate, psychologists inform their clients of the legal limits of confidentiality.

a. Information obtained in clinical or consulting relationships, or evaluative data concerning children, students, employees, and others, is discussed only for professional purposes and only with persons clearly concerned with the case. Written and oral reports present only data germane to the purposes of the evaluation, and every effort is made to avoid undue invasion of privacy.

b. Psychologists who present personal information obtained during the course of professional work in writings, lectures, or other public forums either obtain adequate prior consent to do so or adequately disguise all identifying information.

c. Psychologists make provisions for maintaining confidentiality in the storage and disposal of records.

d. When working with minors or other persons who are unable to give voluntary, informed consent, psychologists take special care to protect these persons' best interests.

Principle 6
Welfare of the Consumer

Psychologists respect the integrity and protect the welfare of the people and groups with whom they work. When conflicts of interest arise between clients and psychologists' employing institutions, psychologists clarify the nature and direction of their loyalties and responsibilities and keep all parties informed of their commitments. Psychologists fully inform consumers as to the purpose and nature of an evaluative, treatment, educational, or training procedure, and they freely acknowledge that clients, students, or participants in research have freedom of choice with regard to participation.

a. Psychologists are continually cognizant of their own needs and of their potentially influential position vis-à-vis persons such as clients, students, and subordinates. They avoid exploiting the trust and dependency of such persons. Psychologists make every effort to avoid dual relationships that could impair their professional judgment or increase the risk of exploitation. Examples of such dual relationships include, but are not limited to, research with and treatment of employees, students, supervisees, close friends, or relatives. Sexual intimacies with clients are unethical.

b. When a psychologist agrees to provide services to a client at the request of a third party, the psychologist assumes the responsibility of clarifying the nature of the relationships to all parties concerned.

c. Where the demands of an organization require psychologists to violate these Ethical Principles, psychologists clarify the nature of the conflict between the demands and these principles. They inform all parties of psychologists' ethical responsibilities and take appropriate action.

d. Psychologists make advance financial arrangements that safeguard the best interests of and are clearly understood by their clients. They neither give nor receive any remuneration for referring clients for professional services. They contribute a portion of their services to work for which they receive little or no financial return.

e. Psychologists terminate a clinical or consulting relationship when it is reasonably clear that the consumer is not benefiting from it. They offer to help the consumer locate alternative sources of assistance.

Principle 7
Professional Relationships

Psychologists act with due regard for the needs, special competencies, and obligations of their colleagues in psychology and other professions. They respect the prerogatives and obligations of the institutions or organizations with which these other colleagues are associated.

a. Psychologists understand the areas of competence of related professions. They make full use of all the professional, technical, and administrative resources that serve the best interests of consumers. The absence of formal relationships with other professional workers does not relieve psychologists of the responsibility of securing for their clients the best possible professional service, nor does it relieve them of the obligation to exercise foresight, diligence, and tact in obtaining the complementary or alternative assistance needed by clients.

b. Psychologists know and take into account the traditions and practices of other professional groups with whom they work and cooperate fully with such groups. If a person is receiving similar services from another professional, psychologists do not offer their own services directly to such a person. If a psychologist is contacted by a person who is already receiving similar services from another professional, the psychologist carefully considers that professional relationship and proceeds with caution and sensitivity to the therapeutic issues as well as the client's welfare. The psychologist discusses these issues with the client so as to minimize the risk of confusion and conflict.

c. Psychologists who employ or supervise other professionals or professionals in training accept the obligation to facilitate the further professional development of these individuals. They provide appropriate working conditions, timely evaluations, constructive consultation, and experience opportunities.

d. Psychologists do not exploit their professional relationships with clients, supervisees, students, employees, or research participants, sexually or otherwise. Psychologists do not condone or engage in sexual harassment. Sexual harassment is defined as deliberate or repeated comments, gestures, or physical contacts of a sexual nature that are unwanted by the recipient.

e. In conducting research in institutions or organizations, psychologists secure appropriate authorization to conduct such research. They are aware of their obligations to future research workers and ensure that host institutions receive adequate information about the research and proper acknowledgment of their contributions.

f. Publication credit is assigned to those who have contributed to a publication in proportion to their professional contributions. Major contributions of a professional character made by several persons to a common project are recognized by joint authorship, with the individual who made the principal contribution listed first. Minor contributions of a professional character and extensive clerical or similar nonprofessional assistance may be acknowledged in footnotes or in an introductory statement. Acknowledgment through specific citations is made for unpublished as well as published material that has directly influenced the research or writing. Psychologists who compile and edit material of others for publication publish the material in the name of the originating group, if appropriate, with their own name appearing as chairperson or editor. All contributors are to be acknowledged and named.

g. When psychologists know of an ethical violation by another psychologist, and it seems appropriate, they informally attempt to resolve the issue by bringing the behavior to the attention of the psychologist. If the misconduct is of a minor nature and/or appears to be due to lack of sensitivity, knowledge, or experience, such an informal solution is usually appropriate. Such informal corrective efforts are made with sensitivity to any rights to confidentiality involved. If the violation does not seem amenable to an informal solution, or is of a more serious nature, psychologists bring it to the attention of the appropri-

ate local, state, and/or national committee on professional ethics and conduct.

Principle 8
Assessment Techniques

In the development, publication, and utilization of psychologi-
cal assessment techniques, psychologists make every effort to
promote the welfare and best interests of the client. They guard
against the misuse of assessment results. They respect the cli-
ent's right to know the results, the interpretations made, and
the bases for their conclusions and recommendations. Psychol-
ogists make every effort to maintain the security of tests and
other assessment techniques within limits of legal mandates.
They strive to ensure the appropriate use of assessment tech-
niques by others.

a. In using assessment techniques, psychologists respect
the right of clients to have full explanations of the nature and
purpose of the techniques in language the clients can understand, unless an explicit exception to this right has been agreed
upon in advance. When the explanations are to be provided by
others, psychologists establish procedures for ensuring the adequacy of these explanations.

b. Psychologists responsible for the development and
standardization of psychological tests and other assessment
techniques utilize established scientific procedures and observe
the relevant APA standards.

c. In reporting assessment results, psychologists indicate
any reservations that exist regarding validity or reliability because of the circumstances of the assessment or the inappropri-
ateness of the norms for the person tested. Psychologists strive
to ensure that the results of assessments and their interpretations are not misused by others.

d. Psychologists recognize that assessment results may
become obsolete. They make every effort to avoid and prevent
the misuse of obsolete measures.

e. Psychologists offering scoring and interpretation services are able to produce appropriate evidence for the validity of

the programs and procedures used in arriving at interpretations. The public offering of an automated interpretation service is considered a professional-to-professional consultation. Psychologists make every effort to avoid misuse of assessment reports.

f. Psychologists do not encourage or promote the use of psychological assessment techniques by inappropriately trained or otherwise unqualified persons through teaching, sponsorship, or supervision.

Principle 9
Research with Human Participants

The decision to undertake research rests upon a considered judgment by the individual psychologist about how best to contribute to psychological science and human welfare. Having made the decision to conduct research, the psychologist considers alternative directions in which research energies and resources might be invested. On the basis of this consideration, the psychologist carries out the investigation with respect and concern for the dignity and welfare of the people who participate and with cognizance of federal and state regulations and professional standards governing the conduct of research with human participants.

a. In planning a study, the investigator has the responsibility to make a careful evaluation of its ethical acceptability. To the extent that the weighing of scientific and human values suggests a compromise of any principle, the investigator incurs a correspondingly serious obligation to seek ethical advice and to observe stringent safeguards to protect the rights of human participants.

b. Considering whether a participant in a planned study will be a "subject at risk" or a "subject at minimal risk," according to recognized standards, is of primary ethical concern to the investigator.

c. The investigator always retains the responsibility for ensuring ethical practice in research. The investigator is also responsible for the ethical treatment of research participants by collaborators, assistants, students, and employees, all of whom, however, incur similar obligations.

d. Except in minimal-risk research, the investigator establishes a clear and fair agreement with research participants, prior to their participation, that clarifies the obligations and responsibilities of each. The investigator has the obligation to honor all promises and commitments included in that agreement. The investigator informs the participants of all aspects of the research that might reasonably be expected to influence willingness to participate and explains all other aspects of the research about which the participants inquire. Failure to make full disclosure prior to obtaining informed consent requires additional safeguards to protect the welfare and dignity of the research participants. Research with children or with participants who have impairments that would limit understanding and/or communication requires special safeguarding procedures.

e. Methodological requirements of a study may make the use of concealment or deception necessary. Before conducting such a study, the investigator has a special responsibility to (i) determine whether the use of such techniques is justified by the study's prospective scientific, educational, or applied value; (ii) determine whether alternative procedures are available that do not use concealment or deception; and (iii) ensure that the participants are provided with sufficient explanation as soon as possible.

f. The investigator respects the individual's freedom to decline to participate in or to withdraw from the research at any time. The obligation to protect this freedom requires careful thought and consideration when the investigator is in a position of authority or influence over the participant. Such positions of authority include, but are not limited to, situations in which research participation is required as part of employment or in which the participant is a student, client, or employee of the investigator.

g. The investigator protects the participant from physical and mental discomfort, harm, and danger that may arise from research procedures. If risks of such consequences exist, the investigator informs the participant of that fact. Research procedures likely to cause serious or lasting harm to a participant are not used unless the failure to use these procedures might expose the participant to risk of greater harm, or unless the research has great potential benefit and fully informed and voluntary consent is obtained from each participant. The participant should be informed of procedures for contacting the investigator within a reasonable time period following participation should stress, potential harm, or related questions or concerns arise.

h. After the data are collected, the investigator provides the participant with information about the nature of the study and attempts to remove any misconceptions that may have arisen. Where scientific or humane values justify delaying or withholding this information, the investigator incurs a special responsibility to monitor the research and to ensure that there are no damaging consequences for the participant.

i. Where research procedures result in undesirable consequences for the individual participant, the investigator has the responsibility to detect and remove or correct these consequences, including long-term effects.

j. Information obtained about a research participant during the course of an investigation is confidential unless otherwise agreed upon in advance. When the possibility exists that others may obtain access to such information, this possibility, together with the plans for protecting confidentiality, is explained to the participant as part of the procedure for obtaining informed consent.

Principle 10
Care and Use of Animals

An investigator of animal behavior strives to advance understanding of basic behavioral principles and/or to contribute to the improvement of human health and welfare. In seeking these ends, the investigator ensures the welfare of animals and treats them humanely. Laws and regulations notwithstanding, an animal's immediate protection depends upon the scientist's own conscience.

a. The acquisition, care, use, and disposal of all animals are in compliance with current federal, state or provincial, and local laws and regulations.

b. A psychologist trained in research methods and experienced in the care of laboratory animals closely supervises all procedures involving animals and is responsible for ensuring appropriate consideration of their comfort, health, and humane treatment.

c. Psychologists ensure that all individuals using animals under their supervision have received explicit instruction in experimental methods and in the care, maintenance, and handling of the species being used. Responsibilities and activities of individuals participating in a research project are consistent with their respective competencies.

d. Psychologists make every effort to minimize discomfort, illness, and pain of animals. A procedure subjecting animals to pain, stress, or privation is used only when an alternative procedure is unavailable and the goal is justified by its prospective scientific, educational, or applied value. Surgical procedures are performed under appropriate anesthesia; techniques to avoid infection and minimize pain are followed during and after surgery.

e. When it is appropriate that the animal's life be terminated, it is done rapidly and painlessly.

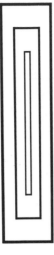

Appendix B

American Association for Counseling and Development: Ethical Standards

Preamble

The American Association for Counseling and Development is an educational, scientific, and professional organization whose members are dedicated to the enhancement of the worth, dignity, potential, and uniqueness of each individual and thus to the service of society.

The Association recognizes that the role definitions and work settings of its members include a wide variety of academic disciplines, levels of academic preparation, and agency services. This diversity reflects the breadth of the Association's interest and influence. It also poses challenging complexities in efforts to set standards for the performance of members, desired requisite preparation or practice, and supporting social, legal, and ethical controls.

The specification of ethical standards enables the Association to clarify to present and future members, and to those served by members, the nature of ethical responsibilities held in common by its members.

The existence of such standards serves to stimulate greater concern by members for their own professional functioning and for the conduct of fellow professionals such as counselors, guidance and student personnel workers, and others in the helping professions. As the ethical code of the Association, this document establishes principles that define the ethical behavior of Association members.

Section A
General

1. The member influences the development of the profession by continuous efforts to improve professional practices, teaching, services, and research. Professional growth is continuous throughout the member's career and is exemplified by the development of a philosophy that explains why and how a member functions in the helping relationship. Members must gather data on their effectiveness and be guided by the findings.

2. The member has a responsibility both to the individual who is served and to the institution within which the service is performed to maintain high standards of professional conduct. The member strives to maintain the highest levels of professional services offered to the individuals to be served. The member also strives to assist the agency, organization, or institution in providing the highest caliber of professional services. The acceptance of employment in an institution implies that the member is in agreement with the general policies and principles of the institution. Therefore, the professional activities of the member are also in accord with the objectives of the institution. If, despite concerted efforts, the member cannot reach agreement with the employer as to acceptable standards of conduct that allow for changes in institutional policy conducive to the positive growth and development of clients, then terminating the affiliation should be seriously considered.

3. Ethical behavior among professional associates, both members and nonmembers, must be expected at all times. When information is possessed that raises doubt as to the ethical behavior of professional colleagues, whether Association members or not, the member must take action to attempt to rectify such a condition. Such action shall use the institution's channels first and then use procedures established by the state Branch, Division, or Association.

4. The member neither claims nor implies professional qualifications exceeding those possessed and is responsible for correcting any misrepresentations of these qualifications by others.

5. In establishing fees for professional counseling services, members must consider the financial status of clients and locality. In the event that the established fee structure is inappropriate for a client, assistance must be provided in finding comparable services of acceptable cost.

6. When members provide information to the public or to subordinates, peers, or supervisors, they have a responsibility to ensure that the content is general, unidentified client information that is accurate, unbiased, and consists of objective, factual data.

7. With regard to the delivery of professional services, members should accept only those positions for which they are professionally qualified.

8. In the counseling relationship, the counselor is aware of the intimacy of the relationship and maintains respect for the client and avoids engaging in activities that seek to meet the counselor's personal needs at the expense of that client. Through awareness of the negative impact of both racial and sexual stereotyping and discrimination, the counselor guards the individual rights and personal dignity of the client in the counseling relationship.

Section B
Counseling Relationship

This section refers to practices and procedures of individual and/or group counseling relationships.

The member must recognize the need for client freedom of choice. Under those circumstances where this is not possible, the member must apprise clients of restrictions that may limit their freedom of choice.

1. The member's *primary* obligation is to respect the integrity and promote the welfare of the client(s), whether the client(s) is (are) assisted individually or in a group relationship. In a group setting, the member is also responsible for taking reasonable precautions to protect individuals from physical and/or psychological trauma resulting from interaction within the group.

2. The counseling relationship and information resulting therefrom be kept confidential, consistent with the obligations of the member as a professional person. In a group-counseling setting, the counselor must set a norm of confidentiality regarding all group participants' disclosures.

3. If an individual is already in a counseling relationship with another professional person, the member does not enter into a counseling relationship without first contacting and receiving the approval of that other professional. If the member discovers that the client is in another counseling relationship after the counseling relationship begins, the member must gain the consent of the other professional or terminate the relationship, unless the client elects to terminate the other relationship.

4. When the client's condition indicates that there is clear and imminent danger to the client or others, the member must take reasonable personal action or inform responsible authorities. Consultation with other professionals must be used where possible. The assumption of responsibility for the client's behavior must be taken only after careful deliberation. The client must be involved in the resumption of responsibility as quickly as possible.

5. Records of the counseling relationship, including interview notes, test data, correspondence, tape recordings, and other documents, are to be considered professional information for use in counseling, and they should not be considered a part of the records of the institution or agency in which the counselor is employed unless specified by state statute or regulation.

Revelation to others of counseling material must occur only upon the expressed consent of the client.

6. Use of data derived from a counseling relationship for purposes of counselor training or research shall be confined to content that can be disguised to ensure full protection of the identity of the subject client.

7. The member must inform the client of the purposes, goals, techniques, rules of procedure, and limitations that may affect the relationship at or before the time that the counseling relationship is entered.

8. The member must screen prospective group participants, especially when the emphasis is on self-understanding and growth through self-disclosure. The member must maintain an awareness of the group participants' compatibility throughout the life of the group.

9. The member may choose to consult with any other professionally competent person about a client. In choosing a consultant, the member must avoid placing the consultant in a conflict-of-interest situation that would preclude the consultant's being a proper party to the member's efforts to help the client.

10. If the member determines an inability to be of professional assistance to the client, the member must either avoid initiating the counseling relationship or immediately terminate that relationship. In either event, the member must suggest appropriate alternatives. (The member must be knowledgeable about referral resources so that a satisfactory referral can be initiated.) In the event the client declines the suggested referral, the member is not obligated to continue the relationship.

11. When the member has other relationships, particularly of an administrative, supervisory, and/or evaluative nature, with an individual seeking counseling services, the member must not serve as the counselor but should refer the individual to another professional. Only in instances where such an alternative is unavailable and where the individual's situation warrants counseling intervention should the member enter into and/or maintain a counseling relationship. Dual relationships with clients that might impair the member's objectivity and profes-

sional judgment (for example, as with close friends or relatives, sexual intimacies with any client) must be avoided and/or the counseling relationship terminated through referral to another competent professional.

12. All experimental methods of treatment must be clearly indicated to prospective recipients, and safety precautions are to be adhered to by the member.

13. When the member is engaged in short-term group treatment/training programs (for example, marathons and other encounter-type or growth groups), the member ensures that there is professional assistance available during and following the group experience.

14. Should the member be engaged in a work setting that calls for any variation from the above statements, the member is obligated to consult with other professionals whenever possible to consider justifiable alternatives.

Section C
Measurement and Evaluation

The primary purpose of educational and psychological testing is to provide descriptive measures that are objective and interpretable in either comparative or absolute terms. The member must recognize the need to interpret the statements that follow as applying to the whole range of appraisal techniques, including test and nontest data. Test results constitute only one of a variety of pertinent sources of information for personnel, guidance, and counseling decisions.

1. The member must provide specific orientation or information to the examinee(s) prior to and following the test administration, so that the results of testing may be placed in proper perspective with other relevant factors. In so doing, the member must recognize the effects of socioeconomic, ethnic, and cultural factors on test scores. It is the member's professional responsibility to use additional unvalidated information carefully in modifying interpretation of the test results.

2. In selecting tests for use in a given situation or with a particular client, the member must consider carefully the spe-

cific validity, reliability, and appropriateness of the test(s). *General* validity, reliability, and the like may be questioned legally as well as ethically when tests are used for vocational and educational selection, placement, or counseling.

3. When making any statements to the public about tests and testing, the member must give accurate information and avoid false claims or misconceptions. Special efforts are often required to avoid unwarranted connotations of such terms as *IQ* and *grade equivalent scores.*

4. Different tests demand different levels of competence for administration, scoring, and interpretation. Members must recognize the limits of their competence and perform only those functions for which they are prepared.

5. Tests must be administered under the same conditions that were established in their standardization. When tests are not administered under standard conditions or when unusual behavior or irregularities occur during the testing session, those conditions must be noted and the results designated as invalid or of questionable validity. Unsupervised or inadequately supervised test-taking, such as the use of tests through the mails, is considered unethical. On the other hand, the use of instruments that are so designed or standardized to be self-administered and self-scored, such as interest inventories, is to be encouraged.

6. The meaningfulness of test results used in personnel, guidance, and counseling functions generally depends on the examinee's unfamiliarity with the specific items on the test. Any prior coaching or dissemination of the test materials can invalidate test results. Therefore, test security is one of the professional obligations of the member. Conditions that produce most favorable test results must be made known to the examinee.

7. The purpose of testing and the explicit use of the results must be made known to the examinee prior to testing. The counselor must ensure that instrument limitations are not exceeded and that periodic review and/or retesting are made to prevent client stereotyping.

8. The examinee's welfare and explicit prior understanding must be the criteria for determining the recipients of the test results. The member must see that specific interpretation

accompanies any release of individual or group test data. The interpretation of test data must be related to the examinee's particular concerns.

9. The member must be cautious when interpreting the results of research instruments possessing insufficient technical data. The specific purposes for the use of such instruments must be stated explicitly to examinees.

10. The member must proceed with caution when attempting to evaluate and interpret the performance of minority group members or other persons who are not represented in the norm group on which the instrument was standardized.

11. The member must guard against the appropriation, reproduction, or modifications of published tests or parts thereof without acknowledgment and permission from the previous publisher.

12. Regarding the preparation, publication, and distribution of tests, reference should be made to:

a. *Standards for Educational and Psychological Tests and Manuals,* revised edition, 1974, published by the American Psychological Association on behalf of itself, the American Educational Research Association, and the National Council on Measurement in Education.

b. "The Responsible Use of Tests: A Position Paper of AMEG, APGA, and NCME," *Measurement and Evaluation in Guidance,* 1972, *5,* 385-388.

c. "Responsibilities of Users of Standardized Tests," APGA, *Guidepost,* October 5, 1978, pp. 5-8.

Section D
Research and Publication

1. Guidelines on research with human subjects shall be adhered to, such as:

a. *Ethical Principles in the Conduct of Research with Human Participants,* Washington, D.C.: American Psychological Association, Inc., 1973.

b. *Code of Federal Regulations,* Title 45, Subtitle A, Part 46, as currently issued.

2. In planning any research activity dealing with human

subjects, the member must be aware of and responsive to all pertinent ethical principles and ensure that the research problem, design, and execution are in full compliance with them.

3. Responsibility for ethical research practice lies with the principal researcher, while others involved in the research activities share ethical obligation and full responsibility for their own actions.

4. In research with human subjects, researchers are responsible for the subjects' welfare throughout the experiment, and they must take all reasonable precautions to avoid causing injurious psychological, physical, or social effects on their subjects.

5. All research subjects must be informed of the purpose of the study except when withholding information or providing misinformation to them is essential to the investigation. In such research the member must be responsible for corrective action as soon as possible following completion of the research.

6. Participation in research must be voluntary. Involuntary participation is appropriate only when it can be demonstrated that participation will have no harmful effects on subjects and is essential to the investigation.

7. When reporting research results, [the investigator must make] explicit mention . . . of all variables and conditions known to [him] that might affect the outcome of the investigation or the interpretation of the data.

8. The member must be responsible for conducting and reporting investigations in a manner that minimizes the possibility that results will be misleading.

9. The member has an obligation to make available sufficient original research data to qualified others who may wish to replicate the study.

10. When supplying data, aiding in the research of another person, reporting research results, or in making original data available, [the investigator must take] due care . . . to disguise the identity of the subjects in the absence of specific authorization from such subjects to do otherwise.

11. When conducting and reporting research, the member must be familiar with, and give recognition to, previous

work on the topic [and must] observe all copyright laws and follow the principles of giving full credit to all to whom credit is due.

12. The member must give due credit—through joint authorship, acknowledgment, footnote statements, or other appropriate means—to those who have contributed significantly to the research and/or publication, in accordance with such contributions.

13. The member must communicate to other members the results of any research judged to be of professional or scientific value. Results reflecting unfavorably on institutions, programs, services, or vested interests must not be withheld for such reasons.

14. If members agree to cooperate with another individual in research and/or publication, they incur an obligation to cooperate as promised in terms of punctuality of performance and with full regard to the completeness and accuracy of the information required.

15. Ethical practice requires that authors not submit the same manuscript or one essentially similar in content for simultaneous publication consideration by two or more journals. In addition, manuscripts published, in whole or in substantial part, in another journal or published work should not be submitted for publication without acknowledgment and permission from the previous publication.

Section E
Consulting

Consultation *refers to a voluntary relationship between a professional helper and help-needing individual, group, or social unit in which the consultant is providing help to the client(s) in defining and solving a work-related problem or potential problem with a client or client system. (This definition is adapted from DeWayne Kurpius, "Consultation Theory and Process: An Integrated Model,"* Personnel and Guidance Journal, *1978, 56.)*

1. The member acting as consultant must have a high degree of self-awareness of his or her own values, knowledge, skills,

limitations, and needs in entering a helping relationship that involves human and/or organizational change, and . . . the focus of the relationship [must] be on the issues to be resolved and not on the person(s) presenting the problem.

2. There must be understanding and agreement between member and client for the problem definition, change goals, and predicated consequences of interventions selected.

3. The member must be reasonably certain that he or she, or the organization represented, has the necessary competencies and resources for giving the kind of help that is needed now or may develop later and that appropriate referral resources are available to the consultant.

4. The consulting relationship must be one in which client adaptability and growth toward self-direction are encouraged and cultivated. The member must maintain this role consistently and not become a decision maker for the client or create a future dependency on the consultant.

5. When announcing consultant availability for services, the member conscientiously adheres to the Association's *Ethical Standards*.

6. The member must refuse a private fee or other remuneration for consultation with persons who are entitled to these services through the member's employing institution or agency. The policies of a particular agency may make explicit provisions for private practice with agency clients by members of its staff. In such instances, the clients must be apprised of other options open to them should they seek private counseling services.

Section F
Private Practice

1. The member should assist the profession by facilitating the availability of counseling services in private as well as public settings.

2. In advertising services as a private practitioner, the member must advertise the services in such a manner as to accurately inform the public [of] services, expertise, profession, and

techniques of counseling in a professional manner. A member who assumes an executive leadership role in the organization shall not permit his or her name to be used in professional notices during periods when not actively engaged in the private practice of counseling.

The member may list the following: highest relevant degree, type and level of certification or license, type and/or description of services, and other relevant information. Such information must not contain false, inaccurate, misleading, partial, out-of-context, or deceptive material or statements.

3. Members may join in partnership/corporation with other members and/or other professionals provided that each member of the partnership or corporation makes clear the separate specialties by name in compliance with the regulations of the locality.

4. A member has an obligation to withdraw from a counseling relationship if it is believed that employment will result in violation of the *Ethical Standards*. If the mental or physical condition of the member renders it difficult to carry out an effective professional relationship or if the member is discharged by the client because the counseling relationship is no longer productive for the client, then the member is obligated to terminate the counseling relationship.

5. A member must adhere to the regulations for private practice of the locality where the services are offered.

6. It is unethical to use one's institutional affiliation to recruit clients for one's private practice.

Section G
Personnel Administration

It is recognized that most members are employed in public or quasi-public institutions. The functioning of a member within an institution must contribute to the goals of the institution and vice versa if either is to accomplish their respective goals or objectives. It is therefore essential that the member and the institution function in ways to (a) make the institution's goals explicit and public; (b) make the member's contribution to insti-

tutional goals specific; and (c) foster mutual accountability for goal achievement.

To accomplish these objectives, it is recognized that the member and the employer must share responsibilities in the formulation and implementation of personnel policies.

1. Members must define and describe the parameters and levels of their professional competency.

2. Members must establish interpersonal relations and working agreements with supervisors and subordinates regarding counseling or clinical relationships, confidentiality, distinction between public and private material, maintenance and dissemination of recorded information, work load, and accountability. Working agreements in each instance must be specified and made known to those concerned.

3. Members must alert their employers to conditions that may be potentially disruptive or damaging.

4. Members must inform employers of conditions that may limit their effectiveness.

5. Members must submit regularly to professional review and evaluation.

6. Members must be responsible for in-service development of self and/or staff.

7. Members must inform their staff of goals and programs.

8. Members must provide personnel practices that guarantee and enhance the rights and welfare of each recipient of their service.

9. Members must select competent persons and assign responsibilities compatible with their skills and experiences.

Section H
Preparation Standards

Members who are responsible for training others must be guided by the preparation standards of the Association and relevant Division(s). The member who functions in the capacity of trainer assumes unique ethical responsibilities that frequently go beyond that of the member who does not function in a training capacity. These ethical responsibilities are outlined as follows:

1. Members must orient students to program expectations, basic skills development, and employment prospects prior to admission to the program.

2. Members in charge of learning experiences must establish programs that integrate academic study and supervised practice.

3. Members must establish a program directed toward developing students' skills, knowledge, and self-understanding, stated whenever possible in competency or performance terms.

4. Members must identify the levels of competencies of their students in compliance with relevant Division standards. These competencies must accommodate the paraprofessional as well as the professional.

5. Members, through continual student evaluation and appraisal, must be aware of the personal limitations of the learner that might impede future performance. The instructor must not only assist the learner in securing remedial assistance but also screen from the program those individuals who are unable to provide competent services.

6. Members must provide a program that includes training in research commensurate with levels of role functioning. Paraprofessional and technician-level personnel must be trained as consumers of research. In addition, these personnel must learn how to evaluate their own and their program's effectiveness. Graduate training, especially at the doctoral level, would include preparation for original research by the member.

7. Members must make students aware of the ethical responsibilities and standards of the profession.

8. Preparatory programs must encourage students to value the ideals of service to individuals and to society. In this regard, direct financial remuneration or lack thereof must not influence the quality of service rendered. Monetary considerations must not be allowed to overshadow professional and humanitarian needs.

9. Members responsible for educational programs must be skilled as teachers and practitioners.

10. Members must present thoroughly varied theoretical positions, so that students may make comparisons and have the opportunity to select a position.

11. Members must develop clear policies within their educational institutions regarding field placement and the roles of the student and the instructor in such placements.

12. Members must ensure that forms of learning focusing on self-understanding or growth are voluntary, or, if required as part of the education program, are made known to prospective students prior to entering the program. When the educational program offers a growth experience with an emphasis on self-disclosure or other relatively intimate or personal involvement, the member must have no administrative, supervisory, or evaluating authority regarding the participant.

13. Members must conduct an educational program in keeping with the current relevant guidelines of the American Association for Counseling and Development and its Divisions.

Appendix C

American Association for Marriage and Family Therapy: Ethical Principles for Family Therapists

1.
Responsibility to Clients

Family therapists are dedicated to advancing the welfare of families and individuals, including respecting the rights of those persons seeking their assistance, and making reasonable efforts to ensure that their services are used appropriately.

    1.1. Family therapists do not discriminate against or refuse professional service to anyone on the basis of race, sex, religion, or national origin.

    1.2. Family therapists do not use their professional relationship to further personal, religious, political, or business interests. Sexual intimacy with clients is unethical.

    1.3. Family therapists continue a therapeutic relationship

Reprinted with permission of the American Association for Marriage and Family Therapy.

only so long as it is reasonably clear that clients are benefiting from the relationship.

1.4. Family therapists make financial arrangements with clients that are consistent with normal and accepted professional practices and that are reasonably understandable to clients.

1.5. Family therapists respect the rights of clients to make decisions consistent with their age and other relevant conditions, while retaining responsibility for assessing the situation according to sound professional judgment and sharing such judgment with the clients. Family therapists clearly advise a client that a decision on marital status is the responsibility of the client.

1.6. Family therapists accept the responsibility for providing services to clients in accordance with AAMFT standards for delivery of family therapy services.

2.
Competence

Family therapists are dedicated to maintaining high standards of competence, recognizing appropriate limitations to their competence and services and using consultation from other professionals.

2.1. Family therapists seek appropriate professional assistance for personal problems or conflicts that are likely to impair their work performance.

2.2. Family therapists, as teachers, are dedicated to maintaining high standards of scholarship and presenting information that is scholarly, up to date, and accurate.

2.3. Family therapists do not attempt to diagnose, treat, or advise on problems outside the recognized boundaries of their competence.

3.
Integrity

Family therapists are honest in dealing with clients, students, trainees, colleagues, and the public, seeking to eliminate incompetence or dishonesty from the work or representations of family therapists.

3.1. Family therapists do not claim, either directly or by implication, professional qualifications exceeding those actually attained, including the presentation of degrees from nonaccredited institutions or programs.

3.2. Family therapists do not use false or misleading advertising or use advertising that in any way violates the AAMFT's "Standards on Public Information and Advertising." Also, they abide by the AAMFT regulations regarding the use of the AAMFT logo.

3.3. Family therapists accept the responsibility to correct wherever possible misleading and inaccurate information and representations made by others concerning the family therapist's qualifications, services, or products.

3.4. Family therapists have the obligation to make certain that the qualifications of persons in their employ are appropriate to the services provided and are appropriately represented.

3.5. Family therapists neither offer nor accept payment for referrals.

3.6. Family therapists accept the responsibility for making informed corrective efforts with other family therapists who are violating ethical principles or for bringing the violations to the attention of the Ethics Committee or other appropriate authority. Proper attention to confidentiality shall be given in such efforts.

3.7. Family therapists do not engage in sexual harassment in their working relationships with clients, students, trainees, or colleagues.

3.8. Family therapists do not use their relationships with students/trainees to further their own personal, religious, political, or business interests. Sexual intimacy with students/trainees is unethical.

3.9. Family therapists use their membership in AAMFT only in connection with their clinical/professional activities.

4.
Confidentiality

Family therapists respect both the law and the rights of clients and safeguard client confidences as permitted by law.

4.1. Family therapists use clinical materials in teaching, writing, and public presentations only when permission has been obtained or when appropriate steps have been taken to protect client identity.

4.2. Family therapists store or dispose of client records in ways that enhance safety and confidentiality.

4.3. Family therapists communicate information about clients to others only after obtaining appropriate client consent, unless there is a clear and immediate danger to an individual or to society, and then only to the concerned individual and appropriate family members, professional workers, or public authorities.

5.
Professional Responsibility

Family therapists respect the rights and responsibilities of professional colleagues and, as employees of organizations, remain accountable as individuals to the ethical principles of their profession.

5.1. Family therapists assign publication credit to those who have contributed to a publication in proportion to their contributions and in accordance with customary professional publication practices.

5.2. Family therapists who are the authors of books or other materials that are published or distributed should cite appropriately persons to whom credit for original ideas is due.

5.3. Family therapists who are the authors of books or other materials published or distributed by an organization take reasonable precautions to ensure that the organization promotes and advertises the materials accurately and factually.

6.
Professional Development

Family therapists seek to continue their professional development and strive to make pertinent knowledge available to clients, students, trainees, colleagues, and the public.

6.1. Family therapists seek to remain abreast of new developments in family therapy knowledge and practice through both formal educational activities and informal learning experiences.

6.2. Family therapists who supervise or employ trainees, family therapists, or other professionals assume a reasonable obligation to encourage and enhance the professional development of those persons.

6.3. Family therapists who provide supervision assume responsibility for defining the relationships as "supervisor-supervisee" and for clearly defining and separating supervisory and therapeutic roles and relationships.

7.
Research Responsibility

Family therapists recognize that, while research is essential to the advancement of knowledge, all investigations must be conducted with full respect for the rights and dignity of participants and with full concern for their welfare.

7.1. Family therapists, as researchers, strive to be adequately informed of relevant laws and other regulations regarding the conduct of research with human participants and to abide by those laws and regulations.

7.2. Family therapists, as researchers, assume responsibility for ensuring that their research is conducted in an ethical manner.

8.
Social Responsibility

Family therapists acknowledge a responsibility to participate in activities that contribute to a better community and society, including devoting a portion of their professional activity to services for which there is little or no financial return.

8.1. Family therapists are concerned with developing laws and legal regulations pertaining to family therapy that serve the public interest and with altering such laws and regulations that are not in the public interest.

8.2. Family therapists affirm that professional services involve both practitioner and client and seek to encourage public participation in the designing and delivery of services and in the regulation of practitioners.

Appendix D

National Association of Social Workers: Code of Ethics

Preamble

This code is intended to serve as a guide to the everyday conduct of members of the social work profession and as a basis for the adjudication of issues in ethics when the conduct of social workers is alleged to deviate from the standards expressed or implied in this code. It represents standards of ethical behavior for social workers in professional relationships with those served, with colleagues, with employers, with other individuals and professions, and with the community and society as a whole. It also embodies standards of ethical behavior governing individual conduct to the extent that such conduct is associated with an individual's status and identity as a social worker.

This code is based on the fundamental values of the social

Reprinted with permission from *Code of Ethics of the National Association of Social Workers,* as adopted by the 1979 NASW Delegate Assembly, effective July 1, 1980.

*work profession that include the worth, dignity, and unique-
ness of all persons as well as their rights and opportunities. It is
also based on the nature of social work, which fosters conditions that promote these values.*

*In subscribing to and abiding by this code, the social
worker is expected to view ethical responsibility in as inclusive
a context as each situation demands and within which ethical
judgment is required. The social worker is expected to take
into consideration all the principles in this code that have a
bearing upon any situation in which ethical judgment is to be
exercised and professional intervention or conduct is planned.
The course of action that the social worker chooses is expected
to be consistent with the spirit as well as the letter of this code.*

*In itself, this code does not represent a set of rules that
will prescribe all the behaviors of social workers in all the complexities of professional life. Rather, it offers general principles
to guide conduct, and the judicious appraisal of conduct, in situations that have ethical implications. It provides the basis for
making judgments about ethical actions before and after they
occur. Frequently, the particular situation determines the ethical principles that apply and the manner of their application. In
such cases, not only the particular ethical principles are taken
into immediate consideration, but also the entire code and its
spirit. Specific applications of ethical principles must be judged
within the context in which they are being considered. Ethical
behavior in a given situation must satisfy not only the judgment
of the individual social worker but also the judgment of an unbiased jury of professional peers.*

*This code should not be used as an instrument to deprive
any social worker of the opportunity or freedom to practice
with complete professional integrity; nor should any disciplinary action be taken on the basis of this code without maximum
provision for safeguarding the rights of the social worker affected.*

*The ethical behavior of social workers results not from
edict but from a personal commitment of the individual. This
code is offered to affirm the will and zeal of all social workers
to be ethical and to act ethically in all that they do as social
workers.*

The following codified ethical principles should guide so-cial workers in the various roles and relationships and at the various levels of responsibility in which they function profes-sionally. These principles also serve as a basis for the adjudica-tion by the National Association of Social Workers of issues in ethics.

In subscribing to this code, social workers are required to cooperate in its implementation and abide by any disciplinary rulings based on it. They should also take adequate measures to discourage, prevent, expose, and correct the unethical conduct of colleagues. Finally, social workers should be equally ready to defend and assist colleagues unjustly charged with unethical conduct.

I.
The Social Worker's Conduct
and Comportment as a Social Worker

A. Propriety: The social worker should maintain high standards of personal conduct in the capacity or identity as social worker.

1. The private conduct of the social worker is a personal matter to the same degree as is any other person's, except when such conduct compromises the fulfillment of professional re-sponsibilities.

2. The social worker should not participate in, condone, or be associated with dishonesty, fraud, deceit, or misrepresen-tation.

3. The social worker should distinguish clearly between statements and actions made as a private individual and as a rep-resentative of the social work profession or an organization or group.

B. Competence and Professional Development: The social work-er should strive to become and remain proficient in professional practice and the performance of professional functions.

1. The social worker should accept responsibility or em-ployment only on the basis of existing competence or the inten-tion to acquire the necessary competence.

2. The social worker should not misrepresent profession-al qualifications, education, experience, or affiliations.

C. Service: The social worker should regard as primary the serv-ice obligation of the social work profession.

1. The social worker should retain ultimate responsibility for the quality and extent of the service that individual assumes, assigns, or performs.

2. The social worker should act to prevent practices that are inhumane or discriminatory against any person or group of persons.

D. Integrity: The social worker should act in accordance with the highest standards of professional integrity and impartiality.

1. The social worker should be alert to and resist the in-fluences and pressures that interfere with the exercise of profes-sional discretion and impartial judgment required for the perfor-mance of professional functions.

2. The social worker should not exploit professional rela-tionships for personal gain.

E. Scholarship and Research: The social worker engaged in study and research should be guided by the conventions of scholarly inquiry.

1. The social worker engaged in research should consider carefully its possible consequences for human beings.

2. The social worker engaged in research should ascertain that the consent of participants in the research is voluntary and informed, without any implied deprivation or penalty for re-fusal to participate, and with due regard for participants' pri-vacy and dignity.

3. The social worker engaged in research should protect participants from unwarranted physical or mental discomfort, distress, harm, danger, or deprivation.

4. The social worker who engages in the evaluation of services or cases should discuss them only for the professional purposes and only with persons directly and professionally con-cerned with them.

5. Information obtained about participants in research should be treated as confidential.

6. The social worker should take credit only for work actually done in connection with scholarly and research endeavors and credit contributions made by others.

II.
The Social Worker's
Ethical Responsibility to Clients

F. Primacy of Clients' Interests: The social worker's primary responsibility is to clients.

1. The social worker should serve clients with devotion, loyalty, determination, and the maximum application of professional skill and competence.

2. The social worker should not exploit relationships with clients for personal advantage or solicit the clients of one's agency for private practice.

3. The social worker should not practice, condone, facilitate, or collaborate with any form of discrimination on the basis of race, color, sex, sexual orientation, age, religion, national origin, marital status, political belief, mental or physical handicap, or any other preference or personal characteristic, condition, or status.

4. The social worker should avoid relationships or commitments that conflict with the interests of clients.

5. The social worker should under no circumstances engage in sexual activities with clients.

6. The social worker should provide clients with accurate and complete information regarding the extent and nature of the services available to them.

7. The social worker should apprise clients of their risks, rights, opportunities, and obligations associated with social service to them.

8. The social worker should seek advice and counsel of colleagues and supervisors whenever such consultation is in the best interest of clients.

9. The social worker should terminate service to clients,

and professional relationships with them, when such service and relationships are no longer required or no longer serve the clients' needs or interests.

10. The social worker should withdraw services precipitously only under unusual circumstances, giving careful consideration to all factors in the situation and taking care to minimize possible adverse effects.

11. The social worker who anticipates the termination or interruption of service to clients should notify clients promptly and seek the transfer, referral, or continuation of service in relation to the clients' needs and preferences.

G. Rights and Prerogatives of Clients: The social worker should make every effort to foster maximum self-determination on the part of clients.

1. When the social worker must act on behalf of a client who has been adjudged legally incompetent, the social worker should safeguard the interests and rights of that client.

2. When another individual has been legally authorized to act in behalf of a client, the social worker should deal with that person always with the client's best interest in mind.

3. The social worker should not engage in any action that violates or diminishes the civil or legal rights of clients.

H. Confidentiality and Privacy: The social worker should respect the privacy of clients and hold in confidence all information obtained in the course of professional service.

1. The social worker should share with others confidences revealed by clients, without their consent, only for compelling professional reasons.

2. The social worker should inform clients fully about the limits of confidentiality in a given situation, the purposes for which information is obtained, and how it may be used.

3. The social worker should afford clients reasonable access to any official social work records concerning them.

4. When providing clients with access to records, the social worker should take due care to protect the confidences of others contained in those records.

5. The social worker should obtain informed consent of clients before taping, recording, or permitting third-party observation of their activities.

I. Fees: When setting fees, the social worker should ensure that they are fair, reasonable, considerate, and commensurate with the service performed and with due regard for the clients' ability to pay.

1. The social worker should not divide a fee or accept or give anything of value for receiving or making a referral.

III.
The Social Worker's
Ethical Responsibility to Colleagues

J. Respect, Fairness, and Courtesy: The social worker should treat colleagues with respect, courtesy, fairness, and good faith.

1. The social worker should cooperate with colleagues to promote professional interests and concerns.

2. The social worker should respect confidences shared by colleagues in the course of their professional relationships and transactions.

3. The social worker should create and maintain conditions of practice that facilitate ethical and competent professional performance by colleagues.

4. The social worker should treat with respect, and represent accurately and fairly, the qualifications, views, and findings of colleagues and use appropriate channels to express judgments on these matters.

5. The social worker who replaces or is replaced by a colleague in professional practice should act with consideration for the interest, character, and reputation of that colleague.

6. The social worker should not exploit a dispute between a colleague and employers to obtain a position or otherwise advance the social worker's interest.

7. The social worker should seek arbitration or mediation when conflicts with colleagues require resolution for compelling professional reasons.

8. The social worker should extend to colleagues of other professions the same respect and cooperation that is extended to social work colleagues.

9. The social worker who serves as an employer, supervisor, or mentor to colleagues should make orderly and explicit arrangements regarding the conditions of their continuing professional relationship.

10. The social worker who has the responsibility for employing and evaluating the performance of other staff members should fulfill such responsibility in a fair, considerate, and equitable manner, on the basis of clearly enunciated criteria.

11. The social worker who has the responsibility for evaluating the performance of employees, supervisees, or students should share evaluations with them.

K. Dealing with Colleagues' Clients: The social worker has the responsibility to relate to the clients of colleagues with full professional consideration.

1. The social worker should not solicit the clients of colleagues.

2. The social worker should not assume professional responsibility for the clients of another agency or a colleague without appropriate communication with that agency or colleague.

3. The social worker who serves the clients of colleagues, during a temporary absence or emergency, should serve those clients with the same consideration as that afforded any client.

IV.
The Social Worker's Ethical Responsibility to Employers and Employing Organizations

L. Commitments to Employing Organization: The social worker should adhere to commitments made to the employing organization.

1. The social worker should work to improve the employing agency's policies and procedures and the efficiency and effectiveness of its services.

2. The social worker should not accept employment or arrange student field placements in an organization which is currently under public sanction by NASW for violating personnel standards, or imposing limitations on or penalties for professional actions on behalf of clients.

3. The social worker should act to prevent and eliminate discrimination in the employing organization's work assignments and in its employment policies and practices.

4. The social worker should use with scrupulous regard, and only for the purpose for which they are intended, the resources of the employing organization.

V.
The Social Worker's Ethical Responsibility to the Social Work Profession

M. Maintaining the Integrity of the Profession: The social worker should uphold and advance the values, ethics, knowledge, and mission of the profession.

1. The social worker should protect and enhance the dignity and integrity of the profession and should be responsible and vigorous in discussion and criticism of the profession.

2. The social worker should take action through appropriate channels against unethical conduct by any other member of the profession.

3. The social worker should act to prevent the unauthorized and unqualified practice of social work.

4. The social worker should make no misrepresentation in advertising as to qualifications, competence, service, or results to be achieved.

N. Community Service: The social worker should assist the profession in making social services available to the general public.

1. The social worker should contribute time and professional expertise to activities that promote respect for the utility, the integrity, and the competence of the social work profession.

2. The social worker should support the formulation, de-

velopment, enactment, and implementation of social policies of concern to the profession.

O. Development of Knowledge: The social worker should take responsibility for identifying, developing, and fully utilizing knowledge for professional practice.

1. The social worker should base practice upon recognized knowledge relevant to social work.

2. The social worker should critically examine, and keep current with, emerging knowledge relevant to social work.

3. The social worker should contribute to the knowledge base of social work and share research knowledge and practice wisdom with colleagues.

VI.
The Social Worker's
Ethical Responsibility to Society

P. Promoting the General Welfare: The social worker should promote the general welfare of society.

1. The social worker should act to prevent and eliminate discrimination against any person or group on the basis of race, color, sex, sexual orientation, age, religion, national origin, marital status, political belief, mental or physical handicap, or any other preference or personal characteristic, condition, or status.

2. The social worker should act to ensure that all persons have access to the resources, services, and opportunities which they require.

3. The social worker should act to expand choice and opportunity for all persons, with special regard for disadvantaged or oppressed groups and persons.

4. The social worker should promote conditions that encourage respect for the diversity of cultures which constitute American society.

5. The social worker should provide appropriate professional services in public emergencies.

6. The social worker should advocate changes in policy

and legislation to improve social conditions and to promote social justice.

7. The social worker should encourage informed participation by the public in shaping social policies and institutions.

Annotated
Bibliography

The reference section contains a list of sources used in the preparation of this book. This list of books, articles, research papers, and professional association statements should be useful to those who wish to pursue a topic further. In addition, the annotated bibliography should give further direction to others who wish to do more extensive study of the topics discussed. The annotated bibliography includes books and articles that we believe cover the topics in this book most comprehensively or most usefully. Several books listed also contain extensive bibliographies, which many readers may find useful.

Amato, J. A. *Ethics: Living or Dead?* Tuscaloosa, Ala.: Portals Press, 1982. A series of essays on how modern thinkers such as Jean-Jacques Rousseau, Karl Marx, Feodor Dostoevsky, Friedrich Nietzsche, and Albert Camus treat the subject of ethics. The book's central theme is that ethical knowledge is tantamount to self-knowledge.

Arieti, S. "Psychiatric Controversy: Man's Ethical Dimension." *American Journal of Psychiatry,* 1974, *132*(1), 39–42. According to Arieti, determinism has had limited influence on the practice of psychiatry; most psychiatrists have rejected Skinnerian concepts and recognize that man's moral values raise him above the level of an animal and enable him to direct his own life. Therefore, effective psychotherapy deals with feelings, emotions, attitudes, choice, and will. In short, therapy must always consider man's ethical dimension.

Barchilon, J. *Malpractice and You.* New York: Ace Books, 1975. This handbook on medical malpractice, written by a physician, shows patients how to sue their doctors. Barchilon provides a list of doctor, nurse, and hospital errors that can lead to malpractice actions. Selecting the right lawyer, preparing for the trial, and finding expert witnesses are among the several topics discussed. Case histories and a glossary of medical terms are provided.

Bayles, M. D. *Professional Ethics.* Belmont, Calif.: Wadsworth, 1981. Considers the obligations of all professionals to their clients, their profession, and third parties. Presents a detailed analysis of how an engineer, a lawyer, an accountant, a physician, and a therapist would rely on similar principles of ethical decision making.

Bazelon, D. L. "The Perils of Wizardry." *American Journal of Psychiatry,* 1974, *131*(3), 1317–1322. Judge Bazelon describes conflicts between patient needs and societal demands and discusses certain ethical challenges faced by psychiatrists as a result of their increasing influence in society. He deals with the role of the psychiatrist in the legal process and points to some major problems between courts and psychiatry. Finally, he warns that psychiatric recommendations may not be so readily accepted in the future.

Bloch, S., and Chodoff, P. (Eds.). *Psychiatric Ethics.* Oxford, England: Oxford University Press, 1981. This volume contains a series of essays on ethical issues related to psychiatric practice, including specific problems in forensics, hospitalization, psychosurgery, psychopharmacology, and other aspects of the profession. Of particular interest is a discussion of psychiatric abuses in politics and society and the professional's responsibility for public welfare.

Brennan, J. G. *Ethics and Morals*. New York: Harper & Row, 1973. An excellent contemporary introduction to the subject of ethics, relating moral theory to such everyday matters as love, war, death, and change. The major approaches, issues, language, and controversies of the field are described in comprehensible style for the introductory student.

Burgum, T., and Anderson, S. *The Counselor and the Law*. Washington, D.C.: American Association for Counseling and Development, 1975. Although this book deals primarily with legal problems in school counseling, the legal principles described are applicable to professional counselors in many settings. The counselor often finds himself in positions where helping clients may lead to civil or criminal liability. Guidelines for avoiding trouble are presented in this book, which presents a good overview of what counselors may and may not do in their relationships with clients.

Cooper, J. C. *The New Mentality*. Philadelphia: Westminster Press, 1969. Cooper argues that in certain eras a new form of man emerges. He believes that we are now living in such an era. Cooper's new generation is more moral and more conscious than its predecessors. The "new mentality" foresees a better form of humanity with a different set of values—and a different goal.

Dawidoff, D. J. *The Malpractice of Psychiatrists*. Springfield, Ill.: Thomas, 1973. Providing a general overview of malpractice in American psychiatry, Dawidoff discusses the legal responsibilities of psychiatrists and gives examples of negligent practices. Several cases are cited in detail.

Dörken, H., and Associates. *The Professional Psychologist Today: New Developments in Law, Health Insurance, and Health Practice*. San Francisco: Jossey-Bass, 1976. This book describes the growth of psychology as a health profession and examines numerous professional problems and issues. The authors provide a wealth of facts and information of interest and importance to all psychologists.

Dunham, B. *Ethics Dead and Alive.* New York: Knopf, 1971. Dunham notes the decline of ethical theory in modern thought but believes that earlier guidelines for making ethical choices can be recovered if we recognize and accept the notion that man is free to make choices and has the capacity for overcoming adversity and defeat. Durham's view of man is optimistic; he believes that mankind can save itself.

Edwards, R. B. (Ed.). *Psychiatry and Ethics.* Buffalo, N.Y.: Prometheus Books, 1982. Articles and essays from journals in psychiatry, psychology, law, and philosophy discuss the ethic of rational autonomy in therapeutic work with clients. Issues such as value questions in mental health, client rights, coercion in therapy, and controversial methodologies are presented by professionals of varied disciplines.

Fish, J. M. *Placebo Therapy: A Practical Guide to Social Influence in Psychotherapy.* San Francisco: Jossey-Bass, 1973. This lively book contains an excellent chapter on ethical issues. Fish succinctly describes therapists' responsibilities to the state, the profession, and the client. He describes the ethical ambiguities facing all members of the helping professions.

Foster, H. M. "The Conflict and Reconciliation of the Ethical Interests of Therapist and Patient." *Journal of Psychiatry and Law,* 1975, *3*(1), 38–48. According to Foster, the medical and legal professions have failed to police themselves, possibly because little attention is given to ethical and moral principles in the training of attorneys and physicians. He discusses the ethical interests of psychiatrists and patients and examines four specific issues: human experimentation, informed consent, confidentiality and privilege, and the professional obligation to exercise due care.

Fretz, B. R., and Mills, D. H. *Licensing and Certification of Psychologists and Counselors: A Guide to Current Policies, Procedures, and Legislation.* San Francisco: Jossey-Bass, 1980.

Provides a clear and concise overview of licensing and certification for both counselors and psychologists. An excellent guide for mental health practitioners.

Fried, C. *Right and Wrong.* Cambridge, Mass.: Harvard University Press, 1979. A philosopher and legal scholar investigates the human structure of morality, with particular focus on the elements of good versus evil, right versus wrong, positive versus negative rights, and the consequences of lying and doing harm.

Goldberg, C. *Therapeutic Partnership: Ethical Concerns in Psychotherapy.* New York: Springer Publishing, 1977. In the tradition of existential philosophy and Szasz's "antipsychiatry," the author examines in detail the alliance between client and therapist. He further describes the process of negotiating a productive and ethical relationship that explicitly details the terms and conditions of services provided.

Herron, W. G., and Rouslin, S. *Issues in Psychotherapy.* Bowie, Md.: R. J. Brady, 1984. The authors discuss several neglected and thorny issues that are threatening to most practitioners—among them, the therapist's narcissism and other occupational hazards of the profession. Suggestions are given for managing countertransference problems and other personal factors that affect therapy outcomes. Particular attention is directed toward the uses and abuses of therapist fantasy, the definition of a "good" clinician, and the uses of contracting.

Huckins, W. C. *Ethical and Legal Considerations in Guidance.* Boston: Houghton Mifflin, 1968. This publication deals primarily with ethical-legal problems of school counseling, but some of the principles discussed are applicable in any setting. Huckins cites several cases to illustrate concepts described in this useful and carefully written monograph.

Johnson, D. "Legal Regulation of the Social Work Profession." *Social Casework,* 1970, *51*(9), 551–555. Legal regulation of the social work profession is occurring through certification and licensure. Johnson discusses the professional implications of certification and licensure in social work and emphasizes the service ideal, technical competence, and professional autonomy as major considerations in licensure and certification.

Jones, W. T., Sontag, F., Beckner, M. O., and Fogelin, R. J. (Eds.). *Approaches to Ethics.* (3rd ed.) New York: McGraw-Hill, 1977. An excellent anthology of ethical writings from such classical philosophers as Plato and Aristotle to the more modern theories of Jean-Paul Sartre, A. J. Ayer, and James T. Smart. In all, the points of view of over forty-five distinguished philosophers are contained in this book. This impressive volume excerpts several passages cross sectioning each of the historical periods in human thought and gives the reader a more than adequate introduction to the significant approaches to ethics. The editors provide concise biographies of each contributor and describe the *Zeitgeist* of each historical period.

Kelley, E. W., Jr. "The Ethics of Creative Growth." *Personnel and Guidance Journal,* 1972, *51*(3), 171-176. According to Kelley, ethical discussions in counseling focus mainly on the familiar concepts of controls, laws, or standards. In his view professional ethics should not be limited to such matters as confidentiality, testing, and report writing but should incorporate the serious business of actively and constructively dealing with the major problems in our society. In this connection the counseling profession can gain valuable knowledge from ethical statements of several great moral leaders.

Kemp, C. G. *Intangibles in Counseling.* Boston: Houghton Mifflin, 1967. In addition to the normal behavior concerns of the psychologist, the author deals with what people hope, feel, believe, and search for. The intangibles are the little-understood or discussed philosophical questions dealing with the nature of man. Kemp, a psychologist-philosopher, discusses such concepts as human freedom and the impact of change, values, and religion and describes the influence of these concerns on the behavior of clients.

Koch, J., and Koch, L. "A Consumer's Guide to Therapy for Couples." *Psychology Today,* 1976, *9*(10), 33-40. Marriage counseling has developed into a booming business, primarily

because of the new freedom of wives. But a couple must be-
ware of quacks and incompetents, particularly in the sex
clinic. Only a few of the four to five thousand new clinics
and treatment centers devoted to sex problems are legitimate.
Hints on how to find the right counselor are provided.

Kurtines, W. M., and Gervitz, J. L. (Eds.). *Morality, Moral Behavior, and Moral Development.* New York: Wiley, 1984.
An overview of the theory and research associated with moral
development. Historical perspectives set the stage for an
understanding of the various theoretical approaches presented by contributors.

Lidz, C. W., and others. *Informed Consent: A Study of Psychiatric Decision Making.* New York: Guilford Press, 1983. A review of how informed consent law affects the daily operation
of outpatient and inpatient mental health services. The authors specifically recommend that practitioners improve their
therapeutic relationships through self-disclosure regulations.

London, P. *The Modes and Morals of Psychotherapy.* New
York: Holt, Rinehart and Winston, 1964. London is a skilled
observer, and his book provides an illuminating discussion of
the kinds of moral choices faced by counselors and psychotherapists. He maintains that therapists must use scientific
knowledge and technical skill in treating clients but that they
will decide the ultimate goals of the treatment on the basis
of moral concerns.

London, P. *Behavior Control.* New York: Harper & Row, 1971.
This comprehensive report describes the various influences—
from persuasion to coercion to technology—that shape human behavior. London discusses the moral and ethical dilemmas resulting from the use of such technology as brain im-
plants, chemotherapy, and thought control. He believes that
one of our major problems is how to use technology without
a corresponding loss of personal freedom.

Moore, G. E. *Ethics.* Oxford, England: Oxford University Press,
1969. (Originally published 1912.) This unimposing little
book contains the basic tenets of Moore's utilitarian ethical

theory. In discussing concepts of moral judgment, free will, intrinsic value, and tests of right and wrong, Moore further develops the ethical theories of his predecessors John Stuart Mill and Henry Sidgwick. Although this classic work is difficult and sometimes dry reading, any serious student is advised to struggle through it.

Mowrer, O. H. (Ed.). *Morality and Mental Health.* Chicago: Rand McNally, 1967. The editor of this volume, one of the luminaries in psychology, has long been interested in the link between morality and mental health. This interest led to the collection of seventy-eight articles, from both popular and professional literature, included in this book. A valuable reference, still timely and lively after almost twenty years.

Pacht, R., and others. "The Current Status of the Psychologist as an Expert Witness." *Professional Psychology,* 1973, *4,* 409–413. A review of court decisions that have helped to establish the psychologist as an expert witness. Guidelines to facilitate the acceptance of the psychologist in this role are suggested.

Pahel, K., and Schiller, M. (Eds.). *Readings in Contemporary Ethical Theory.* Englewood Cliffs, N.J.: Prentice-Hall, 1970. This book is a collection of over thirty papers dealing with contemporary ethical theories. Many of the main controversies and problems in the field are dealt with. The editors introduce each section of the book, offer critiques, and raise questions that are most useful to the reader in examining a certain essay.

Patterson, C. H. "Ethical Standards for Groups." *Counseling Psychologist,* 1972, *3*(3), 93–101. The author raises several questions about possible damages of group therapy and points to the dearth of statistical data on the effects of a group experience. He offers seven guidelines related to the three phases of group work.

Pines, M. *The Brain Changers.* New York: New American Library, 1973. A lucid account of scientific study of experimentation in how the human brain works and in behavior modification. The author believes that within the next few decades scientists will expose to public view man's most private and treasured possession—his brain. People will become powerful and vulnerable as never before. The issue of brain control is as important and as ominous as control of atomic weapons.

Roos, P. "Human Rights and Behavior Modification." *Mental Retardation*, 1974, *12*(3), 3-6. Roos describes ethical and legal questions surrounding behavior modification and provides suggestions for minimizing the criticisms while preserving the viability of behavior modification.

Rosenbaum, M. (Ed.). *Ethics and Values in Psychotherapy.* New York: Free Press, 1982. This comprehensive collection of articles examines the therapist's roles and responsibilities in various aspects of professional practice. It is a good source book for several situation-specific ethical issues, such as work in government and industry, religious settings, and private practice.

Schutz, B. *Legal Liability and Psychotherapy: A Practitioner's Guide to Risk Management.* San Francisco: Jossey-Bass, 1982. Considers several forms of liability pertinent to counselors and examines issues frequently cited in court cases. Discusses implications of day-to-day practices and makes many helpful recommendations to therapists.

Shertzer, B. R., and Stone, S. C. *Fundamentals of Counseling.* (2nd ed.) Boston: Houghton Mifflin, 1975. In several sections of their book, these prolific and highly respected authors deal with professional principles and issues relevant to all counselors. Chapter Sixteen, "Ethical and Legal Considerations," provides a brief introduction to most of the ethical-legal issues in counseling. For each of several areas—such as expert witnesses, libel, malpractice, and privacy—a brief review of the literature, court cases, and issues is presented. In their characteristic style, Shertzer and Stone consolidate relevant data in economical and readable presentations. We recommend this chapter as a good starting point for beginners in the field.

Singer, P. *The Expanding Circle: Ethics and Sociobiology.* New York: Farrar, Straus, and Giroux, 1981. The methods and insight of a philosopher are used to continue the work of sociobiologist Edward O. Wilson in the search for the biological basis of ethical behavior. The book convincingly and carefully makes a case for understanding human morality from an interdisciplinary perspective, combining the social, natural, and philosophical sciences.

Stein, H. *Ethics (and Other Liabilities).* New York: St. Martin's Press, 1982. The columnist on "Ethics" for *Esquire* magazine has collected his favorite essays, mostly humorous, but with insightful, sensitive, and personal moral issues, in this small book with the facetious title. His theme of "trying to live right in an amoral world" is cleverly and beautifully sustained.

Stolz, S., Weinckowski, L., and Brown, B. "Behavior Modification: A Perspective on Critical Issues." *American Psychologist,* 1975, *30*(11), 1027-1047. These authors review current methods of behavior modification and several issues and problems associated with behavior-influencing techniques. Several ethical questions are mentioned, and suggestions for standards of practice are provided.

Szasz, T. S. *The Myth of Mental Illness.* (Rev. ed.) New York: Harper & Row, 1974. Among his dozen books and numerous articles protesting the medical approach to psychiatry, this book most clearly summarizes Szasz's views on ethics in psychiatry. In a convincing tone and with considerable logic, Szasz traces the rise of mental illness and the impact of psychiatry in perpetuating the myth that people are afflicted with "sick" minds. This book is a classic in the field of morality and mental health. It has had considerable influence on several theorists and practitioners.

Taylor, R. L., and Torrey, E. E. "The Pseudo-Regulation of American Psychiatry." *American Journal of Psychiatry,* 1972, *129*(6), 34–39. This article draws attention to some inadequacies in self-regulation of psychiatry and the failure of psychiatrists to ensure competent service providers. The authors maintain that American psychiatry has evolved into a form of professional protectionism that illustrates the pitfalls of professional self-regulation. They call attention to the fact that a number of psychiatrists have only an M.D. and little training in psychiatry.

Viscott, D. S. *The Making of a Psychiatrist.* New York: Arbor House, 1972. All psychological helpers will probably find this best-seller interesting and at times amusing. Viscott describes the training of psychiatrists in a manner that highlights many of the moral and ethical problems of all helping professions. His witty and sometimes frightening accounts of incompetent and unethical behavior provide a vivid image of the psychiatric profession.

Wasserstrom, R. A. (Ed.). *Morality and the Law.* Belmont, Calif.: Wadsworth, 1971. This series of essays begins with John Stuart Mill's "On Liberty" and includes M. T. Louch's "Sins and Crimes" and G. Dworkin's arguments against legal paternalism. Four cases, including the enforcement of morality laws, are summarized.

Wexler, D. "Behavior Modification and Other Behavior Change Procedures: The Emerging Law and the Proposed Florida Guidelines." *Criminal Law Bulletin,* 1975, *11*(5), 600–616. Wexler calls attention to legal controversies surrounding the rights of confined mental patients and to public concern over questionable therapies in use in mental hospitals and prisons. He discusses the legal regulation of behavior modification, including such practices as token economics and deprivation; informed consent and coercion; and the Florida guidelines, which are designed to deal with ethical and legal questions surrounding behavior shaping methods in institutional settings.

Woody, R. H., and Associates. *The Law and the Practice of Human Services.* San Francisco: Jossey-Bass, 1984. An extensive exploration of the interaction between the legal and mental health systems. Specific attention is focused on criminal, juvenile, family, personal injury, and contractual law as well as patient rights and professional responsibilities.

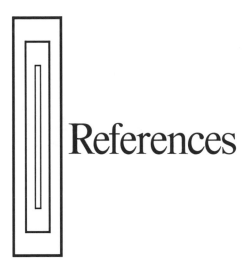

References

Ajzen, R. "Human Values and Counseling." *Personnel and Guidance Journal,* 1973, *52*(2), 77–81.

Alexander, S. "Status of Professional Counseling." Unpublished doctoral dissertation, University of Virginia, 1982.

Amato, J. A. *Ethics: Living or Dead?* Tuscaloosa, Ala.: Portals Press, 1982.

American Association for Counseling and Development. *Ethical Standards.* Washington, D.C.: American Association for Counseling and Development, 1981.

American Association for Marriage and Family Therapy. *Ethical Principles for Family Therapists.* Washington, D.C.: American Association for Marriage and Family Therapy, 1982a.

American Association for Marriage and Family Therapy. *Membership Standards.* Washington, D.C.: American Association for Marriage and Family Therapy, 1982b.

American Association for Marriage and Family Therapy. *Standards on Public Information and Advertising.* Washington,

D.C.: American Association for Marriage and Family Therapy, 1982c.

American Association of Sex Educators, Counselors, and Therapists. *Code of Ethics.* Washington, D.C.: American Association of Sex Educators, Counselors, and Therapists, 1979.

American College Personnel Association. *Guidelines for the Preparation of Professional Group Facilitators.* Washington, D.C.: American College Personnel Association, 1975.

American Medical Association. *Annual Report on Graduate Medical Educators in the U.S.* Chicago: American Medical Association, 1969.

American Medical Association. *Principles of Medical Ethics with Annotations Applicable to Psychiatry.* Chicago: American Medical Association, 1974.

American Psychiatric Association. *The Principles of Medical Ethics.* Washington, D.C.: American Psychiatric Association, 1973.

American Psychiatric Association. *Diagnostic and Statistical Manual of Mental Disorders.* (3rd ed.) Washington, D.C.: American Psychiatric Association, 1980.

American Psychological Association. "Rules and Procedures: Committee on Scientific and Professional Ethics and Conduct." *American Psychologist,* 1974, *29*(9), 703–710.

American Psychological Association. "Board of Social and Ethical Responsibility." *APA Monitor,* 1976, *7*(3), 6–9.

American Psychological Association. *Ethical Principles of Psychologists.* Washington, D.C.: American Psychological Association, 1981.

American Psychological Association, Committee on Scientific and Professional Ethics and Conduct. *Procedures for State Ethics Committees.* Washington, D.C.: American Psychological Association, 1972.

Arbuckle, D. S. *Counseling: Philosophy, Theory, and Practice.* Boston: Allyn & Bacon, 1965.

Argyris, C., and Schön, D. A. *Theory in Practice: Increasing Professional Effectiveness.* San Francisco: Jossey-Bass, 1974.

Association for Counselor Education and Supervision. *Standards for Counselor Preparation.* Washington, D.C.: Association for Counselor Education and Supervision, 1977.

Aubrey, R., and D'Andrea, M. "What Counselors Should Know About High Technology." *Counseling and Human Development,* 1984, *17*(1), 5-11.

Ayer, A. J. *Language, Truth, and Logic.* (2nd ed.) New York: Dover, 1936.

Ayer, A. J. *Logical Positivism.* Westport, Conn.: Greenwood Press, 1978. (Originally published 1959.)

Azrin, N. H., and others. "Ethical Issues for Human Services." *AABT* (Association for the Advancement of Behavior Therapy) *Newsletter,* 1977, pp. 4-11.

Baldwin, J. *Handbook of Psychology: Feeling and Will.* New York: Holt, Rinehart and Winston, 1906.

Bancroft, J. "Ethical Aspects of Sexuality and Sex Therapy." In S. Bloch and P. Chodoff (Eds.), *Psychiatric Ethics.* Oxford, England: Oxford University Press, 1981.

Bandler, R., and Grinder, J. *Frogs into Princes.* Moab, Utah: Real People Press, 1979.

Barchilon, J. *Malpractice and You.* New York: Ace Books, 1975.

Barclay, J. *Counseling and Philosophy: A Theoretical Exposition.* Boston: Houghton Mifflin, 1968.

Bayles, M. D. *Professional Ethics.* Belmont, Calif.: Wadsworth, 1981.

Bazelon, D. L. "The Perils of Wizardry." *American Journal of Psychiatry,* 1974, *131*(3), 1317-1322.

Bazelon, D. L. "A Jurist's View of Psychiatry." *Journal of Psychiatry and Law,* 1975, *3*(2), 137-144.

Becker, H. S. *Outsiders: Studies in the Sociology of Deviance.* New York: Macmillan, 1963.

Bell, D. *The Cultural Contradictions of Capitalism.* New York: Basic Books, 1976.

Benjamin, A. *The Helping Interview.* Boston: Houghton Mifflin, 1974.

Bentham, J. "An Introduction to the Principles of Morals and Legislation." In W. T. Jones and others (Eds.), *Approaches to Ethics.* (3rd ed.) New York: McGraw-Hill, 1977. (Originally published 1810.)

Berger, M. "Ethics and the Therapeutic Relationship: Patient Rights and Therapist Responsibilities." In M. Rosenbaum

(Ed.), *Ethics and Values in Psychotherapy*. New York: Free Press, 1982.

Bergin, A. E. "Psychotherapy Can Be Dangerous." *Psychology Today*, 1975, *9*, 96–104.

Bergin, A. E. "Psychotherapy and Religious Values." *Journal of Consulting and Clinical Psychology*, 1980, *48*, 95–105.

Bolan, R. S. "The Practitioner as Therapist." *Journal of American Planning Association*, 1980, 7(3), 261–274.

Boorstein, S., and Speeth, K. (Eds.). *Exploration in Transpersonal Psychotherapy*. Palo Alto, Calif.: Science & Behavior Books, Inc., 1980.

Boy, A., and Pine, G. *Client-Centered Counseling: A Renewal*. Boston: Allyn & Bacon, 1982.

Brammer, L. M., and Shostrom, E. L. *Therapeutic Psychology*. Englewood Cliffs, N.J.: Prentice-Hall, 1968.

Brandt, R. *Ethical Theory*. Englewood Cliffs, N.J.: Prentice-Hall, 1959.

Brennan, J. G. *Ethics and Morals*. New York: Harper & Row, 1973.

Browne, H. *How I Found Freedom in an Unfree World*. New York: Avon Books, 1973.

Burgum, T., and Anderson, S. *The Counselor and the Law*. Washington, D.C.: American Association for Counseling and Development, 1975.

Callis, R. (Ed.). *Ethical Standards Casebook*. Washington, D.C.: American Association for Counseling and Development, 1982.

Carkhuff, R. R. *The Art of Problem Solving*. Amherst, Mass.: Human Resource Development Press, 1973.

Cohn, B., and others. *Group Counseling: An Orientation*. Washington, D.C.: American Association for Counseling and Development, 1973.

Cooper, J. C. *The New Mentality*. Philadelphia: Westminster Press, 1969.

Corey, G., Corey, M. S., and Callanan, P. *Issues and Ethics for the Helping Professions*. Monterey, Calif.: Brooks/Cole, 1984.

Corey, G., and others. "Ethical Considerations in Using Group Techniques." *Journal for Specialists in Group Work*, 1982, 7 (3), 140–148.

Cottingham, H. "Some Broader Perspectives on Credentialing Counseling Psychologists." *Counseling Psychologist,* 1980, *9* (1), 19-22.

Cottingham, H., and Warner, R. "APGA and Counselor Licensure: A Status Report." *Personnel and Guidance Journal,* 1978, *56*(2), 593-598.

Daubner, E. V., and Daubner, E. S. "Ethics and Counseling Decisions." *Personnel and Guidance Journal,* 1970, *48*(6), 434-442.

Davis, K. L., and Meara, N. M. "So You Think It's a Secret?" *Journal for Specialists in Group Work,* 1982, 7(3), 149-153.

Dawidoff, D. J. *The Malpractice of Psychiatrists.* Springfield, Ill.: Thomas, 1973.

Denes, W. A. "Encounter Group Therapy." *Counseling Psychologist,* 1975, *5*(2), 15-21.

Derner, O. F. "The Ethical Practice of Biofeedback." In M. Rosenbaum (Ed.), *Ethics and Values in Psychotherapy.* New York: Free Press, 1982.

Dörken, H., and Associates. *The Professional Psychologist Today: New Developments in Law, Health Insurance, and Health Practice.* San Francisco: Jossey-Bass, 1976.

Dostoevsky, F. *Crime and Punishment.* New York: Vintage Books, 1950. (Originally published 1866.)

Dove, J. L. "Dynamic Aspects of Success." *British Journal of Medical Psychology,* 1935, *15,* 230-241.

Drane, J. F. "Ethics and Psychotherapy: A Philosophical Perspective." In M. Rosenbaum (Ed.), *Ethics and Values in Psychotherapy.* New York: Free Press, 1982.

Dujovne, B. E. "Sexual Feeling, Fantasies, and Acting Out in Psychotherapy." *Psychotherapy: Theory, Research, and Practice,* 1983, *20*(2), 243-250.

Dunham, B. *Ethics Dead and Alive.* New York: Knopf, 1971.

Dworkin, G. "Paternalism." In R. A. Wasserstrom (Ed.), *Morality and the Law.* Belmont, Calif.: Wadsworth, 1971.

Dyer, W. *Your Erroneous Zones.* New York: Funk and Wagnalls, 1976.

Eber, M., and O'Brien, J. M. "Psychotherapy in the Movies." *Psychotherapy: Theory, Research, and Practice,* 1982, *19* (1), 116-120.

Edelstein, L. "The Hippocratic Oath: Text Translation and In-

238

terpretation." In O. Temkin and C. L. Temkin (Eds.), *Ancient Medicine.* Baltimore, Md.: Johns Hopkins University Press, 1967.

Edwards, R. B. "Mental Health as Rational Autonomy." In R. B. Edwards (Ed.), *Psychiatry and Ethics.* Buffalo, N.Y.: Prometheus Books, 1982.

Ellis, A. *Humanistic Psychotherapy: The Rational-Emotive Approach.* New York: McGraw-Hill, 1974.

Ellis, R. "Human Values and Counseling." *Personnel and Guidance Journal,* 1973, *52*(2), 77–81.

Englehardt, H. T., Jr. "Psychotherapy as Meta-Ethics." In R. B. Edwards (Ed.), *Psychiatry and Ethics.* Buffalo, N.Y.: Prometheus Books, 1982.

Falwell, J. Speech delivered in Charlottesville, Va., Nov. 7, 1984.

Fisch, R., Weakland, J., and Segal, L. *The Tactics of Change: Doing Therapy Briefly.* San Francisco: Jossey-Bass, 1982.

Fish, E. *The Past at Present.* Cambridge, Mass.: Harvard University Press, 1981.

Fish, J. M. *Placebo Therapy: A Practical Guide to Social Influence in Psychotherapy.* San Francisco: Jossey-Bass, 1973.

Fisher, K. "Self-Help Authors' Dark 'How-To' Manual." *APA Monitor,* 1984, *15*(4), 20–21.

Foster, H. M. "The Conflict and Reconciliation of the Ethical Interests of Therapist and Patient." *Journal of Psychiatry and Law,* 1975, *3*(1), 39–48.

Frank, J. *Persuasion and Healing.* (Rev. ed.) New York: Schocken Books, 1974.

Frankel, M. "Morality in Psychotherapy." *Psychology Today,* 1967, *1*(4), 24–30.

Fretz, B. R., and Mills, D. H. "Professional Certification in Counseling Psychology." *Counseling Psychologist,* 1980, *9*(1), 2–17.

Freud, S. *Civilization and Its Discontents.* New York: Doubleday, 1958. (Originally published 1895.)

Fried, C. *Right and Wrong.* Cambridge, Mass.: Harvard University Press, 1979.

Fromm, E. *Man for Himself: An Inquiry into the Psychology of*

Ethics. New York: Holt, Rinehart and Winston, 1947.

Fromm, E. "Values in Hypnotherapy." *Psychotherapy: Theory, Research, and Practice,* 1980, *17*(4), 425–430.

Gazda, G., Duncan, J., and Sisson, P. "Professional Issues in Group Work." *Personnel and Guidance Journal,* 1971, *49*(8), 279–284.

Gill, S. J. "Professional Disclosure and Consumer Protection in Counseling." *Personnel and Guidance Journal,* 1982, *66*(3), 443–446.

Glasser, W. *Mental Health or Mental Illness.* New York: Harper & Row, 1983.

Goble, F. G. *The Third Force.* New York: Pocket Books, 1970.

Goldberg, C. *Therapeutic Partnership: Ethical Concerns in Psychotherapy.* New York: Springer Publishing, 1977.

Goldman, L. "Privilege or Privacy." *Personnel and Guidance Journal,* 1969, *48*(3), 84–88.

Goodman, W. R., and Price, J. J. H. *Jerry Falwell: An Unauthorized Profile.* Lynchburg, Va.: Paris and Associates, 1981.

Graham, P. "Ethics and Child Psychiatry." In S. Bloch and P. Chodoff (Eds.), *Psychiatric Ethics.* Oxford, England: Oxford University Press, 1981.

Gross, D., and Khan, J. "Values of Three Practitioner Groups." *Journal of Counseling and Values,* 1983, *28*(1), 228–233.

Grossack, M., and Gardner, H. *Man and Men.* Scranton, Pa.: International Textbook, 1972.

Gumaer, J. "Ethics and the Experts." *Journal for Specialists in Group Work,* 1982, 7(3), 154–161.

Haley, J. *Problem-Solving Therapy: New Strategies for Effective Family Therapy.* San Francisco: Jossey-Bass, 1976.

Haley, J. "How to Be a Marriage Therapist Without Knowing Practically Anything." *Journal of Marital and Family Therapy,* 1980, *6,* 385–391.

Hall, J. E., and Hare-Mustin, R. T. "Sanctions and the Diversity of Ethical Complaints Against Psychologists." *American Psychologist,* 1983, *38,* 714–729.

Halleck, S. L. "Therapy Is the Handmaiden of the Status Quo." *Psychology Today,* 1971, *5*(2), 31–39.

Hare-Mustin, R. T. "Family Therapy May Be Dangerous to Your Health." *Professional Psychology,* 1980, *11,* 935-938.

Hare-Mustin, R. T., and others. "Rights of Clients, Responsibilities of Therapists." *American Psychologist,* 1979, *34,* 3-16.

Hart, G. M. *Values Clarification for Counselors.* Springfield, Ill.: Thomas, 1979.

Hartley, J., Roback, H. B., and Abramowitz, S. I. "Deterioration Effects in Encounter Groups." *American Psychologist,* 1976, *31,* 247-255.

Hartman, W. E., and Fithian, M. A. *Treatment of Sexual Dysfunction.* Palo Alto, Calif.: Center for Mental and Sexual Studies, 1972.

Hartshorne, H., and May, M. *Studies in the Nature of Character.* Vol. 1: *Studies in Deceit; Studies in Self-Control.* New York: Macmillan, 1928.

Hartshorne, H., and May, M. *Studies in the Nature of Character.* Vol. 2: *Studies in the Organization of Character.* New York: Macmillan, 1930.

Hoffman, M. L. "Moral Development." In P. H. Mussen (Ed.), *Carmichael's Manual of Child Psychology.* New York: Wiley, 1970.

Hogan, R. "Ethical Decision Making." In F. Chu and S. Trotter (Eds.), *The Madness Establishment.* New York: Grossman, 1974.

Holroyd, J. C., and Brodsky, A. M. "Psychologists' Attitudes and Practices Regarding Erotic and Nonerotic Physical Contact with Patients." *American Psychologist,* 1977, *32,* 843-849.

Huckins, W. C. *Ethical and Legal Considerations in Guidance.* Boston: Houghton Mifflin, 1968.

Ivey, A. E. "Counseling and Psychotherapy: Toward a New Perspective." *Counseling Psychologist,* 1981, *9*(2), 83-98.

Jacobs, D. F. "Standards for Psychologists." In H. Dörken and Associates, *The Professional Psychologist Today: New Developments in Law, Health Insurance, and Health Practice.* San Francisco: Jossey-Bass, 1976.

Jeffries, D. "Should We Continue to Deradicalize Children Through the Use of Counseling Groups?" In J. Vriend and W. W. Dyer (Eds.), *Counseling Effectively in Groups.* Englewood Cliffs, N.J.: Educational Technology Publications, 1973.

Jones, W. T., Sontag, F., Beckner, M. O., and Fogelin, R. J. (Eds.). *Approaches to Ethics.* (3rd ed.) New York: McGraw-Hill, 1977.

Katona, G. *Psychological Analysis of Economic Behavior.* New York: McGraw-Hill, 1951.

Keith-Spiegel, P. "Violation of Ethical Principles Due to Ignorance or Poor Professional Judgment Versus Willful Disregard." *Professional Psychology,* 1977, *8,* 288-296.

Kelley, E. W., Jr. "The Ethics of Creative Growth." *Personnel and Guidance Journal,* 1972, *51*(3), 171-176.

Kemp, C. G. *Intangibles in Counseling.* Boston: Houghton Mifflin, 1967.

Kirk, B. "What's in a Name?" *Counseling Psychologist,* 1980, *9* (1), 24-25.

Knapp, S. "A Primer on Malpractice for Psychologists." *Professional Psychology,* 1980, *11,* 606-612.

Koch, J., and Koch, L. "A Consumer's Guide to Therapy for Couples." *Psychology Today,* 1976, *9*(10), 33-40.

Kohlberg, L. "The Development of Modes of Moral Thinking and Choices in the Years 10-16." Unpublished doctoral dissertation, University of Chicago, 1958.

Kohlberg, L. "Development of Moral Character and Moral Ecology." In M. L. Hoffman and L. W. Hoffman (Eds.), *Review of Child Development Research.* Vol. I. New York: Russell Sage Foundation, 1964.

Kohlberg, L. "Moral Development and the Education of Adolescents." In R. Purnell (Ed.), *Adolescents and the American High School.* New York: Holt, Rinehart and Winston, 1971.

Kohlberg, L., and Wasserman, E. R. "The Cognitive-Developmental Approach and the Practicing Counselor: An Opportunity for Counselors to Rethink Their Roles." *Personnel and Guidance Journal,* 1980, *59,* 559-568.

Kottler, J. "Ethics Comes of Age." *Journal for Specialists in Group Work,* 1982, 7(3), 138-139.

Kottler, J. *Pragmatic Group Leadership.* Monterey, Calif.: Brooks/Cole, 1983.

Kottler, J., and Brown, R. *Introduction to Therapeutic Counseling.* Monterey, Calif.: Brooks/Cole, 1985.

Kottler, J. A., and Vriend, J. "How Good Is Your Shrink?" *Detroit Discovery,* Spring 1975, pp. 12-18.

Ladd, E. T. "Counselor, Confidences, and Civil Liberties of Clients." *Personnel and Guidance Journal,* 1971, *50*(4), 261-268.

Lakin, M. "Group Sensitivity Training and Encounter: Uses and Abuses of a Method." *Counseling Psychologist,* 1970, *2*(2), 66-70.

Levy, C. S. "The Context of Social Work Ethics." *Social Work,* 1972, *17,* 95-101.

Lieberman, M., Yalom, I., and Miles, M. *Encounter Groups: First Facts.* New York: Basic Books, 1973.

Lindenberg, S. "Mental Health Counseling: Approaching the 21st Century." *Counseling and Human Development,* 1984, *16*(7), 1-8.

London, P. *The Modes and Morals of Psychotherapy.* New York: Holt, Rinehart and Winston, 1964.

London, P. *Behavior Control.* New York: Harper & Row, 1971.

Lowenthal, M., Thurnher, M., Chiriboga, D., and Associates. *Four Stages of Life: A Comparative Study of Men and Women Facing Transitions.* San Francisco: Jossey-Bass, 1975.

McCandless, B. R., and Evans, E. D. *Children and Youth: Psychosocial Development.* Hinsdale, Ill.: Dryden Press, 1973.

McCully, C. H. "The School Counselor: Strategy for Professionalization." *School Counselor,* 1962, *40,* 681-689.

Madanes, C. *Strategic Family Therapy.* San Francisco: Jossey-Bass, 1981.

Maslow, A. *Toward a Psychology of Being.* New York: Van Nostrand, 1962.

Masters, W. H., Johnson, V. L., and Kolodny, R. *Ethical Issues in Sex Therapy and Research.* Boston: Little, Brown, 1977.

May, R. "Contributions of Existential Psychotherapy." In R. May, E. Angel, and H. Ellender (Eds.), *Existence: A New Dimension in Psychiatry and Psychology.* New York: Basic Books, 1958.

May, R. *Psychology and the Human Dilemma.* New York: Van Nostrand, 1967.

May, R. *The Discovery of Being.* New York: Norton, 1983.

Mill, J. S. *Utilitarianism.* Excerpted in W. T. Jones and others (Eds.), *Approaches to Ethics.* (3rd ed.) New York: McGraw-Hill, 1977. (Originally published 1863.)

Miller, R. B. "A Call to Armchairs." *Psychotherapy: Theory, Research, and Practice,* 1983, *20*(2), 208-219.

Minuchin, S., and Fishman, H. C. *Family Therapy Techniques.* Cambridge, Mass.: Harvard University Press, 1981.

Moore, G. E. *Ethics.* Oxford, England: Oxford University Press, 1969. (Originally published 1912.)

Mowrer, O. H. (Ed.). *Morality and Mental Health.* Chicago: Rand McNally, 1967.

Munk, A. W. *A Synoptic Approach to the Riddle of Existence: Toward an Adequate World View for a World Civilization.* St. Louis: Green, 1977.

Musto, A. "A Historical Perspective." In S. Bloch and P. Chodoff (Eds.), *Psychiatric Ethics.* Oxford, England: Oxford University Press, 1981.

National Association of Social Workers. *Ethical Standards.* Washington, D.C.: National Association of Social Workers, 1978.

O'Connell, W. E. *Action Therapy and Adlerian Theory: Selected Papers.* Chicago: Institute of Alfred Adler, 1975.

Onoda, L. "Ethical and Professional Issues for Psychologists and Counselors Employing Biofeedback in Counseling Settings." *Personnel and Guidance Journal,* 1978, *57*(12), 214-217.

Pacht, C. D., and Soloman, P. "Electroconvulsive Therapy and Other Somatic Therapies." In P. Soloman and C. D. Pacht (Eds.), *Handbook of Psychiatry.* (3rd ed.) Los Altos, Calif.: Lange Medical Publications, 1973.

Pardue, J., Whichard, W., and Johnson, E. "Limiting Confidential Information in Counseling." *Personnel and Guidance Journal,* 1970, *49*(1), 14-20.

Parloff, M. B. "Shopping for the Right Therapy." *Saturday Review,* Feb. 21, 1976, pp. 18-23.

Patterson, C. H. *Theories of Counseling and Psychotherapy.* (3rd ed.) New York: Harper & Row, 1980.

Pearce, J. "God Is a Variable Interval." *Playboy,* Oct. 1975, pp. 144-161.

Perry, R. B. "General Theory of Value." In D. A. Johnson (Ed.), *Ethics Selections from Classical and Contemporary Writers.* (3rd ed.) New York: Holt, Rinehart and Winston, 1974.

Peters, J. J. "Do Encounter Groups Hurt People?" *Psychotherapy: Theory, Research, and Practice,* 1973, *10*(1), 33-35.

Piaget, J. *The Moral Judgment of the Child.* New York: Free Press, 1932.

Piercy, F. P., and Sprenkle, D. H. "Ethical, Legal, and Professional Issues in Family Therapy." *Journal of Marital and Family Therapy,* 1983, *9*(4), 393-401.

Pietrofesa, J., Hoffman, A., and Splete, H. *Counseling: An Introduction.* (2nd ed.) Boston: Houghton Mifflin, 1984.

"A Psychiatrist's Notes." *Newsweek,* Feb. 16, 1976, p. 24.

Raths, L., Hamrin, M., and Simon, S. *Values and Teaching.* (2nd ed.) Columbus, Ohio: Merrill, 1978.

Reamer, F. G. *Ethical Dilemmas in Social Service.* New York: Columbia University Press, 1982.

Reich, W. "Psychiatric Diagnosis as an Ethical Problem." In S. Bloch and P. Chodoff (Eds.), *Psychiatric Ethics.* Oxford, England: Oxford University Press, 1981.

Rice, B. "Call-In Therapy: Reach Out and Shrink Someone." *Psychology Today,* 1981, pp. 39-91.

Roberts, R. W., and Northern, H. *Theories for Social Work with Groups.* New York: Columbia University Press, 1976.

Robitscher, J. "The Impact of New Legal Standards on Psychiatry." *Journal of Psychiatry and Law,* 1975, *3*(2), 410-417.

Rogers, C. R. *Client-Centered Therapy.* Boston: Houghton Mifflin, 1951.

Rogers, C. R. *On Becoming a Person.* Boston: Houghton Mifflin, 1961.

Rogers, C. R. *On Encounter Groups.* New York: Harper & Row, 1970.

Rogers, C. R. "Some New Challenges." *American Psychologist,* 1973, *28*(5), 379-387.

Ross, W. (Trans.). *Aristotle's Ethics.* Book I. Chicago: Contemporary Books, 1954.

Rowe, W., and Winborn, B. B. "What People Fear About Group

Work: An Analysis of Thirty-Six Selected Critical Articles."
In J. Vriend and W. W. Dyer (Eds.), *Counseling Effectively in
Groups*. Englewood Cliffs, N.J.: Educational Technology
Publications, 1973.

Russell, B. *Authority and the Individual*. New York: Simon &
Schuster, 1949.

Russell, B. *The Problems of Philosophy*. Oxford, England: Oxford University Press, 1959.

Sartre, J.-P. *Existentialism and Human Emotions*. New York:
Philosophical Library, 1947.

Sartre, J.-P. *Being and Nothingness*. In R. Cumming (Ed.), *The
Philosophy of Jean-Paul Sartre*. New York: Basic Books,
1965. (Originally published 1943.)

Schutz, B. *Legal Liability and Psychotherapy: A Practitioner's
Guide to Risk Management*. San Francisco: Jossey-Bass, 1982.

Schwebel, M. "Why Unethical Practice?" *Journal of Counseling
Psychology*, 1955, *2*, 122-128.

Serban, G. "Sexual Activity in Therapy: Legal and Ethical Is
sues." *American Journal of Psychotherapy*, 1981, *25*, 76-81.

Shepard, M. *Inside a Psychiatrist's Head*. New York: Dell, 1972.

Shertzer, B. R., and Stone, S. C. *Fundamentals of Counseling*.
(2nd ed.) Boston: Houghton Mifflin, 1975.

Sidgwick, H. *The Methods of Ethics*. Excerpted in W. T. Jones
and others (Eds.), *Approaches to Ethics*. (3rd ed.) New York:
McGraw-Hill, 1977. (Originally published 1874.)

Siegel, M. "Privacy, Ethics, and Confidentiality." *Professional
Psychology*, 1979, *10*(2), 249-258.

Singer, P. *The Expanding Circle: Ethics and Sociobiology*. New
York: Farrar, Straus, and Giroux, 1981.

Snygg, D. "The Psychological Basis of Human Values." In D.
Avila, A. Combs, and W. Purkey (Eds.), *The Helping Relationship Source Book*. Boston: Allyn & Bacon, 1972.

Stefflre, B., and Matheny, K. *The Function of Counseling Theory*. Boston: Houghton Mifflin, 1968.

Stein, H. *Ethics (and Other Liabilities)*. New York: St. Martin's
Press, 1982.

Strupp, H. H. "On Failing One's Patient." *Psychotherapy: Theory, Research, and Practice*, 1975, *12*(1), 39-41.

Strupp, H. H. "Clinical Psychology, Irrationalism, and the Erosion of Excellence." *American Psychologist,* 1976, *31*(8), 561–571.

Stuart, R. B. *Trick or Treatment: How and When Psychotherapy Fails.* Champaign, Ill.: Research Press, 1970.

Sullivan, H. *The Psychiatric Interview.* New York: Norton, 1970.

Szasz, T. S. *The Myth of Mental Illness.* (Rev. ed.) New York: Harper & Row, 1974.

Szasz, T. S. *The Myth of Psychotherapy.* New York: Doubleday, 1978.

Taylor, R. L., and Torrey, E. E. "The Pseudo-Regulation of American Psychiatry." *American Journal of Psychiatry,* 1972, *129*(6), 34–39.

Theroux, A. "The Shrink." *Esquire,* Dec. 1975, pp. 161–186.

Toffler, A. *The Third Wave.* New York: Morrow, 1980.

Trent, C. C., and Muhl, W. P. "Professional Liability Insurance and the American Psychiatrist." *Brief Communications,* 1975, *132*(12), 1312–1314.

Ullmann, L. P., and Krasner, L. *A Psychological Approach to Abnormal Behavior.* (2nd ed.) Englewood Cliffs, N.J.: Prentice-Hall, 1975.

Van Hoose, W., and Miller, H. "Sociocultural Forces and Adult Counseling." *Journal of Counseling and Values,* 1983, *27*(2), 76–83.

Viscott, D. S. *The Making of a Psychiatrist.* New York: Arbor House, 1972.

Wahl, O. "Six TV Myths About Mental Illness." *TV Guide,* March 13–19, 1976, pp. 4–8.

Watkins, C. E. "Counselor Acting Out in the Counseling Situation." *Personnel and Guidance Journal,* 1983, *61*(3), 417–423.

Widiger, T. A., and Rorer, L. G. "The Responsible Psychotherapist." *American Psychologist,* 1984, *39*(5), 503–515.

Wigmore, J. H. *Evidence.* Vol. 3, Sec. 2285. (3rd ed.) Boston: Little, Brown, 1961.

Williams, R. *American Society.* New York: Knopf, 1956.

Wilson, E. O. *On Human Nature.* New York: Bantam Books, 1979.

Woody, R. H., and Associates. *The Law and the Practice of Human Services.* San Francisco: Jossey-Bass, 1984.

Wrenn, C. G. "The Ethics of Counseling." In R. Bernard (Ed.), *Counseling and Psychotherapy.* Palo Alto, Calif.: Science and Behavior Books, 1966.

Wright, A. *The Psychology of Moral Behavior.* New York: Penguin Books, 1971.

Yalom, I. D. *The Theory and Practice of Group Psychotherapy.* New York: Basic Books, 1975.

Yalom, I. D. *Existential Psychotherapy.* New York: Basic Books, 1980.

Yankelovich, D. "New Roles in American Life: Searching for Self-Fulfillment in a World Turned Upside Down." *Psychology Today,* 1981, *15*(4), 35–86.

Zemlick, M. J. "Ethical Standards: Cosmetics for the Face of the Profession of Psychology." *Psychotherapy: Theory, Research, and Practice,* 1980, *17*(4), 448–453.

Zimpfer, D. "Needed: Professional Ethics for Working with Groups." *Personnel and Guidance Journal,* 1971, *50*(4), 14–24.

Zimpfer, D. *Group Work in the Helping Professions: A Bibliography.* Washington, D.C.: American Association for Counseling and Development, 1976.

Index

A

American Board of Psychiatry and Neurology, 83
American Board of Psychological Services, 79
American College Personnel Association, 234
American Educational Research Association, 195
American Medical Association (AMA), 234; standards of, 71, 83, 84
American Mental Health Counselors Association (AMHCA), standards of, 76
American Neurological Association, 83
American Personnel and Guidance Association, 71, 91, 195
American Psychiatric Association (APA), 104, 234; and confidentiality, 48, 49, 54; and malpractice insurance, 64-65; standards of, 71, 83, 84
American Psychological Association (APA): and accreditation, 168; and animal care and use, 186-187; and assessment techniques, 183-184; Board of Social and Ethical Responsibility (BSERP) of, 81, 234; code of, 7, 71, 77, 87, 94, 164, 168, 169, 171-187, 195, 234; Committee on a Directory of Psychological Service Centers of, 79; Committee on Scientific and Professional Ethics and Conduct (CSPEC) of, 87, 172, 234; Committee on Standards for Providers of Psychological Services of, 81; and competence, 174-175; and confidentiality, 179; and consumer welfare, 180-181; Council of Representatives of, 80, 81, 171n; Division 17 (Counseling Psychology) of, 78, 79; Division 22 (Rehabilitation Psychology) of, 79; Division 30 (Hypnosis) of, 150; and human subjects in research, 184-186; and licensure or certifica-

tion, 90, 91; and marketing, 157; and moral and legal standards, 175-176; and professional relationships, 181-183; and public statements, 176-179; and responsibility, 173; Task Force on Standards for Psychologists of, 80
American Society of Clinical Hypnosis, 150
Anderson, S., 50, 51, 62, 63, 223, 236
Animal care and use, standards on, 186-187
Aquinas, T., 22
Arbuckle, D. S., 33, 234
Arcimatheus, 112
Argyris, C., 12, 20, 234
Arieti, S., 222
Aristotle, 22, 26, 31-32, 226
Assessment: ethical issues of, 130-133; standards on techniques of, 183-184
Association for Counselor Education and Supervision (ACES), 75, 234
Association for Specialists in Group Work, 146
Association for the Advancement of Behavior Therapy, 138
Aubrey, R., 101-102, 235
Ayer, A. J., 29, 226, 235
Azrin, N. H., 138, 235

B

Baldwin, J., 37-38, 235
Bancroft, J., 148, 235
Bandler, R., 149, 235
Barchilon, J., 63, 222, 235
Barclay, J., 10, 235
Bayles, M. D., 4, 156, 222, 235
Bazelon, D. L., 57-58, 222, 235
Becker, H. S., 235
Beckner, M. O., 3, 26, 226, 241
Beers, C., 165
Behavior modification: guidelines for, 138; issues of, 137-139
Bell, D., 97, 235
Benjamin, A., 21, 235